Java Virtual Machine

THE JAVA SERIES™

Exploring Java

Java Threads

Java Network Programming

Java Virtual Machine

Java AWT Reference

Java Language Reference

Java Fundamental Classes Reference

Also from O'Reilly

Java in a Nutshell

Java Virtual Machine

Jon Meyer and Troy Downing

O'REILLY™

Cambridge · Köln · Paris · Sebastopol · Tokyo

Java Virtual Machine
by Jon Meyer and Troy Downing

Published by O'Reilly & Associates, Inc., 101 Morris Street, Sebastopol, CA 95472.

Editor: Andrew Schulman

Production Editor: Nicole Gipson Arigo

Printing History:

> March 1997:   First Edition

ISBN: 1-56592-194-1

To my parents.

—Jon Meyer

For my wife, Laura, and my daughter, Morgan—
whose love and understanding have made this book possible.

—Troy Downing

Table of Contents

Preface

This book describes the Java Virtual Machine, the platform-independent engine used to run Java applets and applications. The book is designed for programmers who are familiar with the Java language and know a little C or C++. It includes introductory and tutorial material, as well as a reference section. The book serves as a "how-to" book—it includes lots of practical information, as well as code examples written for the Java Virtual Machine (or the JVM, as it is often referred to in this book). The material presented here is expected to complement the official JVM specifications released by Sun Microsystems.

Readers should be sure to check the "How to Use this Book" section towards the end of this Preface; it describes the structure of the book and explains how to get the most out of it.

Java Books and Resources

O'Reilly & Associates is developing a series of Java books. The series already includes an introductory volume, a quick reference, several tutorial volumes, several reference volumes, and now the Java Virtual Machine book you are holding. The series will be expanded to include a complete set of Java API reference manuals. In addition, the Java series will include additional volumes covering advanced topics in Java programming, such as Java Beans distributed computing. Refer to *http://www.ora.com/info/java* for a complete list of current and upcoming titles in the O'Reilly & Associates Java series.

Sun Microsystems has online reference documentation for the Java API and the Java Virtual Machine that you may find useful in conjunction with this book. You may want to visit *http://www.javasoft.com/* to view or download this API documentation and other useful documents.

The author's own list of documentation related to the Java Virtual Machine can be found at *http://cat.nyu.edu/meyer/jasmin*.

Also, the *comp.lang.java* newsgroup is a central location for discussion of Java. The newsgroup has recently been split into several smaller subgroups, for specialized discussion, so be sure to read the FAQ list to find out which group is most appropriate for your needs.

About This Book

We believe that the Java Virtual Machine is one of the most exciting and important features of the Java technology. It is also one of the least accessible. Writing programs that work on the JVM level is painstaking and complicated, and there is little information available on the subject.

Sun has published a book about the Java Virtual Machine: the *Java Virtual Machine Specification*, by Tim Lindholm and Frank Yellin, available from Addison Wesley, ISBN 0-201-63452-X. The specification is an excellent reference work, and goes a long way to redress the shortfall of information available on the JVM, but it provides little overview material, only has very concise descriptions for many of the JVM instructions, and contains no concrete examples that you can type in and try out. All this is as it should be: the specification is intended as a detailed account of the semantics of the machine, a role it serves well.

This book is written to complement the JVM specification. Where the specification concentrates on giving detailed rules and semantics, in this book we aim to provide more introductory and accessible description, along with lots of actual examples that you can try. For instance, in this book we show how to write a ClassLoader; give pseudo-code showing how instanceof works; present a Web applet as a JVM program; and much more.

In taking this approach, we had to give up something. Our book contains less detail in areas such as the rules of IEEE floating point arithmetic, the checks performed by the class verifier, or the semantics required by threads.

This doesn't mean the book is short on useful information. You will find dozens of examples that illustrate how the JVM actually works; the first part of the book contains a substantial overview of the machine; we've also included lots of notes based on our experiences working with the machine.

We believe the book covers all you need to know in order understand and write programs for the Java Virtual Machine. It also provides implementation notes and performance hints. Of course, some readers (especially systems implementors and language specialists) will want more detail. We encourage those readers to consult the official specification.

Target Audience

This book (and the software accompanying it) is designed for programmers, students, hobbyists, professionals, and anyone else who is interested in Java technology and who wants to learn what goes on under the hood of the Java Virtual Machine. Here are some reader profiles:

Teachers

If you are teaching a compilers course, you might consider using the Java Virtual Machine as a target platform for your student coursework. One advantage of this approach is that students can carry out homework on a large variety of machines (in fact, any machine that runs Netscape with Java enabled). Another advantage is that you can then integrate investigation of some of the features of the Virtual Machine (portability, the verifier, object model, type system) into your coursework.

Hobbyists

This book gives you the tools you need to poke around in Java at the virtual machine level. If you are interested in gaining a real understanding of how Java works and what the Virtual Machine is like, this book is for you.

System Implementors

If you are implementing a Java runtime system, or porting Java to a new platform, this book is a great starting point for learning how everything in the runtime system fits together.

Advanced Programmers

Using this book, and the Jasmin software that comes with it, you can disassemble classes, see how they work, and even implement a critical class or method using the hand-coded Java assembler. Alternatively, you might use this book to gain a better understanding of efficiency issues in Java or to create an application that uses the JVM directly.

Language Implementors

If you want to create an implementation of your favorite programming language that runs on the Java Virtual Machine, this books gives you all the details you need.

Security Wizards

Sun's claim that Java protects you from hostile programs is a pretty strong one. This book helps you assess that claim yourself.

Example Programs

In this book you will find many examples that show you how the Java Virtual Machine works.

We wanted to present these examples in an easy-to-read text format, so that you could quickly type in the examples on your system and try them out. However the Java specification does not include a text format for Java class files (it only describes the underlying binary byte format of Java class files).

For the purposes of writing a book, we created our own Java Virtual Machine assembler, called Jasmin. Jasmin takes text-based descriptions of Java class files, written in a simple easy-to-read syntax, and converts them into the appropriate binary class files. Using Jasmin, it's very easy to poke around, trying things out in the Virtual Machine. All of the VM examples in this book are written using the Jasmin syntax, and the reference section includes notes that describe in more detail the Jasmin syntax and the underlying bytecode format that Jasmin files are converted into.

Jasmin is available for free. If you did not receieve Jasmin with this book, you can download it from the Web. Check *http://www.ora.com/catalog/books/javavm* or *http://www.cat.nyu.edu/meyer/jasmin* for details on how to obtain the latest release of Jasmin.

Request for Comments

We started this book in 1996. At that time, Sun had not released official documentation on the JVM, so much of our early work was based on guesswork and sleuthing. To write the book, we spent a lot of time poking at the internals of the JVM, reading the online material (at *http://java.sun.com*), and writing test programs using Jasmin. This research has enabled us to give you hard-earned insights into the workings of the Virtual Machine.

When Sun released the JVM specification this year, it contained a number of refinements and improvements not present in the earlier software (pre-JDK 1.0.2). We ended up rewriting much of the book to reflect these changes.

During this process, we made every effort to describe the technology fully and accurately, but it is possible we missed something—this is simply one of the drawbacks of working on the cutting edge of new technology.

We invite you to help us find problems and improve this book. If you have an idea that could make this a more useful reference for people working with the JVM, or if you find a bug or an error in the text, please let us know by sending email to *bookquestions@ora.com.*

If we find it necessary to issue an errata for this book, or release updated examples or reference information, you'll find the updated information at *http://www.ora.com/catalog/books/javavm.*

Java Versions

This book was based on Java version 1.02. As the book goes to press, Sun is in the process of releasing JDK 1.1 in beta form. From our preliminary look at this release, there appear to be no major changes to the bytecode format or instruction set of the JVM.

On the other hand, there are new classes in the java.* packages in 1.1, and some new attributes have been added to class files to support new features such as RMI and inner classes. Specifically, an "InnerClasses" attribute has been added to the top-level class file attributes, as well as a "Synthetic" attribute for class members.

We will maintain notes about these and other changes on the Web pages *http://www.ora.com/catalog/books/javavm* and *http://www.cat.nyu.edu/meyer/jasmin.*

How to Use This Book

This book is structured into three parts. The first part contains an overview of the machine; the second part is a guide to the instruction set; and the third part is the reference section.

If you are unfamiliar with the Java Virtual Machine, you will probably want to take this book off to a peaceful place and spend some time reading the first three chapters. Later, you can come back and study the rest of the chapters in the first part.

If you are trying to familiarize yourself with the instruction set of the JVM, take a look at the second part. It contains a quick tour of all of the instructions in the JVM, along with lots of examples.

If, on the other hand, you are trying to find out a specific detail on the operation of the Java Virtual Machine instruction, you will probably find it in the third part.

To help you locate what you are looking for, below is a brief summary of the contents of each of the chapters in this book.

Overview of Machine

Chapter 1, *Overview*

> Introduces the Java Virtual Machine, explaining where it came from, why it is interesting, and what its main characteristics are. After reading this chapter, you will be all set for Chapter 2.

Chapter 2, *Quick Tour*

> Dives in and shows you the Java Virtual Machine in action. This chapter takes four example programs and explains how those programs are run by the Virtual Machine. It introduces you to Jasmin, a low-level assembler used to write programs that run on the Java Virtual Machine. After reading this chapter, you will have practical knowledge of topics such as the operand stack, local variables, class files, and method invocation,

Chapter 3, *Components of the Machine*

> This chapter takes a step back and describes each of the components of the Java Virtual Machine. It shows how the components fit together, and what they are used for. You will learn about concepts such as the constant pool, local variables, registers, data types, signatures, and garbage collection.

Chapter 4, *Classes*

> Contains an overview of how Java manages classes, and introduces the Java class file format. Since many of the Java VM instructions refer to data entities retrieved from a class file, understanding the contents of a Java class file is essential.

Chapter 5, *Security*

> Java is designed as a secure language. Read this chapter to learn more about this claim and to learn about security features in the Java Virtual Machine such as the class verifier.

Chapter 6, *Implementation Notes*

> Outlines some of the things you will need to consider if you are implementing your own Java Virtual Machine.

Instruction Guide

Chapter 7, *Data Operations*

> This chapter tells you how to create and manipulate objects and arrays using the Java Virtual Machine. You will learn more about the instructions provided for creating new arrays and objects, accessing fields, and storing and retrieving values from arrays.

Chapter 8, *Arithmetic*
> Provides an overview of the set of instructions in the JVM for manipulating numeric values. In this chapter you will learn what instructions are provided, how they are organized, and other useful facts about numerical computation using Java.

Chapter 9, *Flow Control*
> Describes all of the instructions for branching, jumping, invoking methods, and performing boolean tests. You will learn how to use subroutines, dispatch methods, and implement switch statements.

Chapter 10, *Exceptions*
> Covers the Java exception mechanism. You will learn how to throw, catch and declare exceptions. You will see how the Java interpreter handles exceptions.

Chapter 11, *Threads*
> Describes instructions not covered elsewhere in the guide section of the book, including thread monitors and debugging instructions.

Reference

Chapter 12, *Class File Reference*
> Describes the Java class file format in detail.

Chapter 13, *Instruction Reference*
> Contains an alphabetical reference for of each of the nearly 200 instructions in the Java Virtual Machine.

Appendix A, *Instructions by Function Group*
> Lists the instructions by function group.

Appendix B, *Instructions by Opcode*
> Lists the instructions by their opcode.

Appendix C, *Jasmin User Guide*
> Contains the Jasmin User Guide, which gives notes on the syntax of the Jasmin assembler.

Appendix D, *The JAS Library*
> A quick tour of JAS—a Java API for creating class files.

Conventions

The following conventions are used in this book:

`Constant Width`
> is used in examples to show contents of files or output from commands.

Constant Bold
> is used in examples to show command lines and options that should be typed literally by the user. (For example, **rm foo** means to type "rm foo" exactly as it appears in the text or the example.)

Constant Italic
> is used in examples to show variables for which a context-specific substitution should be made. (The variable *filename*, for example, would be replaced by some actual filename.)

Italic
> is used to emphasize new terms and concepts when they are introduced.

Quotes
> are used to identify code fragments in explanatory text.

Acknowledgments

A special thanks goes to Andrew Schulman, who was the editor for this book. It's hard work creating a book on a topic never written about before, and Andrew was always there with helpful advice, comments, and interesting perspectives that he dug up on the Web.

Troy Mott was the person behind the scenes who put everything together for us, and kept us awake with his constant barrage of email.

This book would not have been possible without active support and flexible hours of the New York University Media Research Laboratory (*http://www.mrl.nyu.edu*). We also would like to thank the New York University Center for Advanced Technology (*http://www.cat.nyu.edu*) for their support.

Thanks also to the staff at O'Reilly & Associates. Nicole Gipson Arigo was the production editor, project manager, and copyeditor. Frank Willison, Nancy Wolfe Kotary, and Sheryl Avruch performed quality control checks. Madeleine Newell provided production assistance. Seth Maislin wrote the index. Erik Ray, Ellen Siever, and Lenny Muellner worked with the tools to create the book. Chris Reilley fine-tuned the figures. Nancy Priest designed the interior book layout, and Edie Freedman designed the front cover.

1

Overview

Imagine you just purchased a new application from a local computer store, only to discover that in your haste you picked up the IBM PC version, and you own a Macintosh. After your initial frustration fades, you may find yourself wondering why there can't be applications that run on any computer, regardless of their make. After all, software is just a collection of bits and bytes. There isn't all that much difference between a piece of software built for a Macintosh and the same application built for a PC. It would certainly make everyone's life easier if programs came in a single version, rather than in a different version for every platform.

Next, imagine you've just copied what you thought was the latest and greatest interactive video game onto your hard drive, only to discover that the game was in reality a virus, and the contents of your hard drive are quietly being corrupted. The only way to fix this kind of catastrophe is to reinstall all of the programs and data on your computer from scratch. That takes a lot of time, and you may not be able to recover everything. Wouldn't it better if your computer had some built in protection against this malicious waste of your time?

Finally, you've got the right piece of software, and you know it's from a reliable source. Your next horror is the discovery that the computer you bought last year doesn't have enough power and space to run the behemoth application. You will need to spend money buying more RAM, a faster processor, or a bigger disk, before your system is fast enough to support all the new features in the latest version. Why is it that software seems to get bigger and slower every year?

Unfortunately, these stories are very real. They are the sorts of experiences that can happen to anyone. And they are also some of the issues that motivated the Java development team to look for a better solution.

Java Roots

Java is a programming language from Sun Microsystems. It was originally conceived, under the guidance of James Gosling and Bill Joy, by a Sun subsidiary called FirstPerson Inc. and code-named Oak. Oak was intended as a system for programming small consumer electronic devices such as Personal Digital Assistants (PDAs). Later, it was used to run "set-top boxes" for television applications. When neither of these industries really took off, Joy and Gosling found themselves with an impressive technology, but nothing to use it for.

Oak was efficient, robust (it was designed for consumer products), architecture-independent and object-oriented. Sun, whose motto is "The network is the computer," didn't take long to realize that these features were a perfect match for the Internet, which was then just beginning its startling growth and at that point had little in the way of interactive content. With a modest amount of retooling, Oak became Java, and Java has since caught on like wildfire.

The Java Language: Portable, Efficient, Secure

Java offers many tantalizing benefits to the application developer, but probably the greatest strength of Java lies not in any single design feature, but in the elegance of the overall package that the Java designers have put together.

Java is portable. You can run the same Java binary (or class file, as it's more correctly known) on a wide range of computers, from small personal computers up to million-dollar graphics supercomputers. Java's portability is no small feat, and it's something that we will talk about in more detail later in this chapter.

Java is also efficient and relatively lightweight. Java is a byte-compiled language. Byte-compiled languages are much faster than purely interpreted languages (such as JavaScript, Lingo, Perl, and Tcl), and, with work, it is possible to create implementations that run nearly as fast as fully compiled languages (like C and C++).* This means you probably won't have to buy a new computer just to use Java.

Java is a *dynamic* language. In Java, classes are loaded dynamically as they are needed, possibly even over the network. Java can extend its type system on the fly at runtime—something that C and C++ programs cannot do easily. This "late binding" means that programs only grow as large as they need to be at runtime, and it also helps maintain program modularity: Java makes fewer compiled-in assumptions about the implementation of data structures than static, early-binding languages like C or C++.

Even more important is the fact that Java was designed with security and safety in mind. Java was created in the post-Internet era, and it comes with several security layers that protect the host computer from malicious programs. The Java security model was designed to make consumers feel comfortable running programs that have been downloaded over the Internet. Of course, there are no guarantees in the security business, but it is very encouraging that Java takes such a tough stance on security issues.

Other languages offer one or two of these three features. C, for example, is efficient and (to some extent) portable. However, C has very little notion of security. It's very easy to "shoot yourself in the foot" in C, which means that it's very easy for other people to shoot you in the foot, too.

Interpreted languages such as Tcl and JavaScript,† on the other hand, have reasonable security models, and they are also portable and dynamic. But the cost of this is poor performance. Tcl and JavaScript both perform many checks at runtime, and this slows applications down considerably.

Java is one of the first dynamic languages to offer security, portability, and efficiency in a single package, and it also comes with a host of other goodies (read any good book on Java to see the full list), so Java presents an enticing alternative to application developers.

---

* Several companies are creating tools to make Java run faster, by using Just-in-Time code generation techniques or even by creating a chip specially designed to run Java bytecode quickly. There is also plenty of room for optimizing Java, and we expect that implementations will get significantly more efficient over the next few years. Even so, Java programs will never be quite as fast as C code.

† Don't confuse Java with JavaScript: Java is a byte-compiled strongly typed language from Sun Microsystems. JavaScript is a dynamically typed, fully interpreted scripting language from Netscape. Java is closer to SmallTalk and Scheme, whereas JavaScript shares more with languages like Tcl, Perl, or Lingo. JavaScript is intended to be easy for novices to script in, whereas Java is aimed more at the professional programmers community. See Netscape's home page, *http://home.netscape.com*, for more information on JavaScript.

Java and the Web

Java's design strengths certainly contribute to the huge growth in interest that Java has received recently. However, as Don Norman of Apple Computer will quickly point out, good design is, unfortunately, only one small factor when it comes to choosing what technologies society adopts.[*] Many other factors come into play. You only have to look at PAL, Beta, NeXT, or the News Windowing System to see that "better" technologies don't always win acceptance.

Fortunately, Java has a powerful ally. It's called the World Wide Web. When Netscape Inc. announced that it was going to embed Java into its World Wide Web browser, Netscape Navigator, the level of interest in Java increased dramatically. Millions of people use the World Wide Web every day, and the numbers are growing exponentially.

With a Java-enabled Web browser, Web content providers are suddenly able to embed *applets* as part of their online offerings. Applets are mini-applications written in the Java language that are downloaded over the Internet on the fly, and executed on the user's local computer. Applets can be used to create interactive data displays, animations, multimedia games, or database interfaces. They can also be used to create new kinds of Web-aware tools, which are inherently component-based and distributed. For example, you could use Java to create a sophisticated distributed planning and scheduling tool, or an agent-based assistant, or a collaborative writing tool.

The critical point is that these applications are making use of the computing resources available on the user's local computer, and not relying (as CGI scripts and several other Web mechanisms do) on distant servers to carry out the work. This fact is especially significant considering how overloaded many servers are with the crush of Web activity, and how slow most people's Internet connections are.

In this Web-based scenario, the good design decisions made by the creators of the Java language really pay off. It's now possible to create and deliver dynamic applications (i.e., applets) that run securely, efficiently, and on a wide range of platforms. Content providers can also take advantage of Java's modern feature set, including a dynamic object model, strict typing system, packages, threads, exceptions, and much more.

It also helps that major companies like Microsoft and Apple and Symantec have jumped on the Java bandwagon. Given this level of support, the Java programming language looks set to become a popular and well-established language, joining the ranks with older languages like C and C++.

---

[*] Don Norman, *The Design of Everyday Things* (Doubleday).

Even as you have been reading this chapter, several more people have probably been busy downloading a Java-enabled Web browser, and are now ready to start running Java applets.

And underlying each running Java applet, there is a Java Virtual Machine that is doing the all the running.

Java's Virtual Machine

We could continue extolling the benefits and features of the Java programming language for many more pages. However, other books serve that purpose.[*] In this book, we are going to talk about the Java Virtual Machine, which is itself a rich and complex topic. In fact, there are several of aspects of the Java language that you won't find covered in this book. For example, we won't spend much time in this book discussing Java's abstract windowing toolkit (AWT),[†] or Java's handling of strings, vectors, or hashtables, or its input/output mechanisms and networking capabilities. All of these functions are provided by the built-in class library that comes with Java, which in turn is built over the Java Virtual Machine.

In this book, we will look under the hood at the Java Virtual Machine and talk about the mechanisms and components that underlie the standard Java classes.

The Java Virtual Machine is at the core of the Java programming language. In fact, you can't run a Java program without also running an implementation of the Java Virtual Machine. The Java Virtual Machine is the name of the engine that actually executes a Java program and is the key to many of Java's features, including its portability, efficiency, and security. That's a strong claim, so let's expand on it.

Whenever you run a Java program, the instructions that make up the program are not executed directly by the hardware your system uses. Instead, a special piece of software steps through each of the instructions in the program and carries out the action that the instruction represents. In essence, Java programs are not run directly by the central processor (or CPU) in your system, but are instead run by a "virtual" processor, which is itself a piece of software running on your computer.

Virtual Processor's Instruction Set

What do instructions on this virtual processor look like? Many of the instructions are similar to the kinds of instructions you find in a real CPU. This includes the

---

[*] Some good ones are: *Exploring Java*, by Patrick Niemeyer and Joshua Peck (O'Reilly); *Java Primer Plus*, by Gabriel Torok, Troy Downing, and Paul M. Tyma (Waite Group Press); and *Java in a Nutshell*, by David Flanagan (O'Reilly).

[†] For a detailed look at AWT, see *Java AWT*, by John Zukowski (O'Reilly).

fairly typical set of instructions for arithmetic, flow control (branches and jumps), accessing elements in arrays, etc.

To give you a flavor, let's compare some 80x86 instructions with their Java equivalents. Here is the 80x86 code for storing an integer in a work register:

```
mov AX, 10    ;  store the integer 10 in register AX
```

and here is Java's equivalent:

```
bipush 10     ; push the integer constant 10 onto the stack
istore_1      ; store the integer on the top of the stack in local variable 1
```

As a second example, here is the 80x86 code to add two integers:

```
mov AX, 5     ; put the number 5 into AX
mov BX,10     ; put the number 10 into BX
add           ; add the numbers, the result is left in AX
```

and here is Java's equivalent:

```
bipush 5      ; push 5 onto the stack
bipush 10     ; push 10 onto the stack
iadd          ; add top two numbers on the stack, leave the result on the stack
istore_1      ; pop the result off of the stack and store in local variable 1
```

As you can see, Java's virtual processor is stack-based, and it uses numbered "local variables" instead of registers to store working results. But the general "feel" of the instruction set is similar to that of a standard CPU.

In practice, several of the instructions that this virtual processor provides are far more complex than those recognized by real-world processors. For example, there are around 20 instructions for manipulating Java objects (calling methods, getting and setting fields, allocating new objects, etc.), each of which is fairly involved.

Table 1-1 summarizes the categories of instructions, giving the number of instructions in each category, and lists a few examples from each category. (See Appendix A, *Instructions by Function Group*, for a reference list showing instructions by function group).

Table 1–1: Categories of instructions

Category	No. of Instructions	Examples
arithmetic operations	24	iadd, lsub, frem
logical operations	12	iand, lor, ishl
numeric conversions	15	int2short, f2l, d2I

Table 1–1: Categories of instructions (continued)

Category	No. of Instructions	Examples
pushing constants	20	bipush, sipush, ldc, iconst_0, fconst_1
stack manipulation	9	pop, pop2, dup, dup2
flow control instructions	28	goto, ifne, ifge, if_null, jsr, ret
managing local variables	52	astore, istore, aload, iload, aload_0
manipulating arrays	17	aastore, bastore, aaload, baload
creating objects and arrays	4	new, newarray, anewarray, multianewarray
object manipulation	6	getfield, putfield, getstatic, putstatic
method call and return	10	invokevirtual, invokestatic, areturn
miscellaneous	5	throw, monitorenter, breakpoint, nop

Take the multianewarray instruction, which allocates memory for a new multi-dimensional array and initializes the array's elements to zero. As a side effect of using this instruction, objects may get moved around in memory to make room for the new arrays, or, in certain cases, a new Java class may get dynamically loaded from disk. This level of complexity is considerably greater than any single instruction found on a Pentium class CPU. In fact, implementing multianewarray probably requires dozens of Pentium-level instructions, as well as support for things like garbage collection, exception handling, and loading classes from disk.

So Java's virtual processor is more than just a software implementation of a chip. As you will learn, a whole set of interconnected mechanisms are needed to support the virtual processor and run Java programs, and these mechanisms collectively define what's known as the Java Virtual Machine.

Bytecode Interpreters, Runtime Systems

Having gotten this far, it's worth clarifying some terminology. In this book, an implementation of a Java Virtual Machine is usually referred to as a *Java runtime system.* Netscape Navigator, Microsoft Explorer, and other Java-enabled applications all have Java runtime systems embedded within them.

A typical runtime system will include:

execution engine
> the virtual (or maybe even hardware) processor for executing the bytecode in Java methods

memory manager
> for allocating memory for instances and arrays and performing garbage collections

error and exception manager
> for dealing with catching and throwing exceptions

native method support
> for calling C or C++ methods

threads interface
> for supporting threads and monitors

class loader
> for dynamically loading Java classes from Java class files

security manager
> for verifying that classes are safe and controlling access to system resources

In addition, closely coupled to a each JVM implementation is a collection of standard Java classes, which include support for things like strings, numbers, files, and so on. Of these, around 20 are implementation-dependent Java classes that provide support for accessing resources such as the network, the windowing system, threads, and the local filesystem. They act as a Java program's gateway to the underlying operating system, and they contain many native methods (typically implemented in C and closely coupled with the JVM), which are used to call routines provided by the host system. This combination of a JVM and a collection of standard libraries of classes accounts for much of Java's portability.

If you are interested in learning more about the components that make up the Java Virtual Machine, see Chapter 3, *Components of the Machine.*

Why Use a Virtual Machine?

The concept of a virtual machine is hardly new. IBM coined the term in 1959 to describe their pionerring VM operating system. In the 1970s, the SmallTalk programming environment took this to a new level, implementing a virtual machine which supported a very high level object-oriented abstraction of the underlying computer.

Virtual machines have many advantages. They are great for portability. You only have to port the virtual machine and associated support libraries to a new architecture once, and then all of the applications built on top of the virtual machine run unchanged. In SmallTalk, for example, the virtual machine has been ported to numerous computing platforms, and is robust enough that you can save a SmallTalk session on yout HP workstation running HP-UX (Hewlett Packard's version of the UNIX operating system) and restart the same session on a Macintosh running MacOS. For sceptics, I recommend that you try this yourself—when you see the same windows popping up on the Mac that you previously had on the UNIX system, it's impressive.

Another advantage of virtual machines is that they add a layer of abstraction and protection between your computer and the software you run on the computer. With a virtual machine, it's easy to insert protections that prevent a program carrying out malicious acts, such as deleting files on your disk or corrupting memory.

Fully Interpreted Languages

Critics may point out that fully interpreted languages (like Tcl and JavaScript) also have these two benefits of portability and safety. However, there is an important difference between interpreted languages and languages based on a virtual machine. In an interpreted language, the basic representation for a program is textual. To run a program, the interpreter steps through the source code parsing it on the fly. For example, here is the beginning of a Tcl interpreter, written (of course) in Tcl:

```
proc interpreter() {
    while {1} {
        # get next line of program
        set line [get_next_line]

        # parse $line, splitting it into the command name and the arguments
        set command [get_first_word $line]
        set arguments [all_but_first_word $line]

        if {$command == "puts"} {
            puts $arguments ; # print out a message
        }
        #
        # ... insert many more test cases here
        #
         else if {$command == "exit"} {
            return ; # last test case - finished with this program
        }
    }
}
```

As you can see, the interpreter essentially looks at each line of code and performs a series of string comparisions, looking for strings that match certain patterns. When a match is found, some code is executed. Then the next line of code is examined, and so on. In the example above, only very simple programs can be executed—programs containing just puts and exit:

```
puts hello
puts goodbye
exit
```

Implementing an interpreter like this is incredibly easy—you can create a fairly complete high level programming language in an afternoon, using just a few hundred lines of code. Spend a little more time, and you can add error checking, conditionals, file handling, etc.

Unfortunately interpreted programs run very slowly. Consider the following expression:

```
set a [expr cos($angle) * sqrt([magnitude $x $y])]
```

The overhead of parsing this string correctly and determining what it means is probably far greater than the amount of work it takes to actually perform the math involved. In informal tests, Tcl can be up to 200 times slower than C. In some applications, this is not a problem, and there are many good reasons for using an interpreted language like Tcl as a scripting tool. For more complex programs, the slow performance of interpreted languages effectively rules them out, and you have to resort to a more sophisticated tool.

Byte-Compiled Languages

Languages based on a virtual machine typically run faster than fully interpreted languages, because they often employ a bytecode architecture.

The idea is to divide running a program into two steps. In the first step, you parse the program text, perform some analysis, and determine what underlying virtual machine instructions are needed to execute the program. You output this information in an efficient data representation. This is done once, before running the program, either dynamically (in the case of SmallTalk), or as a separate process using a standalone batch compiler (as with Java). Often, byte-based representations are used and hence the name "bytecode." Other representations can also be used—these are often called P-code (short for program code) representations.

Then, in the second step, you iterate over the data (i.e., bytecode) produced by your first step, executing the virtual machine instructions involved. For example, here is an example (written in Java-like code) of a bytecode compiler for the same language we saw earlier:

```
//
// Takes as input an array of strings that contains the program being compiled.
// Uses the append() method to append bytes to the -bytecode-.
// (bytecode is a Vector holding bytes).
//
public static void compile(String lines[]) {
    for (i = 0; i < lines.length. i++) {
        String command = firstWord(lines[i]);  // parse string and
                                                // get command name.
        String argument = otherWords(lines[i]);// get command parameters.

        if (command.equals("puts")) {
            // output bytecode for the PUTS command
            bytecode.append(OPC_PUTS);

            // now output the length of the string that follows puts
            // (in this interpreter, we don't have variables or expressions
            // yet - so this is very basic!)
            bytecode.append(argument.length);  // (string length must be < 256)
            // now output the bytes in the string...
            for (c = 0; c < argument.length; c++) { // bytes in string
                bytecode.append(argument[c]);
            }
        }
        //
        // many more cases go in here
        //
        else if (command.equals("exit")) {
            // output bytecode that tells the interpreter to return
            bytecode.append(OPC_EXIT);
        }
    }
}
```

Now that we have a simple bytecode compiler, let's look at how the interpreter for our very simple virtual machine might work:

```
public static void execute(byte bytecode[]) {
    int pc = 0;     // my 'program counter'
    while (true) {
        int opcode = bytecode[pc];    // get an instruction (or 'opcode')
                                      // from bytecode
        switch (opcode) {             // and switch on its type
        case OPC_PUTS: // Virtual Machine instruction to print a string

            // next byte is a length
            int len = bytecode[pc + 1];

            // print out -len- bytes from the bytecode
            for (i = 1; i <= len; i++) { printChar(bytecode[pc + i]); }
            // force pc to advance to the next instruction in bytecode
            pc = pc + len + 1;
            break; // done
```

```
        // many more cases ...

        case OPC_EXIT: // return from program
            return;
        }
    }
}
```

Our example bytecode interpreter steps through each byte in the bytecode, figures out what instruction the byte represents, possibly takes some extra data from the bytecode, and then carries out the action required. Each time an instruction is executed, the pc (the index keeping track of where you are in the program) is updated to point to the next instruction.

Incidentally, if you went and looked at the bytecode interpreter implementation inside Sun's initial Java runtime system, you might be surprised at how similar it is to the code shown above. The most significant difference is that Sun's interpreter is written in C, and its switch statement is much longer since it has to support the nearly 200 different instructions that make up the virtual machine. Chapter 6, *Implementation Notes*, describes implementation issues in more detail.

Languages based on bytecode interpreters (also known as "semi-compiled" languages, since they are half-way between fully interpreted and fully compiled languages) can be an order of magnitude faster than their fully interpreted cousins. They usually approach speeds in the range of 10 to 20 times slower than C. Given some of the other advantages that languages based on virtual machines offer, that figure is acceptable.

Drawbacks of Virtual Machines

If virtual machines are so all-powerful, you might ask why they are not more common. In fact, they are probably more common than you think. If you have ever used an Apple PowerMac, the chances are you've run some pieces of software using the PowerMac's 68000 emulation mode, which is a form of virtual machine. Similarly, a DOS application in OS/2 or UNIX is also a kind of virtual machine. A surprising number of commercial products have bytecode-interpreter style components to them (e.g., the font rasterizers in TrueType and the Adobe Type Manager are both based on bytecode interpreters). Still, these are special cases. To date, most of the popular programming languages are not based on virtual machines.

One reason that virtual machines aren't a holy panacea for programmers is that they add a lot of additional complexity to a runtime system. Designing, implementing, porting, bug-fixing, tuning, and maintaining a VM-based language is a pretty hefty amount of work. Porting in particular can be arduous, since virtual machines are often very exacting. The Java VM, for example, expects the underlying computer to support 32-bit and 64-bit IEEE floating point numbers and "long long" integers (64-bit integers). Most platforms do, but for the few that don't, porting Java will be extra work.

Social factors must also be taken into consideration. It took several years before C++ (or even ANSI C) procured a large following. Resistance to change is high, especially when the change involves added complexity and reduced speed.

A critical drawback of VM-based languages is that they are not as fast as fully compiled languages. The VM adds a layer between the application and the physical hardware in the computer, and this slows the application down. Given how precious computing resources are, it's not surprising people have shied away from using virtual machines. Yes, a bytecode-interpreted language may only be a few times times slower than C, but it is still slower than C.

Still, it wasn't all that long ago when similar comparisons were made between C and a hand-coded assembly. Most people these days do not program using a hand-coded assembly, which encourages us to believe that as computers get faster, the advantages of using a virtual machine architecture will start to outweigh the performance cost. The day when most programmers are using a dynamic high level language with a virtual machine architecture may be nearer than you think.

Besides, the Java designers added a few more tricks to their virtual machine, as you'll see in the next section.

Magic Beans—Java's Verifier

If other high-level languages based on virtual machines have not won favor, what is different about Java's approach that means that it will do any better?

If there is one clear answer to this question, it's the Java verifier.

Consider the toy bytecode interpreter we looked at earlier. Everything works fine if the bytecode data fed into the interpreter is formatted correctly and the interpreter is also implemented properly. But what happens if the bytecode isn't formatted correctly? For example, what happens if the length of the string stored after the OPC_PUTS instruction is incorrect? Several things could happen: the interpreter could crash, it could print out strange things, or it could by some fluke appear to run everything correctly.

One of the reasons for using a virtual machine is added security. Having the interpreter crash or execute random code because of a badly formatted program is a very serious problem. An obvious way around that is to insert lots of runtime type checks to catch errors that result from badly formatted bytecode, or badly written programs. This approach works well and has been used extensively in bytecode interpreter implementations. SmallTalk, for example, performs numerous runtime checks, making sure, for instance, that each time you carry out a mathematical computation the arguments are indeed valid number types and not instances of some other object class. The VM code for an add must do something along the lines of:

```
if (isinteger(num1) && isinteger(num2)) {
    result = num1 + num2;
} else {
    signal_error();
}
```

The big problem with this approach is that checks slow the system down, and you end up stuck back in the familiar "secure, portable, but slow" domain.

The Java designers opted for another approach. When they were developing the instruction set used by the Java Virtual Machine, they kept two goals in mind. One was to design an instruction set that was simple enough that parts of it could be optimized using hardware (more on this later). The other was to develop an instruction set that was *verifiable*.

In Java, just after a class file is retrieved from disk (or over the Internet), the interpreter can run a "verifier" on it to check that the structure of the class file is correct. The verifier checks all aspects of the class file—it checks that the file has the right magic number, and that all the records in the file are the right length. More importantly, the verifier also runs a "bytecode verifier" that checks that the bytecodes that make up each method in the class are safe to run.

The bytecode verifier is a type of theorem prover. It steps through the bytecode, applying a number of simple rules to determine how the bytecode behaves. For example, it knows that when the bipush instruction is used, then the top item left on the stack will be an integer. If the next instruction is an fneg instruction, the verifier will signal an error, since fneg is used to negate a float.

Knowing this, it's easy to see why the Java Virtual Machine has a comparatively large instruction set. For each different primitive type in Java, there is a set of instructions that operate only with that type. For example, there are separate isub, fsub, dsub, and lsub instructions for subtracting integers, floats, doubles and longs.

Since the resulting bytecode contains so much type information, the theorem prover can (and does) perform a lot of checking at verification time, and then this checking does not need to be carried out by the bytecode interpreter when it is executing the code. In fact, Java performs very little type-checking at runtime. This means it is possible to write arithmetic expressions in Java which are computed nearly as efficiently as in C. For example, to add two floats together, the JVM does something like:

```
(float)stack[-1] += (float)stack[0]; // add top float to second float on stack
stack--;                             // and discard the top float on the stack.
```

This has eliminated the conditional that was needed in the SmallTalk case.

Notice that Java doesn't *require* that the verifier be run on a class file. It is up to the runtime system to decide whether a particular class file needs verification first. If the runtime system decides *not* to verify a class and that class contains methods with invalid bytecode, the runtime system behaves just as you would expect: it crashes miserably. In current implementations, the verifier is run on all classes that are downloaded over the Internet, but not by default on classes that are loaded from a local disk.

Really Fast Java

Even with a verifier, a well-designed instruction set, and an interpreter written in C, current Java interpreters are still not *really* fast. This is likely to change. Several factors are likely to increase the speed of Java programs.

First, the implementations of Java runtime systems are likely to become significantly faster, as vendors spend more time tuning and optimizing their code. Existing Java interpreters have not yet been optimized fully. For example, in Sun's 1.0.2 runtime system, a reference to an object is implemented as a pointer to a handle that points to the object. This means that to retrieve a field from an object, the C code does something like:

```
reference->handle->object->data
```

Microsoft's Java implementation uses a simpler approach (and others are sure to follow). A reference to an object is a pointer to that object. This means that in Microsoft's implementation, to get a field from an object, the C code does:

```
reference->object->data
```

This may not seem like a significant change, until you consider that the extra level of indirection created by using handles slows down every field access or update. If this access or update is happening in a tight loop, the speed difference between these approaches quickly becomes significant.

From an implementation standpoint, also likely to improve are the algorithms used for things such as garbage collection, memory allocation, method lookup, and so on. This will lead to faster implementations down the road.

Also down the road is hardware acceleration. A number of companies, including Sun, have announced plans to build a chip that speeds up Java execution. These chips are being created specifically to run Java bytecode quickly—essentially they will be hardware implementations of a Java interpreter. This is something that the Java designers always planned for, and it explains why they chose to use such a low-level instruction set for the Java VM.

Before everyone rushes out to buy a JavaPC, however, there is help at hand for users of existing processors. The latest Java implementations are now employing what's being called "Just-in-Time" code generation. Just-in-Time (JIT) code generators take the Java bytecode for a method and finish the last stage of the compile— they convert the Java bytecode into the corresponding native code. This happens just before the method is run for the first time (hence the name). The resulting native code then can be executed directly and can run faster than code that is interpreted using a switch statement.

Even so, JIT-compiled Java code still can't quite compete with fully compiled C code. C compilers can take full advantage of the architecture-specific features, whereas Java JIT code generators have to live with some of the design constraints of the the Java VM. For example, many JVM instructions make use of the operand stack to store temporary values. C compilers are more likely to use registers to hold temporary values, since accessing registers is more efficient than accessing a stack stored in memory. Compiled C code is likely to achieve better register usage than JIT-compiled Java, and therefore have a speed advantage. Nevertheless, JIT code generators are likely to reduce the performance gap between Java and C, possibly to a factor less than 5.

If you want to learn more about implementation issues, see Chapter 6.

JVM Shortcomings

Software design involves tradeoffs, and Java is no exception. Since we are looking at the overall nature of the machine, let's take a brief detour to examine some of the less-than-ideal features of the JVM architecture.

Non-Orthogonal Instruction Set

The JVM uses an 8-bit instruction opcode, and in eight bits you can only encode 256 instructions. Consequently, instruction opcodes are in short supply. There aren't enough instruction opcodes to go around, so in the JVM some datatypes (notably shorts, bytes, and chars) are relegated to second class status, and receive less support in the instruction set than other types. This asymmetry makes programming and implementing the JVM more complex.

Lack of orthogonality is hardly a show-stopper; most hardware processors suffer from similar idiosyncrasies. But it is a dent in Java's otherwise clean design.

Hard to Extend

Another drawback of the small instruction opcode size in the JVM is that there is little room for expanding the instruction set. For example, extending the machine to support 96-bit or 128-bit floats and longs cannot be done by simply adding more instructions to the instruction set—a more involved approach would be needed. Fortunately, there are still some unused opcodes, so the JVM team can always add an "escape" opcode and create an extended instruction set.

No Parse Tree

The bytecode representation used by the JVM is simple and flat. By the time a Java method has been converted into bytecode, much of the higher-level information about the structure of the original method is lost. For example, the bytecode does not record information about the lexical blocks in the method, or flow control through the blocks (loops, conditionals, etc.).

This is unfortunate. In a typical compiled language, this sort of structural information plays an important role during optimization, since it allows the compiler to reason about dependencies and flow control. Because method structure is not recorded in class files, it is much harder to write Just-in-Time code generators that perform optimizations to take full advantage of platform-specific features.

Interested readers should look at *http://www.ics.uci.edu/~juice* for a discussion of a system which uses a much richer representation to encode programs.

Doesn't Have <Insert Your Favorite Feature>

Java is still new technology, and many of the features that are found in <your favorite high level language> have yet to become available in Java. This means that porting some languages to the Java Virtual Machine will be hard or impossible.

One particularly frustrating shortcoming in the current version of Java is the lack of "weak references"—references to objects which don't get noticed by the garbage collector. Weak references are very useful if you want to maintain information about an object, but don't want to prevent the object from becoming garbage collected when no one else is using it. They come in especially handy when you are creating persistent databases. (The Java team promises to add weak references in future versions). Another shortcoming is the lack of function closures, such as you find in Scheme.

Some vendors are likely to pick up on these and other shortcomings, and extend their implementations to support additional bells and whistles. In addition, the JavaSoft development team has stated its intention to consider bounded extensions to the JVM to provide better support for languages other than Java.

Uses of the Virtual Machine

Now that you have some idea of what the Java Virtual Machine is, it's worth stepping back a little and looking at some of the things you can and can't do with the Java Virtual Machine.

Bear in mind that, although the Java Virtual Machine was designed specifically to run programs written in the Java programming language, there is nothing preventing you from generating your own Java class files (using a mechanism other than the Java compiler) and running them on a virtual machine. In fact, you can think of the JVM as a new type of computer, with a large and growing installed base. This computer is efficient, dynamic, and net-aware. The default programming tool for this new computer is Java, just as the default programming tool for a UNIX computer is C. Just as some problems call for languages other than C, there will be situations where using something other than Java makes sense on the Java Virtual Machine.

So one thing you can do with the Java Virtual Machine is use it as the target for a compiler. In fact, the Ada programming language has already been ported to the Java Virtual Machine—see *http://www.inmet.com/~stt/adajava_paper* for details.

This isn't the only way you can make use of the Java Virtual Machine. The JVM lets you create new tools for solving programming problems in Java. The Java architecture is very open—it's easy to add programmatic extensions to Java, once you have learned the basic rules of the Java Virtual Machine. And the Java Virtual Machine is portable, so you only have to write the extension once.

For example, if you don't like how a particular feature of the Java language works, you could create an extension library which operates in the way you need it to. It's not as hard as you might think, once you've learned about the machine. Let's say your application has a lot of matrix manipulation code in it—you probably want to write the matrix equations using operators like *, +, / and −. But Java doesn't let you override these operators. The solution? Create a parser that directly compiles matrix expressions into efficient JVM code. You can then call the resulting methods from any Java program, using any JVM implementation.

Alternatively, you might be writing a rule-based application and want to express the rules using easy-to-read syntax. Create a JVM interface that lets you do this quickly, elegantly, and efficiently.

In another scenario, you could create a scripting language which gets converted into JVM. You can use Java and the JVM to create new classes dynamically, on-the-fly, so you could develop authoring tools that let your users create their own scripts and run them directly on the JVM.

In short, the JVM lets you create applications that include operator overloading, user-extensible syntax words, dynamic generation of classes and methods, and much more. You can overcome design features of the Java language, or even create your own languages. And because of the architecture of the Java Virtual Machine, you can do this simply, portably and efficiently. Your work will be accessible from any Java application, in any Java interpreter on nearly any computer.

2

Quick Tour

After the somewhat abstract discussion in Chapter 1, *Overview*, we are now going to dive in, look at some JVM code, and get our virtual hands dirty. This chapter gives you a quick introduction to programming the Java Virtual Machine. It contains the code for four example classes—HelloWorld, Count, HelloWeb, and Malign—shown in Java code and also in the underlying JVM assembly code (using the Jasmin assembler provided with this book), along with detailed explanations.

The chapter introduces a number of important concepts—such as local variables, the operand stack, method invocation, and object initialization—which are covered in more details in later chapters in the book.

After reading this chapter, you will be in a good position to start writing small programs in Jasmin and incorporating them in your applications, and you will also understand more about the components of the Java Virtual Machine and how they fit together.

Hello World!

Consider the canonical Hello World program written in Java:[*]

```
public class HelloWorld {
    public static void main(String args[]) {
        System.out.println("Hello World!");
    }
}
```

---

[*] Section 1 of *Java in a Nutshell* (written by David Flanagan, published by O'Reilly & Associates) gives the same example program along with a fuller explanation.

This program, like every standalone Java program, contains a class definition that supplies a public static main() method. The Java system starts executing the program by calling the main() method. The body of main() contains a single line:

```
System.out.println("HelloWorld!");
```

This line of Java code obtains the object in the field System.out, and calls that object's println method to print out the message:

```
"Hello World!"
```

Before this program can be run by Java, you must first compile it. In Sun's Java Developers Kit (JDK) you use javac[*] to compile Java programs. Save the code in a file called "HelloWorld.java" and then, at the command line prompt, type:

```
% javac HelloWorld.java
```

javac converts Java source code into ".class" files that contain the Java bytecode for the class. As you learned in Chapter 1, bytecode is the name used for Java Virtual Machine instructions when they are encoded as a sequence of binary bytes. The Java runtime system includes an execution engine which knows how to execute the VM instructions contained in the bytecode.

You run the program by typing:

```
% java HelloWorld
Hello World!
```

Now that we have written and run a small Java program, let's look under the hood and see what the class file actually contains and how it is handled by the JVM.

Inside the Class File

The HelloWorld.class file contains all the data about HelloWorld needed by the Java runtime system. The following listing shows the hexadecimal bytes in the file:

```
% dumpfile HelloWorld.class
0000 | CA FE BA BE 00 03 00 2D 00 20 08 00 1D 07 00 0E | ........-.......
0010 | 07 00 16 07 00 1E 07 00 1C 09 00 05 00 0B 0A 00 | ...............
0020 | 03 00 0A 0A 00 02 00 09 0C 00 0C 00 15 0C 00 1A | ...............
0030 | 00 1F 0C 00 14 00 1B 01 00 07 70 72 69 6E 74 6C | .........printl
0040 | 6E 01 00 0D 43 6F 6E 73 74 61 6E 74 56 61 6C 75 | n...ConstantValu
0050 | 65 01 00 13 6A 61 76 61 2F 69 6F 2F 50 72 69 6E | e...java/io/Prin
0060 | 74 53 74 72 65 61 6D 01 00 0A 45 78 63 65 70 74 | tStream...Except
0070 | 69 6F 6E 73 01 00 0F 4C 69 6E 65 4E 75 6D 62 65 | ions...LineNumbe
0080 | 72 54 61 62 6C 65 01 00 0A 53 6F 75 72 63 65 46 | rTable...SourceF
0090 | 69 6C 65 01 00 0E 4C 6F 63 61 6C 56 61 72 69 61 | ile...LocalVaria
00a0 | 62 6C 65 73 01 00 04 43 6F 64 65 01 00 03 6F 75 | bles...Code...ou
00b0 | 74 01 00 15 28 4C 6A 61 76 61 2F 6C 61 6E 67 2F | t...(Ljava/lang/
```

---

[*] If you're using a Java development package from another vendor, follow your vendor's instructions.

```
00c0 | 53 74 72 69 6E 67 3B 29 56 01 00 10 6A 61 76 61 | String;)V...java
00d0 | 2F 6C 61 6E 67 2F 4F 62 6A 65 63 74 01 00 04 6D | /lang/Object...m
00e0 | 61 69 6E 01 00 0F 48 65 6C 6C 6F 57 6F 72 6C 64 | ain...HelloWorld
00f0 | 2E 6A 61 76 61 01 00 16 28 5B 4C 6A 61 76 61 2F | .java...([Ljava/
0100 | 6C 61 6E 67 2F 53 74 72 69 6E 67 3B 29 56 01 00 | lang/String;)V..
0110 | 06 3C 69 6E 69 74 3E 01 00 15 4C 6A 61 76 61 2F | .<init>...Ljava/
0120 | 69 6F 2F 50 72 69 6E 74 53 74 72 65 61 6D 3B 01 | io/PrintStream;.
0130 | 00 10 6A 61 76 61 2F 6C 61 6E 67 2F 53 79 73 74 | ..java/lang/Syst
0140 | 65 6D 01 00 0C 48 65 6C 6C 6F 20 57 6F 72 6C 64 | em...Hello World
0150 | 21 01 00 0A 48 65 6C 6C 6F 57 6F 72 6C 64 01 00 | !...HelloWorld..
0160 | 03 28 29 56 00 01 00 04 00 03 00 00 00 00 00 02 | .()V...........
0170 | 00 09 00 17 00 19 00 01 00 13 00 00 00 25 00 02 | .............%..
0180 | 00 01 00 00 00 09 B2 00 06 12 01 B6 00 08 B1 00 | ................
0190 | 00 00 01 00 10 00 00 00 0A 00 02 00 00 00 05 00 | ................
01a0 | 08 00 03 00 01 00 1A 00 1F 00 01 00 13 00 00 00 | ................
01b0 | 1D 00 01 00 01 00 00 00 05 2A B7 00 07 B1 00 00 | .........*......
01c0 | 00 01 00 10 00 00 00 06 00 01 00 00 00 01 00 01 | ................
01d0 | 00 11 00 00 00 02 00 18                         | ........
```

As you can see, the class file isn't huge (less than 500 bytes), but it's hard to see how this class file relates to the program we typed in earlier. Looking at this listing, you can see several meaningful pieces of data—for example, the "Hello World!" string appears at byte 0x144, and the file starts with the bytes 0xCAFEBABE—a special number identifying the file as a Java class file. But it's hard to really figure out what this data means—it's intended to be read by a computer, not a person! In Chapter 4, *Classes*, there is a detailed breakdown of the data in a class file. For now, let's use the Sun JDK's javap program to disassemble the class file and look at the Virtual Machine instructions it contains. Typing:

```
% javap -c HelloWorld
```

produces a textual description of the class file contents. The "-c" option tells javap to show the Java assembly code in the methods in the file. You will see output like:

```
Compiled from HelloWorld.java
public class HelloWorld extends java.lang.Object {
    public static void main(java.lang.String []);
    public HelloWorld();

Method void main(java.lang.String [])
   0 getstatic #7 <Field java.lang.System.out Ljava/io/PrintStream;>
   3 ldc #1 <String "Hello World!">
   5 invokevirtual #6 <Method java.io.PrintStream.println(Ljava/lang/String;)V>
   8 return

Method HelloWorld()
   0 aload_0
   1 invokespecial #8 <Method java.lang.Object.<init>()V>
   4 return

}
```

Here you can see the class's methods, along with a textual printout of the Java Virtual Machine instructions that make up each method. Surprisingly, the class file contains two methods, even though the original Java program only contained a main() method. The second method in the file, HelloWorld(), contains code to initialize instances of HelloWorld. For historical reasons, in the JVM these methods are known as *instance initialization* methods. In the Java language they are known as constructor methods.

In this case the HelloWorld() constructor uses invokespecial to call java.lang.Object's constructor and then returns—i.e., HelloWorld does not do any initialization itself. All concrete classes contain an instance initialization method (even if it does nothing, as this one does). If you don't define a constructor in your Java code, the `javac` compiler supplies one for you.

Before examining the JVM code for HelloWorld more closely, we are going to rewrite the same program, but this time using Jasmin.

Why Jasmin?

Jasmin is a free Java assembler provided on disk with this book—it is a tool for constructing class files from textual descriptions. Unlike `javap`, which takes a class file and prints out a textual representation of the JVM code in the class file, Jasmin goes the other way—it takes a textual description of a class written using the Java Virtual Machine instruction set and converts this into binary class files. This sort of tool is called an assembler,[*] and equivalent programs exist for most CPUs. Unfortunately, Sun has not defined a standard Java assembler syntax and does not provide an assembler with the JDK, so for the purposes of including examples in this book, we created our own assember.

Using Jasmin, you can try any of the JVM instructions listed in the back of this book. Jasmin also lets you explore the Java Virtual Machine without certain restrictions imposed by the Java language—for example, using Jasmin you can construct "illegal" Java classes and see how a Java runtime system handles them. We will examine such a class later in this chapter.

Jasmin has a simple and readable syntax, and there is usually a close correspondence between what you type in a Jasmin file and what is output in the resulting Java class file. `javap`, on the other hand, tries to present the data in the class file in a way that makes sense to people familiar with the Java programming language, and as a result there are a number of minor differences between the output of `javap` and what you type in Jasmin.

---

[*] There is also a freely available disassembler which takes Java class files and outputs Jasmin syntax. See *http://mrl.nyu.edu/meyer/jasmin*.

HelloWorld in Jasmin

The following listing shows the HelloWorld class written for Jasmin.

```
.class public HelloWorld
.super java/lang/Object

; specify the constructor method for the Example class

.method public <init>()V
    ; just call Object's constructor
    aload_0
    invokespecial java/lang/Object/<init>()V
    return
.end method

; specify the "main" method - this prints "Hello World"

.method public static main([Ljava/lang/String;)V
    ; set limits used by this method
    .limit stack 2

    ; Push the output stream and the string "Hello World" onto the stack,
    ; then invoke the println method:
    getstatic java/lang/System/out Ljava/io/PrintStream;
    ldc "Hello World!"
    invokevirtual java/io/PrintStream/println(Ljava/lang/String;)V

    return
.end method
```

The program looks in many respects like the output from javap in the previous section—you can see the same VM instructions (aload_0, getstatic, return, ...), although Jasmin requires some additional directives (such as the ".limit stack 2" directive) which are not shown in the output generated by javap.

Compiling Jasmin Programs

To compile the Jasmin version of the HelloWorld class, you will first need to install Jasmin—see the README file on the accompanying disk for directions. Then type the above code into a file called "HelloWorld.j", and type the command:

```
% jasmin HelloWorld.j
```

to assemble the program into a Java class file. Running Jasmin produces a new file:

```
HelloWorld.class
```

containing the Java class file for the HelloWorld class. This class file contains the same information as was produced by the Java-compiled version of HelloWorld shown earlier. It is an efficient binary representation of the Java class described by the Jasmin text file. Chapter 4 gives an overview of the class file format used for class files.

You can run the program by typing:

```
% java HelloWorld
Hello World!
```

When you type "java HelloWorld", java looks for a file called HelloWorld.class and loads the class defined in that file. It then looks in that class for method called a "main", and runs that method. The main method is the method you use to start your program—or, in this case, print out a message.

It's a good idea when developing JVM programs to run them using the "-verify" option:

```
% java -verify HelloWorld
Hello World!
```

Giving the "-verify" option to the java command tells it to "verify" the classes it loads and ensure that they are structurally sound. By default, java only verifies classes that are loaded dynamically through a class loader (such as classes obtained over the Net), so classes loaded off a local disk are not checked. The "-verify" option forces java to verify all classes. This is a particularly good idea when testing JVM programs since, without the "-verify" flag, Java will execute programs with almost no checking, and any typos or mistakes in the code are likely to cause the Java process to crash. See Chapter 5, *Security*, for more on class file verification.

A Note on Loading

How does the Java system locate the class files for a particular class? The exact details will vary slightly from one Java vendor to another, but the general picture is the same.

When you reference a class, Java searches for its class file in a number of locations:

1. the current directory (i.e., the directory you were in when you started Java)
2. the Java distribution's class directory or class zip file (e.g., */usr/java/classes/*, *c:\java\classes.zip*)
3. directories and zip files listed in the CLASSPATH environment variable
4. (for applets) in <URL>/<classname>.class, where <URL> is the Uniform Resource Locator of the parent directory for the Web document the applet was on, or the value of the CODEBASE parameter for the applet, if given

Classes are expected to be within a directory hierarchy that corresponds to the package they are in. So the class java.lang.String would be found in *java/lang/String.class* (or *java\lang\String.class* on Windows systems).

Most Java systems can look for classes within zip files. "zip" is an archive format, much like the UNIX "tar" file format. A single zip file can contain many archived files, each stored either as compressed or uncompressed data (Sun's Java expects the data to be stored uncompressed). The zip format supports long filenames, making zip an especially useful tool on platforms such as DOS that don't support long filenames.

HelloWorld, Line by Line

In this section, we'll look at each of the instructions and directives that make up the HelloWorld class.

Header Lines

The first two lines of HelloWorld contain information about the class defined in the file. The first line:

```
.class public HelloWorld
```

is a Jasmin directive that tells Jasmin the name of the class that is being defined. The "public" keyword declares the HelloWorld class as public—the definitions HelloWorld contains can be accessed from other classes and other packages. See *Java in a Nutshell* by David Flanagan (published by O'Reilly) for details about public, private, protected, and other class access keywords.

The second line:

```
.super java/lang/Object
```

indicates that the HelloWorld class is extending the java.lang.Object class—that is, the HelloWorld class is a subclass of the Object class, and inherits methods and fields from it. The Object class is the most primitive class in Java. See *Java in a Nutshell* for more on Object and other classes in Java.

The <init> Method

The first method in HelloWorld is:

```
.method public <init>()V
    ; just call Object's constructor
    aload_0
    invokespecial java/lang/Object/<init>()V
    return
.end method
```

This is an *instance initialization method* for the class—a method called to initialize a new instance of the class. Java constructors all appear at the JVM level as instance initialization methods with the special name <init>. The name <init> is not a valid identifier name in the Java programming language—so Java programmers cannot invoke instance initialization methods directly. The Java language's new keyword automatically generates a call to the appropriate <init> method. At the JVM level, you must do this manually using the invokespecial instruction. See Chapter 7, *Data Operations*, for more details on creating and initializing objects in Java.

The first line of the <init> method is:

```
.method public <init>()V
```

This indicates several things about the method. First, note that it is defined as a "public" method. In Java this means that anyone can call the method—the method is "visible" to all classes and all packages. There are several levels of visibility in Java, as shown in Table 2-1.

Table 2–1: Java visibility modifiers

Modifier	Description
public	available to any class
private	only available inside class
protected	available inside class, one of its subclasses, or in the package the class is defined
private protected	available inside class, or one of its subclasses

After the "public" keyword is the strange label:

```
<init>()V
```

This is actually a two-part token. The first part, "<init>," is the name of the method being defined. The second part, "()V,", is the *type descriptor* for the method.

A type descriptor is a specially formatted string that you use to convey type information to the JVM. For methods, the type descriptor indicates the types of the arguments and return result. In this case, the "()V" means that the <init> method takes no arguments and returns no result (the V stands for Void). See Chapter 4 for a description of type descriptors in Java.

Java supports classes with multiple constructors that take different arguments. For example, you could have:

```
.method public <init>(Ljava/lang/String;)
    ...
.end method
```

which defines a constructor that takes one argument—an instance of java.lang.String. See the instruction reference page for new for an example of using a non-default constructor.

The Body of <init>

The constructor method in the HelloWorld class contains three instructions:

```
aload_0
invokespecial java/lang/Object/<init>()V
return
```

aload_0 pushes the contents of local variable 0 onto the operand stack.

In the JVM, each method invocation has its own set of local variables. The local variables are used to store the arguments that the method was called with, and are also used to store partial results and other useful values—local variables are a bit like registers on a hardware CPU.

Each method invocation also has its own private "operand stack." The operand stack is used to pass data to JVM instructions and also to collect the results of an operation. For example, arithmetic instructions in the JVM such as iadd, imul, idiv, fadd, fmul, fdiv, etc. all take two arguments from the operand stack, perform a computation and then push the result back onto the operand stack, for use by subsequent instructions. There are a collection of instructions in the JVM for managing the contents of the operand stack (e.g., swap, dup, pop, ...). The reference pages in Chapter 13, *Instruction Reference* of this book show what effect each instruction has on the operand stack.

To call a method, you first push its arguments onto the operand stack, and then use one of the four method invocation instructions (more on this soon) to call the method. Method invocation instructions pop arguments off the operand stack and transfer them to the local variables of the new method. When the method returns, any return result is transfered back to the caller's operand stack.

So what is in local variable 0? All non-static methods take an implicit first argument—the object that the method should operate on—known as this in the Java language. The this argument is stored in local variable 0. In the method we are examining, this is the object that is being initialized.

The next instruction in <init> is

```
invokespecial java/lang/Object/<init>()V
```

Here, invokespecial is being used to invoke the method called <init> belonging to java.lang.Object, using the type descriptor "()V" (the same descriptor we saw earlier). This is like the Java statement:

```
super();
```

and calls java.lang.Object's constructor, passing it to the object that is being initialized. All instance initialization methods should first call their superclass's <init> method to let the superclass perform any initialization it needs to.

Even though the descriptor "()V" suggests that the <init> method takes no arguments and returns no results, it's important to remember that all non-static methods take an implicit first argument—the object to apply the method to. When you want to invoke a non-static method, you must first push the object you want it to operate on onto the operand stack—in this case, we used aload_0 to pass the object that is being initialized to the superclass's <init> method.

invokespecial is one of four instructions provided in the JVM to call methods. invokespecial is used to invoke methods in certain "special" cases—for example, when you are calling an instance initialization method. See the instruction reference entry for invokespecial for full details. For normal method invocation, use invokevirtual—this invokes a standard, non-static method. The two other invocation instructions are invokestatic, which is used to invoke static (i.e., class) methods, and invokeinterface, which is used to invoke methods defined by an interface. See Chapter 9, *Flow Control* for more on method invocation.

The invokespecial instruction illustrates another important feature of the JVM: instructions in the JVM obtain the operands they use from two distinct sources:

- the operand stack
- the method's bytecode

invokespecial pops arguments for the method from the operand stack, but it gets the name of the method to invoke directly from the bytecode. In Jasmin, operands that are to be stored inline in the bytecode are written after the instruction, usually on the same line separated by spaces. The reference section shows the Jasmin syntax for each instruction and also how each instruction is laid out in bytecode.

To avoid confusion, in this book we will always refer to items taken from the operand stack as *operands,* whereas items which are stored inline in the bytecode are called *parameters* (this is a little different from the style adopted in the JVM specification, which describes data from either source as operands).

Going back to HelloWorld, the next instruction is:

```
return
```

The return instruction indicates that the method is finished—it has no work to do, so the method returns and control passes back to the caller.

The final line of <init> is:

```
.end method
```

This tells the Jasmin assembler that the method definition is finished.

The main Method

The next method in HelloWorld is called "main". The definition starts with:

```
.method public static main([Ljava/lang/String;)V
```

This indicates that a new method called "main" is being defined as a public static method.

Static methods are treated specially in Java. Unlike their non-static counterparts, static methods are not passed an object as their implicit first argument—you don't need a reference to an object to invoke a static method. Static methods have a number of uses. See *Java in a Nutshell* for a fuller description of static methods.

The type descriptor for this particular static method is "(L[java/lang/String;)V"—this means that main takes an array of strings as a parameter and returns no result. Chapter 4 describes the format of type descriptors in more detail.

The first instruction in "main" is:

```
.limit stack 2
```

In the Java runtime system, each time a method is called, space is set aside for that method's operand stack (each method has its own, isolated operand stack). The ".limit stack" directive is used to tell the system how big the stack should be. In this case, up to two items can be pushed on this method's operand stack during the execution of the method. Note that the Java class verifier (see Chapter 5) checks this limit, and generates an exception if the method exceeds the limit. Also, note that we didn't need a .limit directive in the <init> method—this is because Jasmin uses a default value of 1 for the limit.

The last three instructions in this method are:

```
getstatic java/lang/System/out Ljava/io/PrintStream;
ldc "Hello World"
invokevirtual java/io/PrintStream/println(Ljava/lang/String;)V
```

This is the Java assembler way of writing:

```
System.out.println("Hello World");
```

The getstatic instruction gets the value of the static field called "out" in the java.lang.System class and pushes the value onto the stack. Notice that getstatic takes two parameters—the first identifies the field to fetch, and the second is a type descriptor indicating the type of data held in the field.

The ldc instruction pushes a constant onto the stack—in this case the constant string "Hello World".

Finally, the invokevirtual instruction is used to call the println method. println takes the two arguments—the (implicit) stream object to print to, and the string to print. invokevirtual pops these arguments off the stack and invokes the println method associated with the stream. (The println method takes a string as an argument, prints the string out, and returns no result).

For more information on getstatic, ldc, or invokevirtual, you can consult the reference pages at the back of this book.

A More Extensive Example: Count

How would you rewrite the HelloWorld class to create a Java program which prints out something more complex than just "Hello World"? Let's consider a simple class for printing out the integers 0–9:

```
public class Count {
    public static void main(String args[]) {
        int i;
        for (i = 0; i < 10; i++) {
            System.out.println(Java.lang.String.valueOf(i));
        }
    }
}
```

Here is the same program, this time written using Jasmin:

```
.class public Count
.super java/lang/Object

; the instance initialization method (as for HelloWorld)
.method public <init>()V
    ; just call Object's initializer
    aload_0
    invokespecial java/lang/Object/<init>()V
    return
.end method

.method public static main([Ljava/lang/String;)V

    ; set limits used by this method
    .limit stack 3
    .limit locals 4

    ; setup local variables:

    ;     1 - the PrintStream object held in java.lang.System.out
    getstatic java/lang/System/out Ljava/io/PrintStream;
    astore_1

    ;     2 - the integer 10 - the counter used in the loop
```

```
    bipush 10
    istore_2

    ; now loop 10 times printing out a number

Loop:

    ; compute 10 - <local variable 2>, convert this integer to a string,
    ; and store the string result in local variable 3
    bipush 10
    iload_2
    isub      ; stack now contains (10 - <local variable 2>) - convert to string...
    invokestatic java/lang/String/valueOf(I)Ljava/lang/String;
    astore_3 ; and store in local variable 3

    ; now print the string in local variable 3
    aload_1   ; push the PrintStream object
    aload_3   ; push the string we just created - then ...
    invokevirtual java/io/PrintStream/println(Ljava/lang/String;)V

    ; decrement the counter and loop
    iinc 2 -1
    iload_2
    ifne Loop
    return

.end method
```

Compiling and Running Count

To compile this example, type the code into a file called "Count.j", and then type:

```
% jasmin Count.j
```

to the command line prompt to assemble the program into a Java class file. This produces a file called:

```
Count.class
```

containing the Java class file for the Count class. You can then run the program by typing:

```
% java -verify Count
0
1
2
...
7
8
9
```

Count, Line by Line

The start of the Count class is very similar to the HelloWorld example we saw earlier—until you get to the "main" method, which starts with the two directives:

```
.limit stack 3
.limit locals 4
```

We saw the first of these directives earlier—it tells the JVM how big to make the operand stack for the method.

The ".limit locals" directive tells the JVM how many local variables the method uses. Once again, in Jasmin this defaults to 1, so we didn't need this directive in any previous methods. This example is a little more complex and uses four local variables—numbered 0 through 3 (remember to include local variable 0 when counting the number of local variables used by a method).

Next, the method sets up some of the local variables. Local variable 1 is set using:

```
getstatic java/lang/System/out Ljava/io/PrintStream;
astore_1
```

Here the getstatic instruction gets the PrintStream object reference that is held in the static field called "out" of the class java.lang.System and the astore_1 instruction stores this object reference in local variable 1. This is like the Java expression:

```
PrintStream x = java.lang.System.out;
```

Local variable 2 is set using:

```
bipush 10
istore_2
```

this stores the int 10 in local variable 2. Notice how instructions which are used for ints start with "i", whereas instructions for objects start with "a". This naming convention is a standard practice in the JVM. Chapter 3, *Components of the Machine*, contains a table of all the prefixes used by instructions.

After these setup instructions, the body of the loop in main is defined:

```
Loop:
    ; compute 10 - <local variable 2> ...
    bipush 10
    iload_2
    isub
    invokestatic java/lang/String/valueOf(I)Ljava/lang/String;
    astore_3
    ; ... and print it
    aload_1     ; push the PrintStream object
    aload_3     ; push the string we just created - then ...
    invokevirtual java/io/PrintStream/println(Ljava/lang/String;)V
```

```
    ; decrement the counter and loop
    iinc 2 -1
    iload_2
    ifne Loop
```

The line reading:

```
    Loop:
```

is a *label*. Labels are words followed by a colon and are a special directive telling the Jasmin assembler to remember the current position in the code by giving it a name ("Loop" in this case). Labels then can be referred to later in the code by branch instructions like "goto", or, in this case, "ifne". The label tells the JVM the point in the code to jump to. Labels are provided in Jasmin as a convenience: at the bytecode level, branch addresses are given as integer offsets. Using labels saves you from having to calculate offsets yourself, and they also make reading the code easier. Instead of writing "goto –15", for example, you can write "goto Label".

After the "Loop" label, several actions are performed. Let's break them into chunks—first there is:

```
    bipush 10       ; compute 10 - <local variable 2>
    iload_2
    isub
```

This computes the expression "10 – <local variable>". In more detail, the bipush instruction pushes the int 10 onto the stack. Then the iload_2 instruction pushes the int in local variable 2 onto the stack (local variable 2 is holding the counter we are using) and isub subtracts the two integers, leaving the int result on the stack.

The next two lines of the method are:

```
    invokestatic java/lang/String/valueOf(I)Ljava/lang/String;
    astore_3
```

The invokestatic instruction is used to call the static method valueOf in the java.lang.String class. The type descriptor we are using is "(I)Ljava/lang/String;"—this means that the method expects an int argument and returns a String result. As you probably guessed, valueOf takes an int and converts it into a string. In this case the int is the value of the expression we computed earlier. The String result is stored in local variable 3 using astore_3.

After this, the lines:

```
    aload_1
    aload_3
    invokevirtual java/io/PrintStream/println(Ljava/lang/String;)V
```

call the println method defined by java.io.PrintStream, passing it the output stream we stored in local variable 1 and the string we just created and placed in local variable 3—printing out the counter.

The final statements in the loop are:

```
iinc 3 -1
iload_3
ifne Loop
```

The `iinc` instruction takes two parameters—a local variable number and an amount to change that local variable by. (Note that the local variable must be holding an int for this instruction to work.) In this case, we are decrementing local variable 3 by one.

The `iload_3` instruction then pushes local variable 3 onto the stack, and the "ifne Loop" instruction tells the JVM to jump to the location in the code labeled Loop unless the integer value on the stack is zero—so the program loops until the counter reaches zero. These instructions are essentially like the Java statements:

```
i--;
if (i != 0) goto Loop;
```

except that Java provides no goto instruction. This illustrates one of the differences between the Java language and the Java Virtual Machine—the VM supports several operations (such as branches to an address) that are not made visible at the Java language level.

An Applet Example

Now for a (slightly) more useful program. The next example gives you an idea of what a basic Java applet looks like at the JVM level. Remember that applets are Java programs which can be embedded in an HTML page and then viewed within a Web browser (alternatively you can use appletviewer to view applets).

Below is the Java code for the HelloWeb, a simple applet that draws the string "Hello Web!" in a big font.

```
import java.applet.*;
import java.awt.*;

public class HelloWeb extends Applet
{
    private Font font;

    // during initialization, obtain Helvetica BOLD 48 point
    public void init() {
        font = new Font("Helvetica", Font.BOLD, 48);
    }
```

```
        // to repaint the applet window, draw the string Hello World
        // using the font we created earlier.
        public void paint(Graphics g)
        {
            g.setFont(font);
            g.drawString("Hello Web!", 25, 50);
        }
    }
```

Note that, unlike the HelloWorld and Count programs shown earlier, the HelloWeb is not a standalone program and so doesn't have a main() method (thus it cannot be run directly by the Java command). Instead, the HelloWeb class derives from the java.applet.Applet class, and overrides the init() and paint() methods to tell Java how to repaint the applet's window.

Viewing the Applet

To view the applet, you need to first compile the applet, by saving the code into a file named HelloWeb.java and typing:

```
% javac HelloWeb.java
```

Next, you will need to create an HTML document with a fragment of HTML like:

```
<applet code="HelloWeb.class" width = 400 height = 100>
</applet>
```

The applet tag is used in HTML to indicate a Java applet. An example of a full HTML document using this applet tag is shown below:

```
<HTML>
<HEAD>
<TITLE>The Hello Applet</TITLE>
</HEAD>
<BODY>
<applet code="HelloWeb.class" width=300 height=200>
</applet>
</BODY>
</HTML>
```

If you save this HTML in the file Hello.html, and place the Hello.html and HelloWeb.class in a location which you can reach by your Web browser, then typing in the URL for the Hello.html file should show you the running applet. Alternatively, you can type:

```
% appletviewer Hello.html
```

to see the applet running in appletviewer. Figure 2-1 shows the applet running.

Figure 2–1: The HelloWeb applet

HelloWeb in Jasmin

The following listing shows the HelloWeb applet code rewritten for Jasmin:

```
.class public HelloWeb
.super java/applet/Applet

; declare a private field called font, holding a java.awt.Font object:
.field private font Ljava/awt/Font;

; init() method - creates new font for use in paint() method
.method public init()V
    .limit stack 6      ; up to six items on the stack

    aload_0             ; this
    ;
    ;     new Font("Helvetica", Font.BOLD, 48)
    ;
    new java/awt/Font   ; make a new Font instance
    dup                 ; dup the instance and call its constructor
    ldc "Helvetica"     ; (passing the constructor the font name as a string,
    iconst_1            ; the Font.BOLD flag,
    bipush 48           ; and the font size 48)
    invokespecial java/awt/Font/<init>(Ljava/lang/String;II)V

    ; stack currently contains (this, font).
    ; now use putfield to assign the font item to this.font
    putfield HelloWeb/font Ljava/awt/Font;
    return
.end method

; paint() method - redraws applets window
.method public paint(Ljava/awt/Graphics;)V
    .limit stack 4
    .limit locals 2 ; two locals ( 0 = this, 1 = Graphics object)
    ;
```

```
    ; This is like g.setFont(this.font);
    ;
    aload_1     ; Graphics object g
    aload_0     ; this ...
    getfield HelloWeb/font Ljava/awt/Font;    ; this.font
    invokevirtual java/awt/Graphics/setFont(Ljava/awt/Font;)V

    ; now do:    g.drawString("HelloWorld!", 25, 50);
    aload_1     ; Graphics object g
    ldc "Hello Web!"
    bipush 25
    bipush 50
    invokevirtual java/awt/Graphics/drawString(Ljava/lang/String;II)V
    return
.end method

; standard constructor - just calls Applet's constructor
.method public <init>()V
    aload_0
    invokespecial java/applet/Applet/<init>()V
    return
.end method
```

Much of this code is similar in nature to the HelloWorld and Count programs earlier in this chapter, so we won't go through the code exhaustively step-by-step. Instead, let's just look at how the code handles packages and fields—keen readers may in addition want to look up unfamiliar instructions in the instruction reference section.

Packages

You will have noticed that the Java code for HelloWeb started with:

```
import java.applet.*;
import java.awt.*;
```

whereas there is no mention of packages in the Jasmin equivalent of the code. The Java import statement is purely a convenience mechanism, to save programmers from always having to type class, field and method names in their fully qualified form. At the JVM level inside class files (and also in Jasmin) all references to classes, methods and fields must be written out in full. This means you cannot just write:

```
new Font
```

at the JVM level, but instead have to write:

```
new java/awt/Font
```

Fields

The HelloWeb applet code illustrates the use of Jasmin's .field directive to declare a new field:

```
.field private font Ljava/awt/Font;
```

The "private" indicates that you are declaring a private field, i.e., a field only available within methods belonging to this class. The name of the new field is "font", and the type descriptor of the field is "Ljava/awt/Font;", i.e., the field holds a java.awt.Font object.

The instructions:

```
aload_0
new java/awt/Font
...
putfield HelloWeb/font Ljava/awt/Font;
```

store a font instance in the field, whereas

```
aload_0                                    ; push this
getfield HelloWeb/font Ljava/awt/Font;     ; get this.font
```

retrieves the font object held in the field. Fields are described in more detail in Chapter 7.

Exercising the Verifier

So far our example classes have all been "friendly"—they contained legal Java VM code. What happens if you try to create a class which doesn't behave so nicely? For example, consider the following Java program:

```
class Malign {
    public static void main(String args[]) {
        int x = 100;
        x.clone();
    }
}
```

If you try to compile this program using javac, you will get a compile-time error like:

```
Malign.java:6: Can't invoke a method on a int.
        x.clone();
        ^
```

javac prevents you from performing what would otherwise be a dangerous operation—treating an integer as if it were a pointer to an object (something that in C or C++ you can achieve using a cast). If javac allowed this, hackers would easily be able to construct programs which crash the Java process, or worse.

But even though `javac` does a good job of checking for legal programs, there is no such up-front limitation on programs written directly at the Java Virtual Machine level. The following Jasmin listing shows a similar program written in VM code:

```
.class public Malign
.super java/lang/Object

.method public <init>()V
    aload_0
    invokespecial java/lang/Object/<init>()V
    return
.end method

.method public static main([Ljava/lang/String;)V
    bipush 100
    invokevirtual java/lang/Object/clone()Ljava/lang/Object;
    return
.end method
```

The two critical lines in this example are:

```
bipush 100
invokevirtual java/lang/Object/clone()Ljava/lang/Object;
```

The first line pushes the integer 100 onto the stack and the second calls Object's clone() method—this is clearly an illegal operation, since `invokevirtual` expects the top item on the stack to be an object, not an int.

To try this program, save the code into a file called Malign.j and then use Jasmin as before to assemble it.

Note: Be very wary about the next step! Running the program without verification is very likely to crash your Java system and possibly also your computer (depending on how your resilient your operating system is). Here's what happens if you run the program on a UNIX system without verification:

```
% java Malign
SIGSEGV   11*  segmentation violation
    si_signo [11]: SIGSEGV   11*   segmentation violation
    si_errno [0]: Error 0
    si_code [1]: SEGV_ACCERR [addr: 0x68]

        stackbase=EFFFFB64, stackpointer=EFFFF060

Full thread dump:
    "Finalizer thread" (TID:0xee300370, sys_thread_t:0xef490de0) prio=1
    "Async Garbage Collector" (TID:0xee300318, sys_thread_t:0xef4c0de0) prio=1
    "Idle thread" (TID:0xee3002a0, sys_thread_t:0xef4f0de0) prio=0
    "clock handler" (TID:0xee3001f8, sys_thread_t:0xef5b0de0) prio=11
    "main" (TID:0xee3000a0, sys_thread_t:0x74488) prio=5 *current thread*
Segmentation Fault (core dumped)
```

So how does Java prevent applets from causing this kind of unpleasant behavior? As we've hinted at, Java's verifier is the key player. It is invoked on all classes which are thought to be "untrusted" (usually any class which is downloaded dynamically from a remote site). The Java verifier checks for a wide range of misbehaviors, including the one introduced in the Malign class. Running Malign with verification turned on raises a Java VerifyError exception. The default system response to this exception is to print out an error message and then discard the class that is being loaded:

```
% java -verify Malign
VERIFIER ERROR Malign.main([Ljava/lang/String;)V:
Expecting to find object/array on stack
Can't find class Malign
```

The message "Expecting to find object/array on stack" indicates that the verifier spotted invokevirtual being used with something other than an array or object reference on the stack. The subsequent "Can't find class Malign" message was produced because the JVM rejected the Malign class (since it failed verification) and so couldn't find a Malign class to use.

If you want to learn more about the verifier, see Chapter 5.

3

Components of the Machine

In this chapter, we describe the steps involved in running Java applets and applications and give you an overview of the components that you find under the hood of a Java Virtual Machine.

Java's Compilation Model

When you run Netscape Navigator 3.0 or Microsoft Internet Explorer 3.0, you are running a Web browser which has a Java Virtual Machine embedded within it (see Figure 3-1).

Before an applet can be run on this JVM, you first have to translate your applet's Java source code into a format that the JVM recognizes. This format, known as the Java class file format, is described in detail in Chapter 4, *Classes*.

The Java class file format is closely related to the Java language—many of the programming structures in Java have a related representation within the class files. Compilers such as javac are usually used to compile Java source code into the Java class file format. Of course, as far as the JVM is concerned, any technique used to generate Java class files is acceptable, as long as the resulting class file obeys all the constraints specified by the Java standard. Chapter 5, *Security*, discusses some of these constraints.

Class files are expected to be named "X.class", where X is the name of the class contained in the class file. Each class file contains the definitions for one Java class.

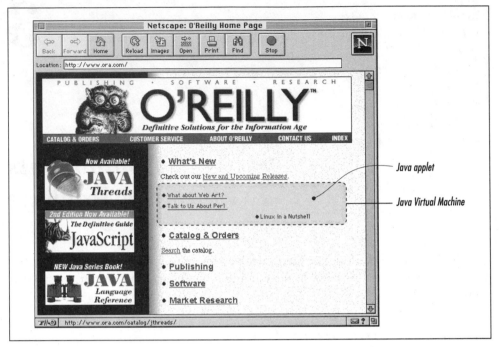

Figure 3–1: Java Virtual Machine and Java applet management

Running Applets

Once a Java applet has been compiled into the Java class file format, your next step is to create an HTML page that incorporates the class file, and then load the HTML document into the Web browser. As we learned in Chapter 2, *Quick Tour*, the <applet> tag is used to embed an applet in an HTML document:

```
<applet code="AAA.class" width=XXX height=YYY></applet>
```

where "AAA.class" is the Uniform Resource Locator of your applet's class file, for example *http://www.me.com/Example.class*, and XXX and YYY are the size of the applet window in pixels.

Figure 3-2 illustrates this process.

Some applets consist of several classes. In this case, each class is compiled into its own class file. Then in your HTML document you name the class file of the toplevel class (the one which extends the Applet class). This class file will be downloaded first. As the JVM comes across references to other classes, their class files are downloaded from the same directory as was the initial class.

Downloading isn't the only way that Java classes are loaded into the Java Virtual Machine. JVMs can also load class files from the local disk. This is how all of the

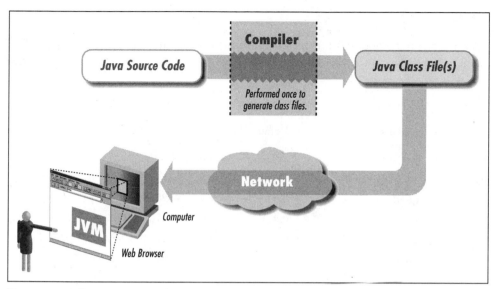

Figure 3–2: A Java applet running in a Java-enabled Web browser

built-in Java classes (java.lang.Object, java.lang.String, etc.) are loaded. Full details of how class files are located and loaded are found in Chapter 4.

Applets vs. Applications

So far we have talked about running applets using a Java-enabled Web browser. What about when you are running a standalone Java application?

Standalone Java applications are very similar to Java applets. However, there are some notable differences:

- Applets subclass java.applet.Applet and override its start() method, whereas standalone applications just define a class that includes a main() method.

- Starting an applet creates a window frame for the applet to draw itself in, whereas standalone applications by default have no graphical appearance (although standalone applications can easily use the AWT to make a graphical user interface).

- Applets can be run within a Web document, whereas standalone applications cannot appear as part of a Web page. Standalone applications are also more often run using a virtual machine that isn't embedded within a Web browser.

Now that we've seen how Java applets and applications are compiled and run, it's time to take a closer look inside the JVM.

Data Types

Java is a strongly typed language. Programmers stringently declare the types of all
storage locations and return values. In Java, you will recall, there are the primitive
types shown in Table 3-1.

Table 3–1: Java primitive types

Type	Contains	Default	Size	Min Value/Max Value
boolean	true or false	false	1 bit	N.A/N.A
char	Unicode character	\u0000	16 bits	\u0000/\uFFFF
byte	signed integer	0.0	8 bits	–128/127
short	signed integer	0.0	16 bits	–32768/32767
int	signed integer	0.0	32 bits	–2147483648/ 2147483647
long	signed integer	0.0	64 bits	–9223372036854775808/ 9223372036854775807
float	IEEE 754/floating-point	0.0	32 bits	{+l–}3.40282347E+38/ {+l–}1.40239846E-45
double	IEEE 754/floating-point	0.0	64 bits	{+l–}1.79769313486231570E+308/ {+l–}4.94065645841246544E-324

Java also supports objects and arrays. These types are often called "reference types"
because they are handled by reference. More on this later.

Data Types in the Java Virtual Machine

You might expect the Java Virtual Machine to offer the same support for data types
as the Java language. While this is true to a large extent, there are some notable
wrinkles that complicate matters. Differences arise for several reasons. One factor
is the byte-wide instruction size adopted by the JVM—there aren't enough instruction opcodes to treat all types equally, so some types receive more support in the
JVM than others. Another factor is the word-oriented design of the JVM: because
local variables and operand stack entries hold one-word (32 bit) quantities, doubles and longs must be handled specially.

In the following sections, we discuss each JVM data type in more detail.

int, long, float, double

The most basic numeric types in the JVM are ints, longs, floats and doubles. A full
set of arithmetic instructions are provided for each of these types. For example,
the iadd instruction adds two integers, the isub instruction subtracts two integers,
and so on.

In addition to arithmetic instructions, there are instructions for comparing two numbers of the same type, and for converting from one of these numeric formats to another.

Floats and doubles use the IEEE 754 numeric representation and adopt the gradual underflow mode. On some platforms, this representation may not be supported at the hardware level and a software emulation may be required—in this (fortunately rare) case, Java programs which perform a lot of floating-point computations may run very slowly.

As we mentioned above, doubles and longs are a little tricky since the most basic working unit in the JVM is a 32-bit word, and doubles and longs are 64 bits wide. To handle this, doubles and longs actually occupy two entries on the operand stack, and the JVM uses two consecutive local variables to store a double or long value. In many situations you can ignore this detail, since the two-word nature of doubles/longs is partly hidden by the JVM. For example, compare the code for adding 1 to an int value in local variable 1, and the code for adding 1.0 to a double value held in local variables 1 and 2 (see Table 3-2).

Table 3–2: Comparison of int and double instructions

Adding one to an int	Adding 1 to a double
iload 1	dload 1
iconst_1	dconst_1
iadd	dadd
istore 1	dstore 1

The code looks nearly identical. But this similarity can be misleading. The code on the left modifies only local variable 1. The code on the right affects both local variable 1 and local variable 2. You must pay particular attention when:

* counting how many arguments a method takes, or counting the number of local variables or stack words used by a method (these counts are measured in words, and doubles/longs take two words each, not one).

* allocating local variables (again, doubles/longs use two consecutive local variables—see dload/dstore and lload/lstore for more details).

* using instructions like dup/pop to manipulate values on the stack—to duplicate a two-word value, you must use dup2. To remove a two-word value from the stack, use pop2.

You can't use instructions that operate on the single-word level with two-word values. Programs can't legally address the upper or lower word of a two-word value independently (i.e., you can't split a double or long into its two constituent words).

byte, short, char

In the Java language, the byte, short, and char types have the same status as, for example, ints or floats. At the JVM level, on the other hand, bytes, chars, and shorts are second-class citizens: they don't enjoy the same level of support in the instruction set as ints or floats. Bytes, chars, and shorts are known as *storage types*. You can declare that a field (or array) stores a byte, short, or char, and there are instructions for creating and manipulating byte, char and short arrays. However, when you retrieve the value of a byte, char, or short field, it is automatically cast into an int, and your program receives this int value. Going the other way, when you want to assign a value to a byte, short, or char field, you pass the JVM an int, and it automatically truncates it to the relevant size before storing it in the field. You can use i2s, i2b or i2c to truncate an int so its value is within the legal range of values of the corresponding type (i2s for shorts, i2b for bytes, i2c for chars).

See Chapter 8, *Arithmetic*, for details on working with numeric types in the JVM.

boolean

In the Java language there is a boolean type, which has either the value *true* or *false*.

At the JVM level, there is no boolean type. Instead, booleans are represented as integers: 0 is used for *false*, and 1 for *true*.

Using the JVM, you can create boolean arrays using newarray. You can also declare that a field holds a boolean value. However, when you retrieve the value of a boolean field or array, the result you get will be either the int 0 or 1. Similarly, to set the value of a boolean field, use the int operand 0 or 1. Conditional branch operations also take int operands rather than booleans, and to return a boolean result in a method you use the ireturn instruction.

You load and store values in boolean arrays using the instructions designated for byte arrays—so to store a value in a boolean array, use bastore. To retrieve a value from a boolean array, use baload. Note that the JVM specification doesn't state how boolean arrays are actually represented in memory in the runtime system. Some implementations may use bit arrays, others (such as Sun's implementation) use byte arrays.

reference

The JVM provides instructions for creating and manipulating Java objects and arrays. Arrays are actually treated as objects in the Java Virtual Machine—you can get the class of an array, and arrays support the same methods as java.lang.Object—though there are some instructions that operate only on arrays (e.g., arraylength tells you the length of an array).

Note that the JVM specification does not indicate how these objects and arrays are laid out in memory in a runtime system—other than saying that all objects are addressed by reference. If you are familiar with C or C++, you can mentally replace the term "reference" with the term "pointer," and you will get the right idea. That is, when you write the Java statement:

```
Object x;
```

this indicates that x is a 32-bit reference to an object. References are very much like pointers in C or C++. As with pointers in C++, at any moment in time there can be many references to the same object. In Sun's implementation of Java, each reference is the index of a special handle, where a handle consists of a pair of pointers: one to the method table of the object, and the other to the object's data. In Microsoft's implementation, on the other hand, a reference really is a pointer which points directly to the object's instance data, and objects have a hidden field which points to their class and method table.

Unlike C and C++, Java provides no equivalent of pointer arithmetic operations—a reference is an opaque type and cannot be treated as a number, or cast into a numeric type, or used to modify an arbitrary location in memory.

Also unlike C and C++, in Java you can *only* address objects by reference. Java does not support call-by-value for objects or arrays (though it does employ call-by-value for numeric types). Neither can objects or arrays be embedded within other objects (though of course one object can refer to other objects). Similarly, there is no way to declare that an identifier (or a field or array) should contain an actual object, rather than a reference to an object. This leads to an important difference between Java and C++. Consider the class definition:

```
class Point {float x, y; };
class Line {Point p1, p2; };
```

In Java, p1 and p2 are both 32-bit fields that contain references to Point instances—in fact, both p1 and p2 could refer to the same Point instance. Allocating a new Line instance will not automatically allocate two new Point instances as well. Instead, p1 and p2 will both default to null—a special object used to indicate an uninitialized object reference.

In C++, p1 and p2 are both embedded objects—so an instance of Line actually contains enough storage for the two Point objects (i.e., each Line instance will be four floats in size). When you create a new Line object, two Point objects are implicitly created as part of that Line object. The objects in p1 and p2 cannot exist in their own right. When the storage for the Line instance is deleted, so is the storage for p1 and p2.

See Chapter 7, *Data Operations*, for details on working with objects in the JVM.

returnAddress

In this book you will come across a few mentions of the returnAddress type. This is a special 32-bit type used by the JVM subroutine mechanism. Subroutines are like lightweight methods—they are provided to facilitate exception handling. Subroutines and the returnAddress type are not exposed at the Java language level—though code which uses try/catch/finally is compiled into subroutines. The `jsr` and `jsr_w` instructions generate a value whose type is returnAddress. This value must be saved in a local variable using `astore`, for later use with the `ret` instruction. See the `jsr` reference page and Chapter 10, *Exceptions*, for more details.

Constant Pools

You will find mentions to the term *constant pool* throughout this book, so let's spend a little time becoming familiar with the constant pool and the kinds of data stored in it.

Every Java class (and interface) has a *constant pool* associated with it. The JVM obtains the constant pool for a class from its class file.

Constant pools serve a role similar to the symbol tables found in shared libraries and executables: they represent a collection of all the symbolic data needed by a class—this includes symbolic references to fields, classes, interfaces, and methods used internally by this class, as well as important symbols such as the name of the class and the names of its fields and methods.

Constant pool entries are ordered. The first constant in a class file is numbered 1, the second is numbered 2, and so on. These numbers are significant because you refer to a constant by using its index number. References to constants get stored in the class file as either 8-bit or a 16-bit unsigned integers, so the maximum number of constant pool entries in any single class is 65535. This puts an upper limit on the complexity of any single class. However, since each Java class has its own constant pool, this is not a severely restrictive limit.

Note that there is no way for a method to access a constant pool belonging to any other class—each constant pool is private to its class.

The constant pool is used to store all the literal constants (e.g., numbers and quoted strings) that appear in the text of methods. These constant values are available inside methods via instructions such as `ldc`, `ldc_w` and `ldc2_w`.

The constant pool also supports dynamic linking. Entries in the pool that refer to things such as methods, fields, or classes do so symbolically— they give the name of the field/method/class rather than an address. When the JVM encounters a use of a symbolic entry, it translates (or *resolves*) the symbolic reference into a concrete reference to a runtime data structure. Classes and interfaces are loaded automatically as necessary. Constant pool resolution is described in detail in Chapter 4.

Table 3-3 summarizes the types of data that can be put in the constant pool, and also lists some example instructions that make use of each type of entry. See Chapter 4 for more details of each entry type.

Table 3–3: Constant pool entry types

Entry Type	Purpose	Contains	Used By
Class	identifies a Java class	full name of class	new, instanceof, ...
Fieldref	identifies a Java field	class, name and type signature.	getfield and putfield.
Methodref	identifies a Java method	class, name, and type signature.	invokevirtual, invokenonvirtual and invokestatic.
InterfaceMethodref	identifies a Java interface method	class, name and type signature	invokeinterface
String	used for constant java.lang.String objects	Utf8 or Unicode string	ldc, ldc_w
Int	used for constant int values	int value	ldc, ldc_w
Float	used for constant float values	float value	ldc, ldc_w
Double	used for constant double values	float value	ldc2_w
Long	used for constant long values	float value	ldc2_w
NameAndType	identifies an identifier name and type	name and type signature	Used by other constant pool entries
Utf8	gives bytes of string in UTF8 format	byte array	Used by other constant pool entries

The Runtime System

In this chapter we've seen how Java source code is compiled into the Java class file format and loaded into a Web browser. We also looked at how the JVM handles data types, and glanced at the concept of constant pools. Now let's look in more detail at the internal structure of the JVM itself.

Strictly speaking, the term "Java Virtual Machine" was coined by Sun to refer to the abstract specification of a computing machine designed to run Java programs. This abstract machine is defined by the Java Virtual Machine Specification, which encompasses topics such as the format of Java class files and the semantics of each instruction. Concrete implementations of the JVM specification are required to support these semantics correctly—these implementations are known as Java runtime systems.

Figure 3-3 shows the components found in a typical Java runtime system.

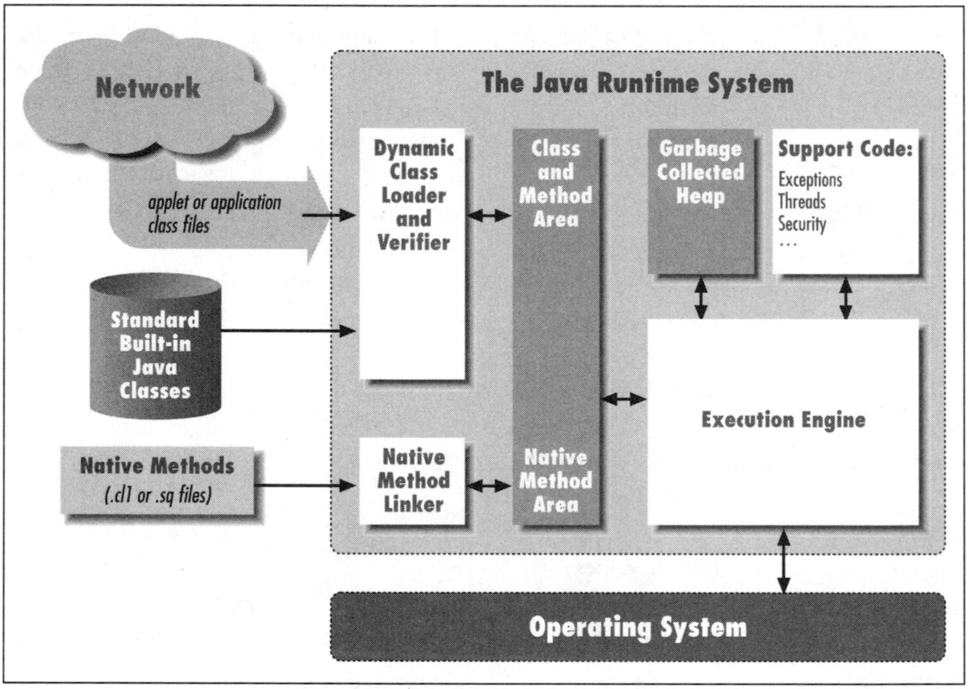

Figure 3–3: Components of a typical runtime system

Let's briefly examine each of these components in turn.

Execution Engine

At the heart of any runtime system is the *execution engine*. This is the piece of software or hardware that actually carries out the instructions contained in the byte-code of Java methods. We'll come back to this component later in this chapter.

Memory Manager

In Java, applications can create new objects and arrays. Objects and arrays are stored in a block of memory known as the *heap*.

Notice that there is no "free" or "delete" method in Java—so an application can never explicitly free memory or delete objects. Instead, the Java runtime system is responsible for reclaiming memory when it is no longer being used, typically using a process known as garbage collection.

Chapter 6, *Implementation Notes*, provides a longer discussion of heap management and garbage collection.

Java runtime systems must also manage the storage space needed for the data structures representing methods and classes. In principle, these form part of the heap and are hence eligible for garbage collection. In practice simple implementations of Java may use a separate area, known in the JVM specification as the *method area*, for storing classes and methods. In implementations that adopt a method area, space used by classes and methods may never get reclaimed.

Error and Exception Manager

Exceptions are Java's way of signaling that something out of the ordinary has happened. Exceptions can signal a recoverable situation – for example, when you try to read past the end of a file, an EOFException is thrown. In some cases, exceptions signal a fatal error, e.g., an OutOfMemoryError is thrown when the Java runtime system runs out of memory and cannot obtain more space from the operating system. Exceptions can also be raised by a Java method, using the athrow instruction—making them a useful mechanism for flow control and error handling.

At the JVM level, each method defines an exception handlers table that lists which exceptions the method catches. The runtime system includes an exception manager that is responsible for processing exceptions. See Chapter 10 for more information on exceptions.

Native Method Support

Classes can contain native method declarations. For native methods, the body of the method is not provided as Java bytecode in a class file, but instead is written using some other language and compiled into native machine code stored in a separate DLL or a shared library.

Runtime systems include code to dynamically load and execute the code in native methods, typically by using operating system calls that use DLLs (in Windows) or shared libraries (in UNIX). Once a native method has been linked into the runtime system, the execution engine traps calls to the native method, and routes these to the underlying native code. This process involves marshaling arguments into a form recognized by the native code and transferring execution control to the native code. When the native code returns, any return result is coerced back into a Java type and left on the operand stack of the caller.

Implementation of native methods is discussed in more detail in Chapter 6.

Threads Interface

Java is a thread-based language. The JVM supports multiple execution threads running concurrently—as if there are multiple execution engines running at once, each with its own call stack and local state.

There are only two instructions (monitorenter and monitorexit) in the JVM instruction set directly related to threads—the rest of the thread support is managed by trapping calls to methods belonging to java.lang.Thread.

Chapter 5 describes some of the implementation issues involving threads.

Class Loader

Java programs are all structured into classes, so an important function of the runtime system is to load, link and initialize classes. These actions are usually carried out dynamically—the first time a class is referenced, its class file is located, the bytes in the class file are loaded into memory, and the class is then linked into the runtime system and initialized.

Some classes, such as built-in classes (java.lang.Thread, java.lang.String, etc.) are loaded from disk. Others may be loaded over the Internet, e.g., by a ClassLoader.

Chapter 4 describes class loading and linking in more detail.

Security Manager

Java uses a series of security mechanisms, designed to make it harder for people to write hostile programs. Each runtime system defines its own security policies, by implementing a SecurityManager. The security manager is an outer shell that protects the JVM—it defines the bounds that a Java program must live within, and limits its access to resources that might be misused.

See Chapter 5 for more information on security in the JVM.

The Execution Engine

The execution engine—the piece of software at the heart of the JVM that acts as the machine's "virtual processor," takes a stream of bytecodes that make up a method and executes the instructions that the bytecodes represent.

The execution engine may be implemented using software, hardware, or both. Sun's initial system emulated the JVM instruction set using a simple bytecode interpreter. More advanced implementations now use Just-in-Time code generation technology in which the instructions that make up a method are first converted into native machine code which is then executed directly by the hardware processor in your computer. The machine code is cached, so the conversion process only needs to be done once for each method.

The JVM execution engine supports object-oriented applications—it includes instructions for creating instances, invoking methods, retrieving fields from objects, and so on. However, it also supports low-level operations such as might be realized in hardware CPU. In the future there are likely to be chips designed to supplement with hardware part or all of the work carried out by the execution engine.

Conceptually, there are multiple execution engines running concurrently in a single runtime system. Each execution engine is associated with a Java thread. In a multiprocessor system, threads may be allocated their own hardware processor. More commonly, time-slicing is used to give the appearance of concurrency. Each execution engine maintains its own state information, though objects in the heap and method area are shared.

Whatever implementation technology or hardware is used, the starting point for all execution engines is always the same—the core set of instructions that appear in the bytecode and whose semantics are defined by the JVM specification.

Bytecode

To execute a Java method, the execution engine retrieves and processes the *byte-code* for the method. Bytecode consists of a sequence of single byte *opcodes*, each of which identifies a specific operation to be carried out. For example, the opcode 96 represents the instruction `iadd`, which adds two integers.

Some opcodes require *parameters*,[*] and these parameters follow the opcode in the bytecode.

---

[*] Formally speaking, the items following an opcode in bytecode are called operands. However, because instructions can also receive values from the *operand stack*, we use the term "parameter" for items which follow an opcode in bytecode, and "operand" for items on the operand stack.

For example, the bipush instruction (opcode 16) takes a single byte parameter: the value to push onto the stack. So:

```
bipush 20      ; push the integer 20 onto the stack
```

is presented in the bytecode as two bytes, the opcode 16 and the parameter 20.

Numeric values are stored in bytecode using the same data format conventions as the java.io.DataInputStream class—for example, a short is stored as two 8-bit bytes, with the most significant byte appearing first. See Chapter 4 for more details.

As a longer example, consider the code:

```
; this is like the Java statement "int y = x + 5;"
    iload  1        ; push integer value held in local variable 1 onto stack
    bipush 5        ; push constant integer 5 onto stack
    iadd            ; add the two integers
    istore 2        ; store the result in local variable 2
```

This translates into the following bytecode:

```
21     1   16      5   96      54       2
iload  1   bipush  5   iadd    istore   2
```

Byte Order

Although the Java VM spec dictates that data in class files is stored in network order (i.e., big endian, with the most significant byte appearing first in the file), the runtime representation of data types can be either big endian or little endian—since the interpreter does not provide any instructions that address memory directly, the byte ordering used for data at runtime is invisible to programs running on the Java Virtual Machine.

Instruction Set

There are over 160 instruction opcodes recognized by the Java interpreter. This seems like a lot of instructions, but many of them differ only in the type of arguments or results they produce—functionally, there is very little difference between, say, iload and fload (in fact, many execution engines will make these two instructions as synonymous). Look at Appendix A, *Instructions by Function Group*, in the reference section to see how these instructions are divided up.

Instruction Prefix

The JVM instruction set is not orthogonal: operations provided for one type are not necessarily provided for other types. The Java designers justify this lack of orthogonality by pointing out that, given an 8-bit opcode for each instruction, there are not enough opcodes to offer the same support to all of Java's runtime types. You can often tell what data type a particular instruction expects by looking at the first letter of its name. For example, all instructions for handling integers start with the letter "i"—iadd, isub, istore, etc. Instructions that aren't associated with a specific type take no prefix—e.g., pop, dup, invokevirtual.

The prefix codes are shown in Table 3-4.

Table 3–4: Prefix codes for instructions

Type	Code
int	i
long	l
float	f
double	d
byte	b
char	c
short	s
reference	a

Table 3-5 shows all of the instructions which take a prefix code, and shows the types that the instruction operates on.

Table 3–5: Instructions and their types

	Int	long	float	double	byte	char	short	reference
?2c	✓							
?2d	✓	✓	✓					
?2I		✓	✓	✓				
?2f	✓	✓		✓				
?2l	✓		✓	✓				
?2s	✓							
?add	✓	✓	✓	✓				
?aload	✓	✓	✓	✓	✓	✓	✓	✓
?and	✓	✓						
?astore	✓	✓	✓	✓	✓	✓	✓	✓
?cmp		✓						
?cmp{gll}			✓	✓				
?const_<n>	✓	✓	✓	✓				✓

Table 3–5: Instructions and their types (continued)

	Int	long	float	double	byte	char	short	reference
?div	✓	✓	✓	✓				
?inc	✓							
?ipush					✓		✓	
?load	✓	✓	✓	✓				
?mul	✓	✓	✓	✓				
?neg	✓	✓	✓	✓				
?newarray								✓
?or	✓	✓						
?rem	✓	✓	✓	✓				
?return	✓	✓	✓	✓				✓
?shl	✓	✓						
?shr	✓	✓						
?store	✓	✓	✓	✓				✓
?sub	✓	✓	✓	✓				
?throw								✓
?ushr	✓	✓						
?xor	✓	✓						

Stack Frames

Whenever you invoke a method, a new activation record (or *frame*) is allocated to store state information about the method invocation. When the method returns, the corresponding frame is discarded.

Frames are maintained on a stack, known as the *Java stack* in the specification. Each thread of execution has its own private Java stack. Invoking a method pushes a new frame onto the top of the stack. Returning from a method causes the top frame to be popped from the stack and discarded. Only the top stack frame in each thread is considered active at any one time.

Within each frame, a number of pieces of information are maintained. Frames are used to store the operand stack and local variables for an executing method. They also hold other state variables, such as the pc (program counter), a pointer to the class of the currently executing method, a pointer to the invoker's frame, etc.

Figure 3-4 illustrates the Java stacks of a runtime system that is executing three threads. The darkened boxes indicate active frames. You can see that the runtime system is current processing three methods: activeMethod, getHour and drawLine.

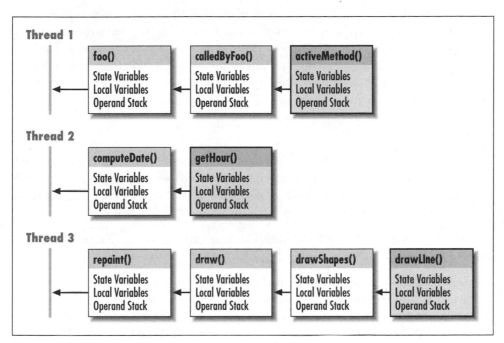

Figure 3–4: Stack frames in a runtime system executing three threads

The method associated with an active frame is called the *current method*. The execution engine also tracks the *current class*—i.e., the class that the current method belongs to—and the *current constant pool*—i.e., the constant pool associated with the class of the currently active method.

Registers

The JVM provides no directly accessible general-purpose registers. Execution engines do maintain state information, including a stack-top index, thread state information, a pointer to the current method being executed, a pointer to that method's class and constant pool, a stack-frame pointer, and a program counter indicating what instruction in bytecode is being executed. These state variables are used internally by the system to execute code, but they are not directly accessible by the code itself.

This is in sharp contrast to hardware processors which have a set of general-purpose registers. One of the reasons the JVM has few registers is to make it easy to port to a wide variety of machines with few or irregular general purpose registers. Instead of using registers, JVM programs use local variables and the operand stack (see below).

In documentation, you will see mentions of pc, the program counter register. This register records the index in bytecode of the instruction the execution engine is currently processing. Branch instructions modify this register indirectly, and the JVM increments the register automatically each time an instruction completes. But there aren't any JVM instructions for querying the register, so it's not what you would describe as a register in the normal sense.

The Operand Stack

The JVM is a stack-based machine.[*] Instructions receive values and return results using an *operand stack*. The operand stack is also used to pass arguments to methods and to receive the return result of a method call. The reference section at the back of this book shows how each instruction affects the operand stack.

The operand stack holds 32-bit quantities. Longs and doubles take two entries on the operand stack.

The operand stack is not a global stack. Instead, each method invocation is given its own operand stack—so a method's operand stack is isolated from other methods that are running. The interpreter is responsible for transferring the return result of a method from its operand stack to the operand stack of the caller.

There is a set of instructions that manipulate values on the operand stack. For example, the pop instruction discards the top item on the stack; the dup instruction takes the top item off the stack and pushes it on twice—giving you an extra copy of the value to work with.

Local Variables

Each method invocation has its own set of local variables. Local variables hold the formal parameters for the method (including the implicit parameter this) and also hold partial results during a computation. For example, in the Java method:

```
void example(int n) {
    int i;
    for (i = 0; i < (n * 2); i++) {
        int j = i + (i-1);
        ...
    }
}
```

The values for n, i, and j are held in local variables during the execution of the method. In addition, the special variable this is held in a local variable, and compilers may also generate temporary unnamed local variables to store useful

---

[*] A stack-based architecture was chosen since it lends itself to machines with few or irregular registers, such as the Intel 80x86.

values—for example, the value (n*2) is a candidate for being stored in a local variable, so that it doesn't have to be recomputed each time around the loop.

In the Java language, variables in a method are referenced by name. At the JVM level, on the other hand, local variables are numbered, and instructions to manipulate local variables take an integer operand indicating which variable to use.

As with the operand stack, each local variable is one word long (32-bits). Two-word values (doubles and longs) take two consecutive local variables, though programs should only address the lower-numbered variable. So when you write in Jasmin:

```
dconst_0    ; push the double 0.0 onto the stack
dstore 1    ; store this in local variable 1
```

then both local variables 1 and 2 will be modified by the dstore instruction (local variable 1 will contain 32 of the 64 bits, and local variable 2 will contain the other 32 bits). Implementations are free to decide how to order these bits, so long as they arc internally consistent and correctly implement the semantics of the JVM instruction set. Since it is illegal for programs to attempt to split two-word values (e.g., by trying to address the upper word in a two-word value), the internal ordering used by an implementation is invisible to a program running on the JVM.

Lexical blocks

The JVM does not have an explicit notion of the block structure of a method. That is, the JVM does not offer a way to mark the start and end of lexical blocks. Instead, it is up to the compiler to allocate local variables so as to implement the correct semantics for lexical variables. When you write in Java:

```
int i = 1;
...
while (true) {
    int i = 10;
...
}
```

the occurrence of i inside the block of code for the while loop is distinct from the one declared outside the loop, and the Java compiler will use a different local variable number for the occurrence of i inside the loop and the one outside of the loop. For example, the compiler might assign the outer occurrence to local variable 2 and the inner to local variable 3.

Note that local variables can be reused. That is, if you have code like:

```
{
    int i;
    ...
}
{
```

```
    int j;
    ...
}
```

then the compiler can reuse the same local variable number for i and j, since the scopes of the two variables do not overlap.

Choosing the mapping between variable names and local variable numbers is much like the problem of assigning registers in a traditional compiler.

Parameters and local variable allocation

The rules for determining which local variable a particular parameter is in are fairly straightforward: the JVM places the first formal parameter of a method to local variable 1, the second to local variable 2, and so on. Remember that longs and doubles take two local variables apiece—so if the first parameter to a method is a long, it is placed in local variables 1 and 2, and the second parameter is placed in local variable 3. Local variable 0 is used for the implicit parameter, this, which is a reference to the object whose method is being invoked.

Static methods are a special case. Since static methods don't have an implicit this parameter, the formal parameters are placed in local variables starting at local variable 0, so the first parameter to a static method is in local variable 0, the second is in 1, etc.

Parameter passing

The JVM always uses call-by-value to pass numeric types and call-by-reference for reference types (i.e., objects and arrays). You can freely change the value of any local variable in a method without affecting the caller. Compilers might use this fact to reduce local variable usage of a method. For example, in the method:

```
void foo(int n) {
    for (int i = 0; i < 10; i++) baz();
}
```

the compiler might recognize that formal parameter n (in local variable 1) is unused, and so use its local variable as the loop variable for i instead, reducing the local variable count by one.

Local variables and hardware registers

Good JVM implementations are likely to try to use hardware registers to hold at least the first few local variables. Keeping more frequently used values in lower-numbered local variables may improve performance.

4

Classes

In this chapter, we give an overview of how Java manages classes and of the Java class file format. You will learn more about important concepts such as the constant pool, resolving, type descriptors, and class file attributes. You will also learn more about the structure and representation used in the class file format. Toward the end of the chapter, we step through the contents of an example class file byte-by-byte.

This chapter concentrates on providing high-level overview information on classes. See Chapter 12, *Class File Reference*, for reference material describing the format of class files.

Loading Classes

Before a JVM can run any program, the first thing it has to do is load the classes that make up the program.

Loading is the process of obtaining (in bytes) the Java class file that defines a class. This can be done either by reading a file from disk, or over a network, or even by dynamically generating a byte array.

The JVM uses two mechanisms for loading classes. First, each runtime system has a "primordial" or "system" class loader—a built-in class loader used to load all the standard Java classes (i.e., classes in the java.* packages) as well as classes named on the command line to the Java executable. This loader typically searches for classes using the CLASSPATH environment variable. For example, when you type:

```
% java MyClass
```

the file "MyClass.class" will be loaded by the system loader from one of the directories listed in the CLASSPATH environment variable (see Chapter 2, *Quick Tour*, for a longer discussion of CLASSPATHs).

In addition to the system class loader, classes can be loaded using an instance of a ClassLoader. Java programmers can define their own ClassLoaders, so it is possible to customize the method Java uses to locate and load classes. Note that ClassLoaders are one of the resources protected by Java's SecurityManager; the SecurityManager in most Web browsers does not allow applets to create custom class loaders.

The JVM remembers how each class is loaded. When a class loaded by a Class-Loader tries to access another class, the same ClassLoader is invoked to obtain the new class. Effectively, each ClassLoader defines its own namespace—so classes that were loaded through one class loader are not necessarily available in others.

Let's look in more detail at the API to class loaders.

Class Loaders

Java programmers subclass java.lang.ClassLoader to define custom methods for locating and loading class files. The programming interface to ClassLoader is:

```
package java.lang;

public abstract class ClassLoader {
    // system methods, implemented by the JVM:
    protected final Class defineClass(byte[] data, int offset, int length)
    throws ClassFormatError;
    protected final Class findSystemClass(String name)
    throws ClassNotFoundException, NoClassDefFoundError;
    protected final void resolveClass(Class c);

    // provided by subclasses:
    protected abstract Class loadClass(String name, boolean resolveIt)
    throws ClassNotFoundException;
}
```

The JVM calls the loadClass method whenever it needs to load a class. In fact, it calls loadClass more often than that. For historical reasons, loadClass is expected to do a good bit more than just load classes. It also has to:

- call defineClass whenever it has loaded a class
- use findSystemClass to load system classes
- call resolveClass whenever the second parameter to loadClass is true.

loadClass is also expected to keep track of the classes it has loaded and resolved, and to only call defineClass or resolveClass once for each class.

Implementing these actions correctly takes a lot of extra boilerplate code, so Class-Loaders are larger than you would expect them to be. The good news is that Sun recognizes that this is an overcomplicated role for loadClass, and we can expect that future Java versions will offer a simplified interface for class loaders.

An example ClassLoader

In the following Java code, you see an example of a simple class loader, called, appropriately enough, SimpleClassLoader. When we say simple, we are referring to the way it locates and loads classes: it just takes the name of the class it is expected to load, converts the class name into a file name (by replacing "." characters with file path separators and appending the extension ".class"), and then attempts to load that file from disk. Unfortunately, as we mentioned above, ClassLoaders also have to do a lot more than just load classes, so the code is more involved than you might expect:

```
import java.io.*;
import java.util.Hashtable;

public class SimpleClassLoader extends ClassLoader {
    //
    // getClassFile actually loads the class. It takes the class name,
    // converts the name into a filename (e.g., "foo.Bang" -> "foo/Bang.class")
    // and attempts to read the contents of that file into a byte array.
    // If it succeeds, the bytes are returned in an array. If something
    // goes wrong, an IOException is thrown.
    //
    private byte[] getClassFile(String className) throws IOException {
        FileInputStream fin;
        byte classBytes[];

        // open the appropriate file
        fin = new FileInputStream(className.replace('.', File.separatorChar)
                                  + ".class");

        // read the bytes in the file into an array called classBytes
        classBytes = new byte[fin.available()];
        fin.read(classBytes);
```

```
        // return the bytes
        return classBytes;
}


// The rest of this code implements the semantics for ClassLoaders
// defined in the JVM specification.

// we use hashtables to remember the classes we've loaded and resolved.
//
private Hashtable loadedClasses   = new Hashtable();
private Hashtable resolvedClasses = new Hashtable();

// loadClass is the method called by the system to do all the work
//
protected Class loadClass(String className, boolean resolveIt)
                        throws ClassNotFoundException {
    print("loadClass(\"" + className + "\", " + resolveIt + ") :");
    printIndent(1);

    // loadClass does two jobs. The first is to load the class. This
    // may entail obtaining the bytes using getClassFile, though we
    // must also check for classes that are already loaded, and for
    // system classes.

    try {
        Class gotClass = null;

        if (loadedClasses.containsKey(className)) {
            // already loaded - don't do anything
            print("(already loaded class " + className + ")");

        } else if (className.startsWith("java")) {
            // wants a system class - call findSystemClass

            print("findSystemClass " + className);
            printIndent(1);

            gotClass = findSystemClass(className);

            printIndent(-1);
        } else {
            // Some other class name - need to obtain the class as an array
            // of bytes. In our case, we call getClassFile to do this.

            byte classBytes[] = getClassFile(className);

            // now call defineClass, passing it classData
            print("defineClass " + className);
            printIndent(1);

            gotClass = defineClass(classBytes, 0, classBytes.length);

            printIndent(-1);
        }
```

```
            // ensure that the className is registered in the hashtable
            if (gotClass != null) {
                loadedClasses.put(className, gotClass);
            }
        } catch (IOException ioe) {    // couldn't read the file
            System.err.println(ioe);       // so throw a ClassNotFoundException
            throw new ClassNotFoundException();
        }


        // The second job of loadClass is to call resolveClass on classes
        // whenever it is told to do so (i.e., when resolveIt is true), but only
        // once per class.

        if (resolveIt && !resolvedClasses.containsKey(className)) {
            print("resolveClass " + className);
            printIndent(1);

            // call resolveClass, passing it the class we have
            // in the hashtable
            resolveClass((Class)loadedClasses.get(className));

            printIndent(-1);

            // remember that we've resolved it
            resolvedClasses.put(className, "true");
        }

        printIndent(-1);

        // return the class we loaded
        return (Class) loadedClasses.get(className);
    }

// printing mechanism
//
int indentLevel = 0;

void print(String str) {
    for (int i = indentLevel; i > 0; i--) System.out.print("    ");
    System.out.println(str);
}
void printIndent(int level) {indentLevel += level; }

// test program
//
public static void main(String arg[]) {
    try {
        //
        // To test the class loader, we need to load a class - so we load
        // the SimpleClassLoader class itself! We borrowed this idea from
        // http://magma.Mines.EDU/students/d/drferrin/Cool_Beans. Thanks!
        //
```

```
            System.out.println("Testing the class loader");

            SimpleClassLoader loader = new SimpleClassLoader();

            Class myself = loader.loadClass("SimpleClassLoader", true);

            System.out.println("Making an instance of the loaded class");
            myself.newInstance();

        } catch (Throwable t) {
            t.printStackTrace(System.err);
            System.err.println(t);
        }
    }

}
```

We've divided SimpleClassLoader into two major methods. The first, getClassFile, is the method responsible for actually locating class files and obtaining the bytes in the file. You could easily rewrite this method to obtain classes from places other than your local hard disk—e.g., over the Net or by some other process.

The second method in SimpleClassLoader is loadClass—this implements the semantics for class loaders documented by the JVM specification. We've also added some print statements and a main() method so that we can see what the program does. To test the class loader, we need a class to load—so we just load the Simple-ClassLoader class itself, and make an instance of it. Here is a copy of the output from running the program:

```
% java SimpleClassLoader
Testing the class loader
loadClass("SimpleClassLoader", true) :
    defineClass SimpleClassLoader
        loadClass("java.lang.ClassLoader", false) :
            findSystemClass java.lang.ClassLoader
    resolveClass SimpleClassLoader
        loadClass("java.lang.ClassNotFoundException", false) :
            findSystemClass java.lang.ClassNotFoundException

Making an instance of the loaded class
loadClass("java.lang.ClassLoader", true) :
    (already loaded class java.lang.ClassLoader)
    resolveClass java.lang.ClassLoader
loadClass("java.util.Hashtable", true) :
    findSystemClass java.util.Hashtable
    resolveClass java.util.Hashtable
```

From this output, you can actually see some of the machinery in the JVM being exposed. Notice that, inside loadClass, calls to defineClass may call loadClass recursively. Internal classes are also passed to the ClassLoader for loading. Let's look at the stages that the JVM goes through to make a class ready for use.

Linking, Preparation, Initialization

Even after a class has been loaded, it isn't quite ready for use. The JVM spec describes a number of phases that a class undergoes:

Loading

As we mentioned above, this is the process of obtaining the bytes that make up the class's class file.

Linking

This phase involves taking the binary form of the class file and converting it into a runtime representation suitable for use within the Java Virtual Machine. Note that when a class is linked, this may cause the JVM to recursively load and link other classes (e.g., the superclass of the class). Linking is also the stage during which class file verification is performed.

Verification

Verification checks that the bytes in a class file are structurally sound, and that the class defined in the file is "safe." See Chapter 5, *Security*, for a description of the verification process. Note that, in Sun's JDK, verification is only performed on classes loaded via a ClassLoader. Classes loaded via the internal system class loader are assumed to be safe, and they are not verified by default.

Preparation

After linking, a class is prepared. Preparing a class performs various checks and initializations. During preparation, static fields are given their initial values, and the system checks the methods in the class, making sure that the class does not contain abstract methods unless it is marked as an abstract class.

Initialization

Finally, after all of the stages above, the class is initialized. To initialize a class, first the JVM checks that all the superclasses have been initialized. Then the class's static initializers are called. In the JVM, class initializers have the special name <clinit>. For example, if you define a class:

```
class Foo {
    static {/* some actions here */ }
}
```

this is compiled into a class like:

```
.class Foo
.super java/lang/Object

.method <clinit>()V
    // some actions here
.end method
```

The actions in <clinit> are executed when the class is first initialized.

Resolution

> During the execution of the methods in a class, the JVM will encounter refer-
> ences to entries in the class's constant pool. The first time that an entry in the
> constant pool is referenced, that entry is *resolved*. We'll talk about resolution
> when we discuss the constant pool below.

Finalization

> In some JVM implementations, classes may also become eligible for garbage
> collection. For example, if the JVM detects that there are no instances of a
> given class (or any of its subclasses), then the class itself may be marked as
> garbage and unloaded.

> The JVM specification doesn't currently dictate a standard mechanism for
> unloading classes, except to say that if a class contains a method like:

```
static void classFinalize() {... }
```

> this method will be invoked before the class is unloaded.

Exceptions During Loading, Linking, and Preparation

During any of the phases listed above, the JVM may encounter problems with the
class it is trying to obtain. If the JVM encounters a problem, it marks the relevant
class as invalid, and throws an exception. Briefly, the JVM can raise the following
exceptions.

During loading

ClassCircularityError

> A class is its own superclass, or an interface is its own superinterface.

ClassFormatError

> The data in a class file contains the wrong class, or is malformed.

NoClassDefFoundError

> The class loader could not find the relevant class or interface.

During linking and preparation

VerifyError

> The verifier found an error in a class file.

AbstractMethodError

> A method is declared as abstract but it appears in a class which isn't marked as
> abstract.

During initialization

ExceptionInInitializerError
> A static class initializer threw an exception.

Runtime errors

OutOfMemoryError
> Not enough memory available to complete an operation.

The Java Class File Format

We've seen many references to Java class files so far in this book. Now it's time to take a closer look at the data in class files.

The Java class file format is the format that a compiled Java class or interface is saved in. Class files have the extension ".class". You can think of class files as the Java equivalent of object files produced by other compilers, although Java class files are not tied to a particular processor or operating system, so the programs they contain can be run on many different computers.

The Java class file contains all the information needed by a Java runtime system to define a single class (or abstract class, or interface). See *Java in a Nutshell* for a description of classes, abstract classes, and interfaces.

A number of applications use the information in Java class files:

- The Java compiler javac reads files in this format to see what fields and methods are defined by the class.

- Java runtime systems (including Java-enabled Web browsers) read class files to obtain declarations and the bytecode for methods defined by the class.

- The javap program reads class files and prints out useful information found in the files.

- Java debuggers use information in class files to map bytecode to the corresponding line numbers in source, or to tell the programmer the symbolic name of a local variable.

A Java class file contains several critical pieces of data:

- virtual machine code for methods provided by the class

- a symbolic reference to the superclass of the class

- a list of the fields defined by the class

- a "constant pool" containing literals and symbols used by the class

- other data required by the runtime system

The Java class file format is the data format used to transmit Java programs over the Internet. As you can see, class files play a pivotal role in Java.

Representation

Information in class files is stored in an efficient binary format, which is treated by Java systems as a stream of 8-bit bytes. 16-bit, 32-bit, and 64-bit quantities are written in network order (also known as MSB or big-endian order), so the high-byte comes first. For example, the first item in a class file is the magic number 0xCAFEBABE. This integer is written in the class file as the bytes:

```
0xCA, 0xFE, 0xBA, 0xBE
```

in that order (if this was a little-endian format, the bytes would appear in the reverse order).

Streams using this format can be written and read in Java using classes which follow the DataInput and DataOutput interface, such as java.io.DataInputStream and java.io.DataOutputStream.

Structure

Class files are organized as a set of nested tables. The exact structure of the tables in a class file is described in Chapter 12. The essential tables are:

Top-level table
> The outermost table in a class file defines information relating to the class as a whole, including the name of the class, its superclass, and the access permissions for the class. The top-level table starts with the special magic number 0xCAFEBABE.

Constant-pool table
> This contains an ordered set of symbols and literals—strings, numeric constants, references to other classes, method names, field names, and type descriptors are stored in the constant pool.

Interfaces table
> An interface table contains a list of the interfaces this class implements.

Fields table
> A fields table contains a list of the fields that this class adds.

Methods table

A methods table contains a list of the methods that this class defines.

Attribute tables

Attribute tables appear at all levels in class files. They provide additional information associated with the class and with fields and methods. Attributes are named—for example, the "SourceFile" attribute is used to tell the Java runtime system the name of the source file the class file was generated from.

Note that, although class files provide definitions for fields and methods implemented by a class, they do not include definitions for fields or methods provided by any of its superclasses. To obtain these definitions, the Java system must load the class files of each of the superclasses.

The following code listing gives you an idea of what the top-level table in a class file looks like:

```
class ClassFile {
    int magic;
    short minor_version;
    short major_version;

    short constant_pool_count;
    ConstantPool cp[];

    short access_flags;
    short this_class, super_class;

    short interfaces_count;
    Interfaces interfaces[];

    short fields_count;
    Definition fields[];

    short methods_count;
    Definition methods[];

    short attributes_count;
    Attribute attributes[];
}
```

Classes and Interfaces

Note that both Java classes and Java interfaces use the same file format. In fact, the only difference between classes and interfaces at the file format level is that interfaces set the ACC_INTERFACE access flag in the top-level table (see the section called "Access Flags" later in this chapter for a description of access flags).

Interfaces are also more constrained than classes in what they contain. For example, you cannot have private or protected fields/methods in an interface. These constraints are described in full in the Java specification. In this book, we often use the term *class* to refer to either classes or interfaces.

Type Descriptors

The Java VM is a strongly typed machine, so a standard method for specifying the types of data locations (fields, arguments to methods, local variables, array elements, etc.) is essential. Type specifications in the JVM are done using type descriptors. Type descriptors are represented as string constants in the constant pool. They are constructed using a simple grammar, which we describe informally below.

Note that, unlike C and C++, Java does not provide unsigned datatypes, or datatypes representing functions or methods (so you cannot pass a method as an argument to another method).

Basic Type Descriptors

A single location in Java can store either a primitive value, a reference to a class, or a reference to an array. Let's first look at the type descriptors for primitive types.

Primitive types

All of the primitive types in Java are specified using a single-character descriptor, as shown in Table 4-1.

Table 4–1: Primitive type descriptors

Descriptor	Type	Meaning
B	byte	signed byte
C	char	character
D	double	double-precision IEEE float
F	float	single-precision IEEE float
I	int	integer
J	long	long integer
S	short	signed short
Z	boolean	true or false

For example, the descriptor for field holding a signed short is simply the string "S".

Class types

A class type is indicated using a string of the form:

```
L<fullclassname>;
```

i.e., the letter L, followed by the full name of the class, followed by a semicolon. Note that in class files, a "/" character is used to separate package names in a class name instead of the "." character used in the Java language. For example, to indicate that a field holds a java.lang.String, use the descriptor "Ljava/lang/String;".

Array types

An array type is specified using a descriptor with the form:

```
[<type>
```

i.e., an open square bracket, followed by a type descriptor, which is itself either a primitive type, a class type, or an array type (if you are specifying a multi-dimensional array).

It's a little strange seeing an opening brace but no closing brace—but it makes descriptors a little more compact and you will quickly become accustomed to it. Examples of array descriptors are shown in Table 4-2.

Table 4–2: Examples of array type descriptors

Descriptor	Type	Meaning
[C	char[]	single-dimensional array of 16-bit Unicode chars
[[F	float[][]	two-dimensional array of floats
[Ljava/lang/Thread;	Thread[]	single-dimensional array of threads

Methods

The type descriptors given above suffice for fields and arrays. For methods, a more elaborate type descriptor is required. Method type descriptors have the form:

```
(<argument_types>)<return_type>
```

where <argument_types> is a sequence of zero or more descriptors indicating the types of the arguments to the method, and <return_type> indicates the return type of the method. It can be any one of the descriptors listed above, or the special descriptor "V" to indicate that the method returns no value.

For example:

```
()V
```

is the type descriptor you use for a method that takes no arguments and returns no result, whereas:

```
()I
```

is the descriptor of a method that takes no arguments and returns an integer result. Taking a more complex example:

```
(SF[Ljava/lang/Thread;)I
```

is the type descriptor of a method that takes a short, a float, and an array of Threads as arguments, and returns an integer result.

Notice that type descriptors don't encode the name of a field or a method—only the type of data used in conjunction with the field or method. So the descriptor we saw above could be used for a method like:

```
class Example1 {
int doSomething(short x, float y, Thread z[]) {... };
}
```

or for a static method like:

```
class Example2 {
    static int doAnotherThing(short x, float y, Thread z[]) {... };
}
```

Descriptors in Jasmin

Descriptors appear in Jasmin when you use instructions like invokevirtual, getstatic, or anewarray, and also when you use Jasmin directives like .method or .field. See the Jasmin Guide in Appendix C, *Jasmin User Guide*, for a description of the syntax used by Jasmin, as well as the instruction reference pages for per-instruction details.

For example, to call the doSomething method we saw just above, you would use:

```
invokevirtual Example1/doSomething(SF[Ljava/lang/String;)I
```

Here you can see the "(SF[Ljava/lang/String;)I" type descriptor tacked onto the end of the name of the method—Jasmin parses the method name, extracts the type descriptor and stores it in the class file for you.

As another example, to set the value of a field, you might use something like:

```
bipush 10
putstatic Session/historyLength I
```

The "I" given as the second parameter to putstatic is the type descriptor for the field—in this case, the "I" indicates that the field holds an int.

The Constant Pool

We've mentioned the constant pool several times in this book, so you probably already know that the constant pool contains an eclectic mix of entries—from the names of classes, methods, and fields, to string and integer constants—that provide much of the essential information needed by a class.

The constant pool is a heterogeneous array. Many JVM instruction parameters and class file fields contain integers which are the index of an entry in the constant pool array.

In a class file, each entry in the constant pool starts with a one-byte tag field that identifies the type of the entry. The JVM specification currently defines the type tags shown in Table 4-3.

Table 4–3: Constant pool tag types defined by the JVM

Tag Name	Value	Used For
CONSTANT_Utf8	1	String in "Utf8" format (a derivative of ASCII)
CONSTANT_Integer	3	32-bit signed int
CONSTANT_Float	4	32-bit floating point number
CONSTANT_Long	5	64-bit long
CONSTANT_Double	6	64-bit double-precision floating point number
CONSTANT_String	7	Literal java.lang.String object
CONSTANT_Classref	8	Symbolic reference to a class
CONSTANT_Fieldref	9	Symbolic reference to a field
CONSTANT_Methodref	10	Symbolic reference to a method
CONSTANT_InterfaceMethodref	11	Symbolic reference to an interface method
CONSTANT_NameAndType	12	Name and type descriptor pair

After the tag field, entries in the constant pool have one or more additional fields, depending on the tag type.

For example, to refer to a Java method in a class file, you must add an entry tagged CONSTANT_Methodref in the constant pool. These entries have three fields:

- tag (a single byte)
- class_index (a two-byte unsigned integer)
- name_and_type_index (a two-byte unsigned integer)

The tag must contain CONSTANT_Methodref (i.e., the value 10). The class_index gives the index of an entry in the constant pool tagged CONSTANT_Class. The name_and_type_index field is the index of an entry in the constant pool which is tagged a CONSTANT_NameAndType—as you can see, constant pool entry indices are used a lot in class files. See Table 4-4 for a listing of the data associated with each constant pool type, or Chapter 12 for more details on the format of constant pool entries.

The constant pool usually contains a lot of string data. Literal strings, type descriptors, class names, method and field names—they are all stored in the constant pool. String data is stored in the pool using Utf8 entries (i.e., entries tagged CONSTANT_Utf8). Utf8 is a character encoding which is compatible with ASCII, but can also encode 16-bit Unicode characters. See Chapter 11, *Threads*, for a description of the Utf8 encoding.

The constant pool also acts as a symbol table. If in a class you want to reference some other class, or a method, or a field, you will need to create appropriate entries (CONSTANT_Class, CONSTANT_Method, etc.) in the constant pool. These entries contain symbolic information.

Table 4–4: Constant pool contents

Reference Type	Contains
CONSTANT_Utf8	array of bytes making up a string
CONSTANT_Integer	an int
CONSTANT_Float	a float
CONSTANT_Long	a long
CONSTANT_Double	a double
CONSTANT_String	index of a CONSTANT_Utf8 entry giving the bytes in the String
CONSTANT_Classref	index of a CONSTANT_Utf8 entry giving the name of a class
CONSTANT_Fieldref	index of a CONSTANT_Class entry and a CONSTANT_NameAndType entry
CONSTANT_Methodref	index of a CONSTANT_Class entry and a CONSTANT_NameAndType entry
CONSTANT_InterfaceMethodref	index of a CONSTANT_Class entry and a CONSTANT_NameAndType entry
CONSTANT_NameAndType	index of a CONSTANT_Utf8 entry containing the name of a field or method, and a CONSTANT_Utf8 entry containing a type descriptor

Constant Pool Resolution

The constant pool is designed to support dynamic linking. When the Java Virtual Machine encounters a use of a constant pool entry for the first time (e.g., when you first use new to create a new object of a class, or in the first use of getfield to get a field), the constant pool entry it *resolved*.

The actions the JVM performs to resolve a constant pool entry depend on its type. Resolution involves two basic steps: checking that the item you are trying to access exists (possibly loading or creating it if it doesn't already exist), and checking that you have the right permissions to access the item—i.e., making sure that you don't access private fields in other classes, etc.

Let's briefly look at how the JVM resolves each constant type:

Classes

> When the JVM encounters a use of an unresolved entry tagged CON-
> STANT_Class, it checks if the named class has been loaded and setup already.
> If it hasn't, then the JVM tries to load, link, prepare and initialize the class,
> using the phases we described earlier in this chapter. Any of the exceptions
> listed at the start of the chapter may be thrown if there is a problem loading
> and setting up the class.

> After the class has been loaded and set up successfully, the JVM checks that the
> current use of the class is valid. For example, if you are running a method in
> class A, and it is trying to make an instance of a class B, the runtime system
> checks that A has permission to access B, and that B is not an abstract class. If
> B is marked private and is in a different package from A, or if there is some
> other access violation, an exception is thrown.

Fieldrefs

> A CONSTANT_Fieldref entry contains pointers to two other items in the con-
> stant pool: a CONSTANT_Class entry (which is resolved first, as described
> above) indicating the class that the field is defined by, and a CON-
> STANT_NameAndType entry giving the name and type descriptor of the field.

> To resolve a Fieldref, the JVM checks all aspects of the named field—it checks
> that the named field exists in the indicated class, that it has the same type as
> the one given in the CONSTANT_NameAndType entry, that the current
> method has permission to access the field, and that the field is the correct stor-
> age type (e.g., if it's a static field, the instruction using the constant pool entry
> must be a getstatic or putstatic, not getfield or putfield). During this process,
> any of the exceptions listed below may be thrown.

Methodref and InterfaceMethodrefs

A CONSTANT_Methodref (or CONSTANT_InterfaceMethodref) entry contains pointers to two other items in the constant pool: a CONSTANT_Class entry (which is resolved first, as described above) indicating the class that the method is defined by, and a CONSTANT_NameAndType entry giving the name and type descriptor of the method.

To resolve a Methodref or InterfaceMethodref, the JVM checks all aspects of the named method—it checks that the named method exists in the indicated class, that it has the same type descriptor as the one given in the CONSTANT_NameAndType entry, that the current method has permission to access the named method, and that the method is the correct kind of method (e.g., if it's a static method, the instruction using the constant pool entry must be invokestatic, not invokevirtual) and so on. During this process, any of the exceptions listed below may be thrown.

Strings

Entries tagged CONSTANT_String contain a pointer to a CONSTANT_Utf8 entry in the constant pool containing the bytes that make up the string. To resolve a CONSTANT_String entry, the JVM constructs an instance of java.lang.String containing the characters encoded in the Utf8 entry. Strings built this way are maintained in a hashtable, so if many classes use CONSTANT_String entries which use the same sequence of characters, only one String object is constructed by the JVM for those classes. The strings in this hashtable are available to the Java programmer by calling the String.intern() method—for example, if you have the code:

```
String x = "Foo";
String y = ("F" + "o" + "o").intern();
```

then x and y will refer to the same underlying string object (i.e., x == y).[*]

Other Types

There are no special actions to perform when resolving any of the following types:

CONSTANT_Integer
CONSTANT_Long
CONSTANT_Float
CONSTANT_Double
CONSTANT_NameAndType
CONSTANT_Utf8

---

[*] Sun's JDK 1.02 implements this incorrectly. If you are using this version of Java, String instances generated by resolving CONSTANT_String entries are never == to the Strings returned by intern().

Note that entries in the constant pool are resolved only once. The runtime system caches the information it obtains after resolving the item. For example, after resolving a CONSTANT_Class entry, the JVM maintains a pointer directly to the class that was resolved. Similarly, after resolving a CONSTANT_String entry, the JVM caches a pointer to the String instance that was built. Because of this, the overhead of resolving constant symbols during runtime is reduced considerably.

Exceptions During Resolution

During the resolution of classes, fields and methods, any of the following exceptions can be thrown by the Virtual Machine:

IncompatibleClassChangeError
> Attempt to operate on a static field or method using an instruction designated for non-static fields or methods (or vice versa)

IllegalAccessError
> Attempt to access a private or protected field or method

InstantiationError
> Attempt to create an instance of an abstract class

NoSuchFieldError
> Attempt to retrieve the value of a non-existent field

NoSuchMethodError
> Attempt to call a non-existent method

Unlike exceptions generated by linking, preparation or initialization, these exceptions do not indicate that the class itself is invalidated—only that a particular *use* of the class is invalid.

Attributes

Attributes are named pieces of data that appear in class files. Attribute names are given as strings in the constant pool. The runtime system looks at the attribute name to decide how to interpret the data in the attribute.

Attributes always have a bytes_count field, which tells the class file reader how much data there is. Class file readers are required to ignore the data in attributes they don't recognize. Because of this behavior, attributes are a handy way to extend the data stored in a class file without breaking existing class file readers.

Attributes appear at all levels in a class file; you can add attributes to methods, fields, and the top-level class structure. The standard currently defines six attributes (see Table 4-5), although more are being added.

Table 4–5: Constant pool of class "out"

Attribute Name	Purpose
SourceFile	Gives the name of the source file that the class file was created from.
Code	Contains a block of bytecode holding the Java Virtual Machine instructions that implement a method.
ConstantValue	Indicates the value of a constant field, so when you write `public static final int N = 10;` the integer 10 is specified in the class file as a ConstantValue attribute associated with the field.
Exceptions	Provides a list of the classes of exception that a method can throw.
LineNumberTable	Contains a mapping between instructions in the bytecode and lines in the source file that the bytecode was derived from. Used by debuggers.
LocalVariableTable	Tells the Java runtime system the textual names of local variables in a method. Used by debuggers.

Some attributes give essential information to the class file reader. For example, a "Code" attribute is used in a method definition record to give the bytecode for a method. Other attributes, such as the "SourceFile" attribute, give non-essential information which can be safely ignored by the reader.

Attributes may also used to provide implementation-specific data. Some implementations extend the basic set of attributes. For example, an implementation might use a "MIPS-Code" attribute to hold a version of the bytecode of a method which has been compiled for the MIPS architecture.

Naturally, if you decide you want to add your own kind of attribute to a class file, you'll have to choose a name for the attribute. Sun recommends that people use the package naming conventions described in the Java Language Specification when choosing attribute names. For example, use a name like "COM.mycompany.MyAttributeName".

Methods and Fields

Class files of course contain method definitions (including abstract, class and instance methods) and field definitions (including private, static and instance fields).

Fields and methods both use a similar structure in the class file:

```
class Definition {
    short access_flags;
    short name_index;
    short type_index;
```

```
        short attributes_count;
        Attribute attributes[];
    };
```

access_flags defines the access permissions for the field or method (more on this later). The name_index and type_index fields give the indexes of Utf8 strings in the constant pool—one defining the name of the field or method, the other indicating the type descriptor. After that, an array of attributes is supplied.

The JVM specification lists only one attribute that you can give for fields, the "ConstantValue" attribute, which is used to provide the initial value for a static field. See Chapter 12 for more details on this attribute.

Methods have more attributes associated with them—of which perhaps the most important is the "Code" attribute, that actually gives the bytecode of the method (assuming the method is not an abstract method).

Access Flags

Classes, interfaces, methods, and fields all have *access flags* associated with them. Access flags are given as a 16-bit unsigned integers in the class file. The meaning of the bits in the access flags is given in Table 4-6.

Table 4–6: Access flags

Name	Value	Meaning	Used By
ACC_PUBLIC	0x0001	Visible to everyone	class, interface, field, method
ACC_PRIVATE	0x0002	Visible only to the defining class	field, method
ACC_PROTECTED	0x0004	Visible to this class and subclasses	field, method
ACC_STATIC	0x0008	A static field or method	field, method
ACC_FINAL	0x0010	No further subclassing or assignment	class, field, method
ACC_SUPER	0x0020	Use new invokespecial semantics	class, interface
ACC_SYNCHRONIZED	0x0020	Use monitor lock when method is invoked	method
ACC_VOLATILE	0x0040	Can't cache value	field
ACC_TRANSIENT	0x0080	Not to be written/read by persistent object manager	field

Table 4–6: Access flags (continued)

Name	Value	Meaning	Used By
ACC_NATIVE	0x0100	Implemented using "native" code (e.g., "C")	method
ACC_INTERFACE	0x0200	File contains an interface	interface
ACC_ABSTRACT	0x0400	Class cannot be instanced	class, interface

Note that not all access flags are relevant in all cases. For example, the ACC_TRANSIENT flag should only be set on a field. ACC_INTERFACE can only be set on a class.

There are also other constraints imposed by the Java language:

- ACC_FINAL and ACC_ABSTRACT are mutually exclusive—they cannot both be set.

- On the other hand, if ACC_INTERFACE is set, then ACC_ABSTRACT must also be set for the class and for all the methods in the class.

- If ACC_INTERFACE is set, ACC_FINAL cannot be set.

- Only one of ACC_PUBLIC, ACC_PRIVATE, or ACC_PROTECTED can be set.

- In interfaces, fields must be given the access ACC_PUBLIC, ACC_STATIC, and ACC_FINAL.

- For methods, ACC_ABSTRACT cannot be used in conjunction with ACC_FINAL, ACC_NATIVE, ACC_SYNCHRONIZED, or ACC_STATIC.

The ACC_SUPER flag exists for backwards compatibility. In early versions of the JVM, the `invokespecial` instruction was called `invokenonvirtual` and had more relaxed semantics. When the specification was released, Sun tightened the semantics of `invokenonvirtual`, and renamed it `invokespecial`. All modern compilers should set the ACC_SUPER bit in the class's access flags, to indicate that they follow the new semantics. Runtime systems should also use the newer semantics—see the reference page for `invokespecial` in Chapter 13, *Instruction Reference.*

In many cases, the meanings and uses of access flags are derived directly from the Java Language specification. See the JVM Specification for more details.

Limits

Class files do impose some limitations on how large a class, field, or method can grow. Table 4-7 summarizes these limits.

Table 4–7: Class file limitations

Description	Limit	Units
Constant pool entries	65535	word entries per class
Fields	65535	fields per class
Methods	65535	methods per class
Bytecode length	65535	bytes per method
Local variables	65535	words per method
Arguments to a method	255	words (including the implicit this)
Operand stack	65535	words per method
Array dimensions	255	dimensions per array

An Example Class File: The out Class

In this section, we take a brief look at the contents of an example class file, for a class called "out".

The "out" class is defined by the Jasmin code:

```
.class public out
.super java/lang/Object

.method public <init>()V  ; just call Object's initializer
    aload_0
    invokespecial java/lang/Object/<init>()V
    return
.end method

; specify the "main" method - this prints "Hello World"
.method public static main([Ljava/lang/String;)V

   ; set limits used by this method
   .limit stack 2

   ; Push the output stream and the string "Hello World" onto the stack,
   ; then invoke the println method:

   getstatic java/lang/System/out Ljava/io/PrintStream;
   ldc "Hello World"
   invokevirtual java/io/PrintStream/println(Ljava/lang/String;)V

   return
.end method
```

You probably recognize this class—it's the HelloWorld class we saw in Chapter 2.

The hex dump of the class file is shown below:

```
0000 CA FE BA BE 00 03 00 2D 00 19 01 00 07 70 72 69    Ê_º_...-.....pri
0010 6E 74 6C 6E 09 00 07 00 16 0C 00 01 00 09 01 00    ntln............
0020 13 6A 61 76 61 2F 69 6F 2F 50 72 69 6E 74 53 74    .java/io/PrintSt
0030 72 65 61 6D 01 00 04 43 6F 64 65 07 00 0A 07 00    ream...Code.....
0040 14 01 00 03 6F 75 74 01 00 15 28 4C 6A 61 76 61    ....out...(Ljava
0050 2F 6C 61 6E 67 2F 53 74 72 69 6E 67 3B 29 56 01    /lang/String;)V.
0060 00 10 6A 61 76 61 2F 6C 61 6E 67 2F 4F 62 6A 65    ..java/lang/Obje
0070 63 74 07 00 04 0A 00 0B 00 03 01 00 04 6D 61 69    ct...........mai
0080 6E 0C 00 10 00 17 01 00 16 28 5B 4C 6A 61 76 61    n........([Ljava
0090 2F 6C 61 6E 67 2F 53 74 72 69 6E 67 3B 29 56 01    /lang/String;)V.
00A0 00 06 3C 69 6E 69 74 3E 01 00 15 4C 6A 61 76 61    ..<init>...Ljava
00B0 2F 69 6F 2F 50 72 69 6E 74 53 74 72 65 61 6D 3B    /io/PrintStream;
00C0 0A 00 06 00 0E 07 00 08 01 00 10 6A 61 76 61 2F    ...........java/
00D0 6C 61 6E 67 2F 53 79 73 74 65 6D 08 00 18 0C 00    lang/System.....
00E0 08 00 11 01 00 03 28 29 56 01 00 0B 48 65 6C 6C    ......()V...Hell
00F0 6F 20 57 6F 72 6C 64 00 01 00 13 00 06 00 00 00    o World.........
0100 00 00 02 00 01 00 10 00 17 00 01 00 05 00 00 00    ................
0110 11 00 01 00 01 00 00 00 05 2A B7 00 12 B1 00 00    .........*·....
0120 00 00 00 09 00 0D 00 0F 00 01 00 05 00 00 00 23    ...............#
0130 00 03 00 04 00 00 00 17 B2 00 02 4C 12 15 4D 10    ........2..L..M.
0140 05 3E 2B 2C B6 00 0C 84 03 FF 1D 9A FF F7 B1 00    .>+,¶.._|__.ÿ._ÿ.
0150 00 00 00 00 00                                      .....
```

Top-Level Fields

The first 10 bytes in the class file define the magic number, the minor_version, the major_version and the constant_pool_count fields for the class:

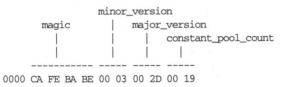

```
                    minor_version
      magic          |    major_version
        |            |      |    constant_pool_count
        |            |      |      |
    ----------- ----- ----- -----
0000 CA FE BA BE 00 03 00 2D 00 19
```

magic
> the value 0xCAFEBABE, in network (MSB first) order

minor_version
> the minor version number (3)

major_version
> the major version (0x2D = 45)

constant_pool_count
> the number of items in the constant pool (0x19 = 25)

The magic field identifies the file as a Java class file—it is the hex integer 0xCAFEBABE.

The minor_version and major_version identify the version number of the runtime system that the class file is designed for. The Java Virtual Machine is currently at major version 3, minor version 45. If you use other values for these two fields, a Java runtime system may refuse to load the class.

The constant_pool_count of 25 indicates that there are 25 items in the constant pool. Note that this number is misleading, since it is one more than the number of constants written out in the class file. For historical reasons, the first constant pool entry (the entry with index 0) is reserved for use by the runtime system—JVM class files do not write out a value for constant pool entry 0, and they must also never refer to index 0 in constant pools.

Constant Pool

The next 24 items in the file constitute the constant pool. The constant pool provides a heterogeneous collection of items needed by the class—including constants, references to fields, methods and classes, and other important pieces of data. The constant pool is treated as an ordered array by Java, and many VM instructions take an index into the constant pool as a parameter.

As we noted above, only 24 items are given even though the length of the constant pool is 25. Here is a breakdown of the first two entries in the constant pool:

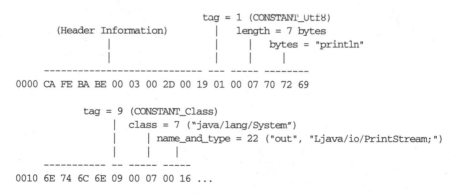

```
                                    tag = 1 (CONSTANT_Utf8)
            (Header Information)      |    length = 7 bytes
                  |                   |      |   bytes = "println"
                  |                   |      |   |
        ----------------------------  ---  -----  --------
  0000  CA FE BA BE 00 03 00 2D 00 19 01 00 07 70 72 69

            tag = 9 (CONSTANT_Class)
              |    class = 7 ("java/lang/System")
              |      | name_and_type = 22 ("out", "Ljava/io/PrintStream;")
              |      |   |
        -----------  --  -----  -----
  0010  6E 74 6C 6E 09 00 07 00 16 ...
```

Table 4-8 shows a decoded list all of the entries in the constant pool, along with their types and the values of their fields. Numbers in parentheses indicate that there is a field which references another entry in the constant pool by index—for convenience the value for that entry is shown after the number.

Table 4–8: Constant pool entries

Entry	Type	Value
1	Utf8	bytes = "println"
2	Fieldref	class = (7) "java/lang/System" name_and_type = (22) "out", "Ljava/io/PrintStream;"
3	NameAndType	name = (1) "println" descriptor = (9) "(Ljava/lang/String;)V"
4	Utf8	bytes = "java/io/PrintStream"
5	Utf8	bytes = "Code"
6	Class	name = (10) "java/lang/Object"
7	Class	name = (20) "java/lang/System"
8	Utf8	bytes = "out"
9	Utf8	bytes = "(Ljava/lang/String;)V"
10	Utf8	bytes = "java/lang/Object"
11	Class	name = (4) "java/io/PrintStream"
12	Methodref	class = (11) "java/io/PrintStream" name_and_type = (3) "println", "(Ljava/lang/String;)V"
13	Utf8	bytes = "main"
14	NameAndType	name = (16) "<init>" descriptor = (23) "()V"
15	Utf8	bytes = "([Ljava/lang/String;)V"
16	Utf8	bytes = "<init>"
17	Utf8	bytes = "Ljava/io/PrintStream;"
18	Methodref	class = (6) "java/lang/Object" name_and_type = (14) "<init>", "()V"
19	Class	name = "out"
20	Utf8	name = "java/lang/System"
21	String	index = (24) "Hello World"
22	NameAndType	name = (8) "out" descriptor = (17) "Ljava/io/PrintStream;"
23	Utf8	bytes = "()V"
24	Utf8	bytes = "HelloWorld"

Class, Superclass, and Interfaces

The constant pool extends up to byte 0xF7 in the file. After that, the class contains some additional top-level fields, as shown in the following diagram.

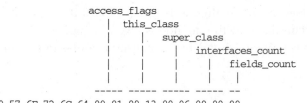

```
                        access_flags
                         |  this_class
                         |   |  super_class
                         |   |   |  interfaces_count
                         |   |   |   |  fields_count
                         |   |   |   |   |
                        ----- ----- ----- ----- --
        00F0 6F 20 57 6F 72 6C 64 00 01 00 13 00 06 00 00 00
```

```
              methods_count
                   |
               ------
        0100 00 00 02  ...
```

access_flags
> specifies the class access information. 0x1 = ACC_PUBLIC, so the class is a public class.

this_class
> is an index into the constant pool: constant pool entry 0x13 (19) is an item tagged CONSTANT_Class, and has the name "out"—so the file is defining the "out" class.

super_class
> is another index into the constant pool. Entry 0x06 is a CONSTANT_Class item whose name is "java/lang/Object"—specifying that the superclass of "out" is java.lang.Object.

interfaces_count
fields_count
> are both zero—this class does not implement any new interfaces or add any additional fields.

methods_count
> is 2, indicating that there are two methods associated with this class.

Methods

The out class file then contains the definition and implementation details for two methods. The breakdown for the start of the first method is shown below:

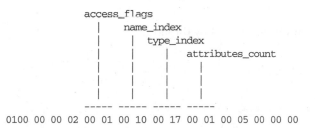

```
                 access_flags
                   |    name_index
                   |     |  type_index
                   |     |   |  attributes_count
                   |     |   |   |
                   |     |   |   |
                   |     |   |   |
                 ----- ----- ----- -----
        0100 00 00 02 00 01 00 10 00 17 00 01 00 05 00 00 00
```

The access_flags for the method is 0x1 (ACC_PUBLIC)—i.e., the method is a public method. The name of the method is given by name_index, which is the index of the Utf8 string item "<init>" in the constant pool—this is the definition of the <init> method:

```
.method public <init>()V
    aload_0
    invokespecial java/lang/Object/<init>()V
    return
.end method
```

The descriptor of the method is given by type_index, which is the index of the Utf8 string containing "()V" in the constant pool.

The method has one attribute—as specified by the attribute_count. This attribute is the next entry in the class file:

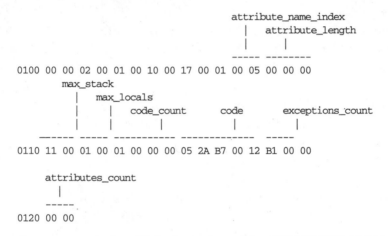

The attribute_name_index (5) is the index of the CONSTANT_Utf8 item "Code" in the constant pool—indicating that this is a "Code" attribute. The overall length of the attribute, attribute_length, is 0x11 or 17 bytes. After this are the fields for the code attribute:

max_stack
    The maximum number of items pushed on the stack by this method is 1.

max_locals
    The number of local variables used by the method is 1.

code_count
    There are 5 bytes of bytecode.

code

> The actual bytecode for the method (hurrah!). We leave it to you to decode the instructions in the bytecode.

exceptions_count
attributes_count

> These are both 0—the method does not catch any exceptions, and the Code attribute has no further attributes.

The Rest

We will skip the second method defined by the class, and move onto the last entry in the class file—these are the final two bytes:

```
0150 00 00 00 00 00
     -----
```

These two bytes indicate the length of the last table in the class file—the attributes table for the class. In this case, the attribute table is empty, so bytes 0x153 and 0x154 are zero. Other class files may contain attribute tables—for example, a "SourceFile" attribute defining the name of the source file that the class file was generated from.

As you can see, it takes quite a bit of work to decode a class file. Fortunately, it's not something that you have to do very often—class files are usually read by a computer, not a person.

5

Security

This chapter examines security issues in the Java Virtual Machine, and unveils some of the features and mysteries of the class file verifier. It explains the verification process and tells you how to create Java applications that pass verification. It gives you insights into how Java can run applications securely and efficiently.

In this chapter, we assume you've read some of the earlier chapters and have some knowledge of the instructions and structure of the Java Virtual Machine.

Security: A Layered Approach

Security is extremely important in Java. If people are going to download third-party programs and run them on their computers, they need to be certain that the third-party program won't cause any damage. For instance, downloaded applets must not:

- damage the computer hardware or file system

- cause the computer to crash or go so sluggishly that it becomes unusable.

- transmit details about the computer or contents of its files to third parties.

If an applet could do any of these things, people would be unwilling to run applets downloaded from an external source.

Java employs a number of techniques to manage security. For example, calls for system resources, such as sockets and files, are monitored by Java. Java runtime systems can trap many of the operations that an applet or an application wants to perform.

For example, applets are generally prevented from doing any of the following:

• Read or write, create or delete or otherwise modify or examine the local file system.

• Create network connections to computers, other than the computer that the applet was downloaded from.

• Listen to or accept network connections on the local system.

• Create top-level windows that masquerade as windows created by a local application. (Applet windows are given a title indicating their nature.)

• Obtain information about the user, such as the user's name or home directory.

• Execute programs on the local system.

• Cause the runtime system to exit.

• Load dynamic libraries or native methods.

• Create or manipulate threads outside of the applet's ThreadGroup.

• Specify a ClassLoader, SecurityManager, ContentHandlerFactory, SocketImplFactory, or URLStreamHandlerFactor for the system.

• Load classes except from the packages java.applet, java.awt, java.awt.image, java.awt.peer, java.io, java.lang, java.net, java.util.

• Extend local packages.

Implementation of all of these security measures is done using a SecurityManager. This Java object implements much of Java's security policy. See the Java Language Specification for details about SecurityManager.

In this chapter, we focus on the JVM's role in Java's security model, namely the class file verifier. The verifier is a key component of the security strategy. In fact, none of the restrictions listed above would be worth much if Java didn't employ a class file verifier. It's the verifier's job to make sure that the classes loaded by an applet are well behaved on a much deeper level—to prevent classes from forging pointers to memory, or branching to arbitrary locations in a program, or otherwise abusing the Java runtime system.

The Class File Verifier

Whenever Java downloads a class file from a remote (or "untrusted") site, it "verifies" the class file. Verification is mostly concerned with ensuring that loading and running the code in the class file will not crash the JVM interpreter, leave the interpreter in an undefined state, or crash the host computer.

Verification involves applying a number of "structural constraints" to the class file. For example, the verifier checks the layout of the data in the class file, making sure that:

- The data format of the class file is correct: It has the right magic value 0xCAFEBABE at the start, all the tables' length fields are within allowable limits, all class entries in the constant pool provide a string constant naming the class, etc.

- All type descriptors are well-formed and consistent.

- All named fields, methods and classes exist.

- More importantly, the verifier performs "bytecode verification" using the Java bytecode verifier.

The Bytecode Verifier

The Bytecode verifier is a sophisticated program that checks the bytecode within a method to ensure that it is well-behaved.

The bytecode verifier performs a range of basic checks. For example, it checks that:

- All goto and branch instructions refer to a valid bytecode address (one that is the start of an instruction in the code).

- The types of all instruction parameters are correct—for example, if an instruction references an entry in the constant pool, the bytecode verifier checks that the entry exists and that it is the right kind of entry.

In addition, the class file verifier runs a "theorem prover" on the virtual machine code in each method. The theorem prover checks the code at a much deeper level. After running the theorem prover, the verifier knows that:

1. The operand stack is used consistently and doesn't overflow or underflow. For example, if you write:

```
pop          ; pop top single-word item off the stack and discard it
```

and the stack is empty, the verifier will complain. Similarly, if you write:

```
dconst_0     ; push the double-precision float 0.0 onto the stack
pop          ; pop top single-word item off the stack and discard it
```

the verifier will complain again—you cannot use pop to remove one word of a two-word double from the stack since you are not allowed to split two-word items in two (you must use pop2 instead).

2. The local variables are used consistently and correctly, so if you write:

```
iconst_0        ; push the integer 0 onto the stack
astore_1        ; store the object on the stack in local variable 1
```

the verifier will fail the class file—astore expects a reference to an object, not an integer. Similarly, if you write:

```
.method public example()V
    aload_1
    ...
.end method
```

the verifier will fail—you are trying to access the value of a local variable before you have assigned it a value.

3. Methods are called with the right number and types of arguments. For example, if you write:

```
fconst_0
invokestatic java/lang/String/valueOf(I)Ljava/lang/String;
```

the method will not pass verification—you are calling a method, called valueOf, that has the type descriptor:

```
(I)Ljava/lang/String;
```

i.e., it takes an integer as an argument and produces a string as a result, but the top item on the stack (left there by fconst_0) is a float.

The Catch: Flow Control and Verification

Of course, you have probably noticed the catch by now: it's easy to see how the verifier knows that you have done something illegal when you have a method like:

```
.method public example()V
    aload_1
    ...
.end method
```

Clearly, if the aload_1 instruction is the first instruction in the method, the verifier can deduce that the program is trying to retrieve the value of a variable before it has been assigned a value. But what about a more complex example, which has branch instructions. Take the method:

```
.method public example()I
    .limit locals 2

    goto Label2

Label1:
    iload_1
    ireturn
```

```
Label2:
    iconst_0
    istore_1
    goto Label1

.end method
```

If you follow the flow of instructions here, the code is actually doing the following:

```
(branch)
iconst_0
istore_1
(branch)
iload_1
ireturn
```

This is in fact a legal program: local variable 1 is assigned an integer value, then the integer value is retrieved and returned as the result of the method (which is declared as a method that takes no arguments but returns an integer result).

But if a verifier looked at this program naively, the `iload` instruction does appear in the bytecode before the `istore` instruction. A naive implementation of a byte-code verifier might fail this program.

Now imagine how much harder things get when you start adding conditional branches—as you get with instructions like ifne or if_icmpeq.

One solution to this problem might be to have the verifier follow all of the possible routes in a program—checking that each route is valid. However, checking that a program is valid in the general case is a very costly process—in fact, it's a famous problem, called the halting problem, that was studied by Alan Turing and Kurt Gödel in the 1930s. It's been shown that, in the general case, it is not possible to take a description of a program and decide whether or not the program will complete, let alone whether it behaves well or not.

Java's Solution: A Midway Approach

The Java verifier doesn't attempt to solve the general case problem—instead it expects the person generating the Java VM code to help out a little. The verifier's theorem prover checks only a limited number of routes through the program, applying the following restriction:

- For each alternative way in a method for reaching an instruction X, the stack state and the local variable state must be equivalent.

    For example, if you have the code:

    ```
    .method public example()I
        ...
    ```

```
        iconst_1
        goto Mylabel

        ...
        iconst_2
        goto Mylabel
        ...

Mylabel:        ; several parts of the method jump here ...
        istore_1
        ...
```

The verifier checks that, for every place in the code that contains a branch instruction to Mylabel, the stack contains one integer item. In this case, both of the ways of reaching Mylabel meet this constraint, so the program passes.

Now consider the program:

```
        iconst_4
        istore_1      ; store 4 in local variable 1 (used as a counter)

Loop:
        aconst_null ; push null onto the stack
        iinc 1 -1    ; decrement the counter
        iload_1
        ifne Loop    ; repeat this until the counter reaches zero
```

This code tries to push null onto the stack four times using a loop. It is a reasonable thing to do, but this program will fail verification. Compare the two stack states:

–   when the program first runs:

```
        iconst_4
        istore_1
                    <- stack is empty
Loop:
        aconst_null
```

–   and, after the branch back to Loop:

```
Loop:    <------------|
    aconst_null       |
    iinc 1 -1         |   <- stack contains one item - null
    iload_1           |
    ifne Loop      -----
```

these stack states are not equivalent—in one case the stack is empty, in the other the stack contains a reference to an object. The verifier will detect this and fail the code.

As you can see, the verifier prohibits certain ways of writing code. However this isn't usually a problem—it's normally straightforward to rewrite code so that the branches and gotos don't muddle the stack.

In this case, one alternative is simply:

```
aconst_null
aconst_null
aconst_null
aconst_null
```

or you could allocate a temporary array:

```
    iconst_4
    istore_1    ; store 4 in local variable 1

    iconst_4
    anewarray java/lang/Object
    astore_2    ; store a 4-element array of objects in local variable 2

Loop:
    ; at this point the stack is empty. Now fill the array ...

    aload_2     ; load array onto the stack
    iload_1     ; load counter onto the stack
    aconst_null ; push null onto the stack
    aastore     ; store the value in array[counter]

    iinc 1 -1   ; decrement the counter
    iload_1

    ; the stack is empty again - so the branch will pass verification
    ifne Loop   ; jump back to the Loop label unless the counter is zero
```

Passing Verification

From the previous section, it should be clear that when you are writing tools that target the Java Virtual Machine, you have to follow certain rules to ensure your classes pass verification. In this section, we look at those rules from the perspective of someone generating code which passes verification. For full details, you should consult the JVM Specification.

Verification issues can be thought of on three levels: structure, environment and content.

Structure

The verifier checks that the class file is "structurally sound" at all levels. This means that class files must follow all the constraints described in the class file format specification (see Chapter 4, *Classes*, and Chapter 11, *Threads*).

All aspects of a class file are subject to structural checks. Any deviation from the class file format constitutes a breach of structural soundness, and the class file will be rejected.

For example, the this_class field in the top-level structure of a class file must be the index of a CONSTANT_Class entry in the constant pool. If it's not, the class will fail verification. Similarly, the magic field of a class file must be the value 0xCAFEBABE, written out in big-endien order (i.e., the bytes 0xCA, 0xFE, 0xBA, 0xBE in that order). If the magic field is not correct, the class file will not pass verification.

Structural soundness extends to the contents of the bytecode for methods. The bytecode verifier checks that all bytecode offsets (including offsets for exceptions, jumps, conditional branches, and so on) reference the start of an instruction; branches to the middle of an instruction or to an offset before the start of the code or beyond the end of the code are not allowed. Additionally, all instructions which include parameters referencing the constant pool must reference a valid offset in the constant pool and the reference must be of the correct type. For example, ldc must be used only for constants using the CONSTANT_String, CONSTANT_Float or CONSTANT_Integer tags; putfield must be given a CONSTANT_Fieldref entry, etc.

There are some gray areas—for example, setting the ACC_VOLATILE bit (0x0040) in a class file's access_flags may be ignored by some JVM implementations. It is important not to rely on this behavior. As a general rule, be conservative: even if something isn't checked by the class file verifier in Netscape 2.0, say, it may be checked in future versions, or by other verifiers. If you want to be really sure, it's worth checking in the JVM specification—it lists several hundred checks that the verifier performs.

Using a program like Jasmin or JAS to generate class files makes it much harder to create structural errors. With Jasmin, many of the structural constrains are handled for you. For example, if you write:

```
ldc "hello world"
```

or:

```
goto Label
```

in a Jasmin file, then Jasmin automatically creates the right entries in the constant pool for ldc, and uses a valid offset for the goto instruction. (It's still up to you to check that you use well-formed names for classes, methods, fields and type descriptors.)

Environment

When writing JVM code, you need to be aware of the "environment" that the class will be used in—in other words, the other classes that your class depends on, and the methods and fields of those classes.

When the verifier comes across, for example, a CONSTANT_Fieldref item in the constant pool, it performs structural checks to ensure that the field name is well formed (it contains no spaces, starts with a non-numeric character, etc.) and that the type descriptor is a well-formed type descriptor. However, it doesn't immediately check if the field really exists in the indicated class. This means the constant pool can contain items which are correctly formed, but which refer to make-believe classes, fields or methods. The constant pool can also contain references to classes that haven't been loaded yet.

The first time a Java runtime system comes across a *use* of a constant pool entry, it *resolves* the entry. This involves checking whether the relevant classes have been loaded, loading/verifying classes if necessary, and then checking that the reference in question is valid. We discussed resolving in Chapter 4.

The verifier checks for type conflicts and for access conflicts. A type conflict occurs when a method is called with one type descriptor, but is declared with another. Access conflicts occur when a program tries to access a field, method or class which is declared as private or protected, and the code doing the accessing is not within a class or a subclass. So if you write:

```
invokestatic foo/baz/mymethod()V"
```

the class verifier will check that foo.baz is an existing class, that mymethod is a static method belonging to the foo.baz class, that the type descriptor of the method is ()V, and that the caller has the right access permissions. (So if the method is private, then the caller must belong to the same class as the method).

The JVM verifier tries to delay these checks until they are necessary. This can speed up the initial loading time for a class.

For example, if you write:

```
; call the method "funmethod" which returns an instance of a FunClass,
; then immediately assign the instance to a field of the same type:

invokenonvirtual myclass/funmethod()LFunClass;
putfield myclass/myfield LFunClass;
```

the verifier will not bother to check that the FunClass exists—it knows that, assuming FunClass exists, it is valid to assign it to the field myfield. Then, when the code is executed, the interpreter will notice that FunClass has not been loaded, and will load FunClass (or produce an exception if FunClass cannot be found and loaded).

On the other hand, if you write:

```
; call the method "funmethod" which returns an instance of a FunClass,
; then assign the instance to a field of a DIFFERENT type:
invokenonvirtual myclass/funmethod()LFunClass;
putfield myclass/myfield LAnotherClass;
```

the verifier is forced to load FunClass so that it can check that FunClass is indeed a subclass of AnotherClass.

Content

Generating a class file which is structurally and environmentally correct does not guarantee that it will pass verification—compilers could easily generate class files which follow the file format but which contain bytecode instructions that are designed to cause the system to crash. For example, consider the code:

```
label1:
    push 10
    goto label1
```

This would quickly cause Java's operand stack to overflow, with possibly nasty consequences. Another hostile program might try to jump to a computed address, using something like:

```
ipush 1234
astore_1          ; store an integer is local variable 1
ret 1             ; return to the address stored in local variable 1
```

To prevent methods like this, the class file verifier runs a theorem prover to examine the contents of the bytecode of each method.

From the perspective of writing code that passes the bytecode verifier, you need to be concerned with three things:

1. Each instruction should be invoked with the correct types for its operands and stack values. This can be quite subtle. For example, the code:

   ```
   lconst_1     ; push the two-word long integer 1 onto the stack
   pop          ; pop the first word off the top of the stack
   pop          ; pop the second word off the top of the stack
   ```

   will cause the verifier to complain: pop can only be called when the top item on the stack is a single-word value. To pop a two-word value from the stack, you need to use pop2.

2. The maximum stack length must not be exceeded. Each method in Java has its own local operand stack. The size of the operand stack is specified in the "Code" attribute and should not be exceeded in each method. This means that you will need to calculate the maximum size of the operand stack yourself, set it to an arbitrary value which is sufficient for the code you generate, or determine it manually.

3. Finally, you must consider the contents of the stack and local variables when you use branch instructions. It's tempting to use the stack to store all sorts of temporary pieces of data, but if you use the stack in complex ways, you are likely to run into trouble with verification.

For example, if you write or generate code that looks like:

```
iconst_1        ; push the integer 1 onto the stack

... <insert several dozen other instructions here> ...

ipush_2         ; push local variable 2
isub            ; now compute (<the 1 pushed earlier> - <local variable 2>)
istore_1        ; store the result in local variable 1
```

then you can easily forget that there was a 1 lying on the stack from near the top of the code, change or delete the code in between in some way, and introduce a stack error. Try to keep the use of the stack as small as possible, and group instructions together so that at the end of each group the stack is empty again. In the case above, it would be better to write:

```
... do lots of stuff ...

iconst_1        ;  now- push the integer 1 onto the stack
ipush_2         ; push local variable 2
isub            ; now compute (<the 1 pushed earlier> - <local variable 2>)
istore_1        ; store the result in local variable 1
```

In general, only push items onto the stack just before they are needed. That way, you are less likely to insert branch instructions that introduce inconsistent stack states.

How the Bytecode Verifier Works

The theorem prover used by Java's bytecode verifier is complex, and you will not require a deep understanding of it unless you are implementing your own Java interpreter. However, a brief description is given below in case you are interested.

The theorem prover works by modeling the contents of the operand stack and local variables at all points in the execution of a method. To do this, the theorem prover emulates the effect that each instruction has on the stack and on local variables. It tracks the types of each item on the stack and in each local variable, as well as the length of the stack. It also keeps track of when local variables contain illegal values (e.g., before they have been assigned a value).

The theorem prover is only concerned with types—it doesn't check how many times a loop is done, what the loop does, or the specific values of fields that the loop accesses—it only checks that the loop treats the stack types and the local variable types consistently. When the theorem prover encounters an instruction for the first time, it stores in a table the stack state and local variable state at the point just before the instruction is executed. A separate entry is maintained in the table for every instruction in the bytecode.

The theorem prover then checks that the instruction is being run with the correct types—for example, if the instruction is istore_0 then the item on top of the stack must be an integer. If the instruction is being run with invalid argument types, the class fails verification.

Next, the theorem prover emulates the instruction's effect on the stack and local variables, checking that the stack does not overflow or underflow. Finally, it moves onto the next instruction and continues verification.

When a branch instruction is met, the theorem prover looks at all the possible destinations for the branch instruction. If a destination has not been seen previously by the verifier, the verifier recursively examines that destination. If a destination has been seen previously, the verifier compares the current stack and local variable types with the information recorded for the instruction before. One of three things can happen:

a. If the two states are identical, then the destination doesn't need any further checking—the verifier moves on to another possible destination, or the next unchecked instruction.

b. If the two states are incompatible—for example, if in one state the stack contains:

    ```
    int
    int
    ```

    and in the other it contains:

    ```
    int
    float
    ```

    then the verifier complains. The verifier also complains if the stacks are of different lengths, or if the local variables contain different types.

c. If the two states are "compatible," then the verifier "merges" the two states, and goes back to the first step described above: it records the current stack and local variable state in a table, emulates the instructions effect on the stack, checks the next instruction—and so on.

The point of step (c) is to deal with the situation where the two states differ, but in a way that is not dangerous. For example, consider the two stack states:

```
int          <- stack state recorded for the instruction earlier
Object
```

and

```
int          <- the current stack state
String
```

all the methods that can be applied to objects can also be applied to Strings, so the difference between these two stack states is not likely to be of great importance (a change in the other direction would not be safe).

We mentioned that step (c) above tests if two states are "compatible." What does "compatible" mean? If the only difference between them is the types of references to objects, they may be compatible. For example, the stack states:

```
| int                 |          | int                   |
| float               |   and    | float                 |
| DataInputStream     |          | BufferedInputStream   |
```

are compatible, whereas the states:

```
| int                 |          | int                   |
| float               |   and    | float                 |
| Vector              |          | int                   |
```

are not.

If the theorem prover notices that two states are compatible but not identical, it "merges" the states—it creates a new state by substituting the nearest common ancestor for each class that is different, so:

```
| int                 |          | int                   |
| float               |   and    | float                 |
| DataInputStream     |          | BufferedInputStream   |
```

becomes the new state:

```
| int                 |
| float               |
| FilterInputStream   |
```

It then acts as though it has not seen the instruction before—it continues verification using the new merged state, following the first step we described.

Verification in the Future

In principle, as a side effect of using a class file verifier, JVM implementations can run code that passes verification significantly faster, without compromising safety. This is because the runtime interpreter can avoid performing all of the checks that have already been done during verification. Since verification includes fairly comprehensive checking of the bytecodes for methods, a large amount of runtime checking can be avoided. For example, the interpreter does not need to perform runtime checks for the following three types of items.

- stack limits (overflows or underflows)

- types of arguments to JVM instructions

- accesses or assignments to local variables

Is this the whole story? Unfortunately not.

One downside of verification is that the verification process itself can be slow. A large amount of checking is done before the class is made available for use, and this checking is computationally expensive.

Another downside of verification is that it is very hard to verify the verifier—i.e., to test whether the class file verifier really is catching all the illegal programs. Already we've seen scares in the press where hackers have discovered a previously unknown loophole. We'd like to think that all the loopholes are now known, but experience teaches us that this is never the case.

Fortunately, there are some other alternatives that may offer better solutions. Future implementations of Java are moving towards techniques such as public key encryption to identify class files that are from a trusted registered source. These "trusted" class files don't need to be verified. Depending on the level of trust, other security mechanisms may be lifted as well—the day when applets can be as functional as full-blown applications may not be that far away.

6

Implementation Notes

In a book of this size, we don't have space to give you a step-by-step account describing how to implement a Java runtime system. On the other hand, we can examine some of the important issues that you will encounter and explore some possible solutions and strategies.

In this chapter we look at a few of the components of a Java runtime system from a system-implementor's standpoint. This will give people who are developing a runtime system an idea of the nature of the task they are involved in. It should also help programmers working with Java to understand the technology they are relying on.

Implementing a JVM runtime system isn't trivial, although we know of several students who have built simplified runtime systems as student projects. Of course, developing a system that works efficiently and supports all the features in Java is a much larger undertaking.

Choosing a System Language

To implement a Java runtime system, your first step is to select a language in which to implement it. The language will need to be powerful enough to support the various features of the Java language (e.g., garbage collection, threads, efficient bytecode interpretation, objects and methods, and so on). Sun's Java interpreter, for example, is implemented in C. This means that at its most basic level, a Java statement is executed by running a piece of C code. Other choices are possible—you might decide to implement an interpreter in a high-level language such as Scheme or SmallTalk. This approach is attractive since it saves you having to reimplement every aspect of the JVM (for example, you wouldn't need to write your own garbage collector, since both Scheme and SmallTalk support automatic memory management). SmallTalk is particularly interesting since it has its own Virtual Machine that you could target.

A more radical approach would be to implement your own batch compiler that compiles Java-like statements directly into machine code for a particular platform, producing an executable module that can be run directly. You could then use Java itself as the system language, and implement things like the runtime bytecode interpreter, the garbage collector, and the various built-in classes using your compiled version of Java. You could then even write the system compiler as a Java program, so that your whole system is Java-based. This idea may seem a little mind-bending at first, but it's common practice in compiler writing (and how C compilers first got started).

Class Files and Java Primitive Types

One of the early hurdles you will face is implementing a class loader. The runtime system needs to be able to read programs stored in the Java Class File format, described in Chapter 4, *Classes*. You may decide to adopt your own file format as well, but for compatiblity you will need to support the standard format.

Reading class files is straightforward. Once you have a function for reading a byte from a stream, you can quickly construct functions for reading shorts, ints, floats, etc. If your system supports 32-bit IEEE floats (as most do), you can convert four bytes into a float by doing:

```
float convert_to_float(unsigned char *bytes)
{
    float f;
    unsigned char *buf = (unsigned char *)&f;
    // We can't rely on the -bytes- array being aligned in memory correctly,
    // so we transfer the data to a piece of memory we know is correctly aligned
    // correctly (because buf points to a float, and the compiler will align
    // the float for us)
    buf[0] = bytes[0];
    buf[1] = bytes[1];
    buf[2] = bytes[2];
    buf[3] = bytes[3];

    return f;
}
```

Similar conversion functions will be needed for the other Java types (32-bit integers, 64-bit integers and doubles, etc.). In Ansi C, a 64-bit integer is usually declared as a "long long," and a 64-bit float is usually a "double." You will need to check with your compiler supplier to determine which types to use for these quantities on a particular system. If no 64-bit integer arithmetic is supported, you can emulate it yourself using two 32-bit integers and manually computing overflow and sign.

Some CPUs use little-endian representation (e.g., Intel x86 chips) for data. The first byte in memory is used to store the least significant bits of data. On these systems, conversion functions will need to perform byte swapping, since Java bytestreams are stored in big-endian (most significant byte first) order, also known as network order. So on a little-endian system, convert_to_float would be written as:

```
float convert_to_float(unsigned char *bytes)
{
    float f;
    unsigned char *buf = (unsigned char *)&f;

    buf[0] = bytes[3];
    buf[1] = bytes[2];
    buf[2] = bytes[1];
    buf[3] = bytes[0];

    return f;
}
```

In case you are unclear, the following simple program will print out the byte ordering used by the computer on which it is compiled and run:

```
#include <stdio.h>

int main(int argc, char **argv)
{
    int i = 1;
    unsigned char *buf = (unsigned char *)&i;

    if (buf[0] == 1) {
        /* least significant bits appear first ... */
        printf("little-endian\n");
    } else {
        printf("big-endian\n");
    }

    return(0);
}
```

In practice, most runtime systems on little-endian machines will swap the order of bytes in a class file once, when the class file is loaded. This avoids the runtime overhead of constantly performing byte swapping.

The Interpreter

The core of any JVM implementation is the execution engine that executes the instructions in the bytecodes of a method. Java interpreters step over the Virtual Machine instructions in a method, executing each in turn. They include a few state variables for remembering things such as the current program counter (pc), the top of the stack (optop), the class of the method that is being executed, as well as pointers to storage for local variables (vars) and the stack frame.

A simple way to implement an interpreter is using the equivalent of the "switch" statement in C. For example, the start of an interpreter might look like:

```
void interpret(unsigned char *bytecodes)
{
    StackFrame frame;    /* the stack frame for the method */

    /* setup the registers ... */

    unsigned char *pc  = bytecodes;
    Item *optop         = frame.operand_stack;
    Item *vars          = frame.local_variables;

    while (1) {

        unsigned char opcode = *pc; /* get current instruction */

        switch (opcode) {/* switch on current instruction */

            case OPCODE_dup: /* duplicate item on stack */
                optop[0] = optop[-1];

                /* update registers */
                pc += 1; optop += 1;
                continue;

            case OPCODE_pop: /* remove item from stack */
                pc += 1; optop -= 1;
                continue;

            case OPCODE_iadd: /* add two items on the stack */

    ...

            case OPCODE_return: /* return from method */
                return;

        }
    }
}
```

The `interp.c` code provided on the disk with this book contains a fleshed-out version of the above code.

Bytecode Verification

The Java Virtual Machine is designed so that the content of a class file can be "verified" to ensure that it follows a number of restrictions. Chapter 5, *Security*, provides details on bytecode verification and a description of Sun's verifier.

From an implementation standpoint, there are several options. You may choose not to include any form of verification, since bytecode verification is not a prerequisite for running Java programs. It's easier to implement a Java runtime system which doesn't perform verification. Note that this approach is no less safe than creating an executable using, say, C or C++ and then running that executable. Sun's Java compiler performs a lot of compile-time checks to ensure that the code will run safely and pass verification, so a Java program is less likely to crash the runtime system than a C or C++ program.

On the other hand, if you ever intend to embed your runtime system in an application that downloads classes over the Internet, some form of security is essential. You may opt to license Sun's verifier, or implement your own verifier, or use a third-party solution such as one based on public keys. More options will become available in the near future, as the Java technology matures.

Built-In Classes

All implementations of JVM need to provide a standard set of built-in classes for use by Java applications. The Java language specification dictates that the classes in the following packages will be available:

*   java.lang
*   java.io
*   java.util

You will also need to consider support for:

*   java.net
*   java.awt
*   java.applet

Many of the classes in these packages have been implemented by Sun purely in Java, so you could obtain initial versions of the code by licensing the Sun implementation. This will save you from writing all the classes from scratch. Because of Sun's licensing policies, it makes sense to use Sun's class files but re-implement the native methods necessary to run them (this isn't as hard as it might seem—several

implementations we know of have followed this route). Sun has a very liberal
license covering the use of their class files, but this just covers the compiled Java
bytecode (not the native code necessary to run these classes). Native code falls
under the stricter terms of the VM license.

Given that many of the methods for these classes will be written in the native system language—the language that the runtime system is implemented with—you
need to determine how to call native system methods in Java early in your design
process.

Native Methods

Java allows applications to dynamically load and then execute "native methods."
These are methods which are implemented in a language other than Java.

Supporting native methods introduces a number of complexities. Issues include:

- Mapping Java types and classes into native types

- Mapping Java identifier names into native names

- Trapping errors and signalling exceptions from native methods

- Resolving differences in procedure calling mechanisms

- Interacting with Java features such as threads, the garbage collector, type
  checking, etc.

The Java specification does not yet offer a standard solution to these issues.
Although Sun supports native methods in its implementation, the details for this
interface are undergoing changes.* However, it is worth describing some of the
mechanisms you will need to work with.

You can think of native methods on three levels:

- Linking methods into the executable

- Calling native methods from Java

- Calling Java methods from native code

The native method mechanism must be able to "link" the native code into the Java
runtime system. This involves locating any symbols and libraries needed by the
native code and then mapping that code into the running Java process's memory.
On many UNIX systems, the C procedures dlopen and dlsym can be used to link in
a dynamic shared library and load objects from the library. On older systems, it is
possible (although clumsy) to use fork and ld to achieve the same effect.

---

* JDK 1.1 includes a new Java Native Interface (JNI). See *http://java.sun.com* for more details.

Once you have loaded the code into the running executable, you need to be able
to call the code from Java. In C, you use type casting to cast a pointer to a function
pointer, and then call the underlying function.

Suppose you had a C routine declared as:

```
int my_function(int);
```

The example code below shows how to use dlopen, dlsym, and casting to dynamically load and call my_function:

```
void *handle;
int i;
int (*fptr)(int); /* pointer to a function which takes an
                      int and returns an int */

/* open the needed object */
handle = dlopen("libmylibrary.so", RTLD_LAZY);

/* set fptr to the address of my_function */
fptr = (int (*)(int))dlsym(handle, "my_function");

/* invoke my_function, passing integer value as a parameter */
i = (*fptr)(10);
```

In Windows, there is also run-time dynamic linking. The key functions are Load-
Library and GetProcAddress. Here is a simple program that loads a library and
calls a function in the library:

```
main(int argc, char *argv[])
{
    HMODULE lib = LoadLibrary(argv[1]);
    int (*proc)(char *) = GetProcAddress(lib, argv[2]);
    int retval = (*proc)(argv[3]);       // or just "proc(argv[3])" in ANSI C
    FreeLibrary(lib);
    return retval;
}
```

As well as calling C code from within Java, you will need to be able to go the other
way: calling Java methods from C. This requires a C API for native methods. The
Java Specification does not currently dictate a standard for the API, though Sun's
Java native method API is fairly comprehensive. For example, Sun provides a C
routine:

```
long execute_java_static_method(ExecEnv *ee, ClassClass *jclass,
                                char *method_name, char *signature,
                                ...)
```

to execute a static Java method. For this procedure, ee is an "execution environment," giving details of the current method being run by Java. You can use the
function EE() to obtain the current execution environment. jclass is a pointer to
a Java class, usually obtained by calling the C routine FindClass. method_name and

signature are the name and signature of the method to call. Additional arguments to the method are given after the signature (the execute_java_static_method takes a variable number of arguments).

For example, for the class:

```
class Example {
    public static void callme() {...}
};
```

you can invoke the callme() method from C using:

```
(void)execute_java_static_method(EE(),
                FindClass(EE(), "Example", TRUE),
                "callme", "()V");
```

Garbage Collection

In Java, an object is never explicitly deleted. Instead, Java uses a memory model known as "automatic storage management." Java implementations keep track of when each object is still in use and automatically free an object only when there are no more references to it. The specific details of how this mechanism operates are left up to the implementor of the Java Virtual Machine.

Garbage collection is a rich and large topic. There are hundreds of possible garbage collection algorithms. This section provides a quick overview. For more information, see *Garbage Collection, Algorithms for Automatic Dynamic Memory Management,* by Richard Jones, published by John Wiley & Sons, Ltd. Or see Jones's page, *http://stork.ukc.ac.uk/computer_science/Html/Jones/gc.html,* on garbage collection.

No-Brainer Storage Manager

One approach to storage management is simply to never free the memory for an object. This idea may horrify experienced programmers, but if you are trying to create an implementation of the JVM quickly this may be an initial starting point. On modern operating systems, if an area of memory is never referenced by a program, it eventually gets swapped out, so programs can in fact grow quite large before they run into memory problems. However, this is not a recommended approach!

Reference Counting

The next step up is to perform "reference counting" storage management. The idea is that every object has a hidden slot which acts as a counter used to remember how many "references" there are to that object. References originate from local variables, object fields, entries on the stack, static variables, and so on.

For example, if you wrote the code:

```
String x = Myclass.mystring;
```

the assignment operator would need to increment the counter for the object held in Myclass.mystring before assigning it to "x". If you then did:

```
x = null;
```

the counter for the string object would need to be decremented. When the counter reaches zero, the memory for the object is released.

Reference counting systems are fairly straightforward to implement, and incur a fairly low fixed penalty on all assignment operations. However, reference counting breaks down in some circumstances—for example, circular data structures are hard to deal with, since if an object A refers to B, and B refers to A, then the reference count for both objects will never reach 0 and the objects will not be freed. There are ways to detect some of these situations, but mark-and-sweep garbage collection offers a more general and bullet-proof alternative.

Mark-and-Sweep

The most common way to implement automatic storage management is called *mark-and-sweep garbage collection*. Objects are allocated from a single, large, "heap." Each object in the heap includes a tag field that identifies what class of object it is. From this information, the system can determine what fields the object has, and therefore how large it is and where the next object starts.

Intermittently, a "garbage collector" is run. In a copying garbage collection, the garbage collector first obtains a new, empty heap. It then marches over all known references to objects—objects stored in local variables, or on the stack, or in static class variables. For each object referenced, the garbage collector first checks if the object is "marked" (marking is usually done by setting a bit in one of the object's fields). If it is marked, the object is ignored and the next object is examined. If it is not marked, the object is copied to the new heap, a bit is set in the original object to "mark" that it has been copied, and the new memory address for the object is stored somewhere in the original.

Then the garbage collector examines all of the fields of the new copy, updating references to objects to point to their new locations, and running the garbage collector recursively on unmarked objects to copy them as well. Eventually a new heap containing only live objects is generated, and the old heap can be discarded.

Optimizations on Mark-and-Sweep

A major drawback of mark-and-sweep is that the garbage collector tends to be "hungry." As the heap grows larger, the collector takes a noticeable time to run and uses large amounts of memory and processing power. Scanning several megabytes of data may take a few seconds, and the copying algorithm described above temporarily doubles the size required by the process.

There are a number of strategies for reducing the impact of the garbage collector. One is to use a non-copying algorithm, which moves objects around in the existing heap rather than copying them into a new heap. This saves space but increases complexity and processing time.

In Sun's Java system, the garbage collector is run as a low-priority thread. When the system appears to be idle, the garbage collector is run, making better use of the idle cycles on the CPU and reducing the number of garbage collections needed during non-idle times.

Other high-level environments (e.g., Apple's Dylan) utilize multiple heaps and a "generational" garbage collector. The idea is that, as objects age (i.e., remain in use) they are moved to heaps that are garbage collected less often, until eventually they get moved into a heap that is hardly ever examined by the garbage collector. These systems take advantage of the fact that objects in a program have different kinds of life cycles, depending on their use. Many of the objects created in an application are transitory—they are generated as the side effect of a computation, and then are immediately discarded and become eligible for garbage collection. For example, in the statement:

```
"a" + "b" + "c"
```

the string "ab" is created, then the string "abc" is created and the intermediate "ab" string immediately becomes garbage.

On the other hand, some objects in an application remain in the heap for long periods—for example, the object representing an applet window remains in the heap until the applet is quit. Separating objects of different lifespans into different heaps is a simple strategy for improving the focus of garbage collection efforts.

Threads

Threads empower the Java programmer, but from the JVM implementor's standpoint, threads are an added nuisance.

To write a runtime system that supports threads, there are a number of issues to consider.

- You must correctly maintain the state variables and stack frames for multiple execution engines, one per thread.

- Data that is shared between threads must be synchronized properly. In particular, uses of shared resources in the VM must be properly synchronized. For example, the table of available classes is a shared resource. Changes to the table must be done using a synchronizing mechanism, such as a mutex lock.

- Some implementations tie Java threads to the native operating system's thread mechanism. Doing this involves more work (though the results scale up better).

- The native code in the runtime system must be aware of threads—it must be "thread safe." Writing thread-safe code involves steps such as protecting the use of global or static variables and playing by the rules described in the JVM Specification.

For more information on threads, see *Java Threads*, by Scott Oaks and Henry Wong (published by O'Reilly & Associates, Inc.).

Performance Enhancements

This section outlines two methods for improving the speed of Java programs—quick instructions and just-in-time compilation.

Quick Instructions

If you look at the Java VM instruction opcodes, you will notice that opcodes above 202 are currently undefined (of course, in future versions it's possible these opcodes will be used for new instructions). As an implementor, you might decide to take advantage of the 53 undefined opcodes to implement a few additional special purpose instructions. Then, when you first run the bytecode for a method, you might substitute some of the standard instruction opcodes in the method with your equivalent alternatives—in some cases you can use this to perform a basic level of optimization. This is completely hidden from the program running on the JVM.

Sun, for example, has implemented a number of "quick" instructions using unassigned opcodes. The "quick" instructions shadow instructions which reference items in the constant pool, such as getfield, putfield, getstatic and putstatic. The first time that one of these non-quick instructions is executed, it resolves the entry in the constant pool, and then replaces itself in the bytecode with its quick (non-checking) version, which then performs the intended operation. Subsequent execution of the same piece of bytecode runs faster since the quick varient of the instruction is used, and this performs less checking than the non-quick alternative.

The "quick" opcodes are listed in Table 6-1.

Table 6–1: Quick opcodes

Number	Opcode
203	ldc_quick
205	ldc2_w_quick
206	getfield_quick
207	putfield_quick
208	getfield2_quick
209	putfield2_quick
210	getstatic_quick
211	putstatic_quick
212	getstatic2_quick
213	putstatic2_quick
214	invokevirtual_quick
215	invokenonvirtual_quick
216	invokesuper_quick
217	invokestatic_quick
218	invokeinterface_quick
219	invokevirtualobject_quick
221	new_quick
222	anewarray_quick
223	multianewarray_quick
224	checkcast_quick
225	instanceof_quick
226	invokevirtual_quick_w
227	getfield_quick_w
228	putfield_quick_w

See the JVM specification for more details on these opcodes.

Just-in-Time Code Generation

Performing tricks such as using quick instructions can slightly improve the speed of a Java program. However, Java interpreters cannot compete with C programs ... or can they?

It is conceivable to create a standalone compiler for Java which acts just like the C compiler—it takes Java code and compiles it into an executable format that can be run by the hardware directly. You could then produce Java programs that run just as quickly as their C counterparts, but you would lose some of the nice features of Java (portability, added security, etc.).

An alternative is to implement a *just-in-time code generator*. Just-in-time code generation is a technique for speeding up the execution of interpreted programs. The idea is that, just before a method is run for the first time, the machine-independent Java bytecode for the method is converted into native machine code. This native machine code can then be executed by the computer directly, rather than via an interpreter. Certain optimizations are possible during this conversion process, and the result is a method that runs far quicker than its interpreted cousin.

The most basic implementation of just-in-time code generation uses the idea of *inlining*. Instead of using a giant switch statement to interpret the instructions in a method, the machine code needed for each JVM instruction is concatenated together into one long stream of data. This data can be executed directly by the CPU.

An easy way to explore how this might be implemented is to write a simple interpreter in C (or use the toy interpreter provided with this book) and then use your C compiler to compile it into assembler code. Most C compilers provide an option for outputting assembler rather than native object code. On UNIX systems, you use the "-S" flag to turn on this mode, so doing:

```
cc -S toy-interpreter.C
```

produces a file called "toy-interpreter.s" that contains the assembly code generated by the compiler. You can then look at this code to see how the compiler deals with the C version of each JVM instruction. On an Intel system, the OPCODE_dup instruction in the interpreter we saw at the start of the chapter becomes the following (comments have been added to make the code easier to read):

```
L23:
    movl eax, -4(ebx)    ; eax = optop[-1]
    movl (ebx), eax      ; optop[0] = eax
    addl ebx, 4          ; optop = optop + 1 word (i.e., 4 bytes)
    incl esi             ; pc = pc + 1
    jmp L16              ; jump back to the top of the interpreter's loop
                         ; to process the next instruction
```

In this example, you can see that the register ebx is used for Java's optop (the pointer to the top of the stack). Register eax is used as a temporary working register. Register esi holds the program counter (pc).

Note that optop[-1] is the top item on the stack, since optop always points to the next available slot on the stack. Also note that the stack is addressed in units of 4 bytes (1 word is 4 bytes).

Now we can inline this code. The inlined version of the dup instruction is simpler, since in the inlined code, each JVM instruction is placed consecutively in memory, and we no longer have to maintain a pc register (the CPU handles the program counter register for you). We also don't need to jump back to the top of the interpreter's main loop after executing each instruction. So the incl and jmp can be omitted, leaving:

```
movl eax, -4(ebx)        ; move optop[-1] into eax
movl (ebx), eax          ; move eax into optop[0]
addl ebx, 4              ; increment optop by 1 word
```

You can continue this type of examination for each of the JVM instructions. Eventually you will have a list of the assembler code needed for each JVM instruction. The next stage is to find a way of turning these assembler descriptions into actual machine code at runtime. Unfortunately, this is rather tedious. It involves writing a runtime assembler that takes a description of the code and creates the appropriate data in memory for that code. Since each chip has its own set of conventions for alignment, addressing, modes, and so on, writing a runtime assembler is fairly arduous. Fortunately, you don't have to support every instruction provided by the CPU, only the subset required by the JVM instructions.

Optimizing Just-in-Time

Inlining by itself buys a certain amount of performance improvement, but more significant gains can be made by analyzing the Java bytecode and looking for more efficient ways to achieve the same results. Many of the optimizations can be made by looking at how the method uses the stack. A full discussion of optimizing code generators is outside the scope of this book, but let's look at a few simple examples.

Take the case of a method containing:

```
pop
pop
pop
```

You can replace this with a single instruction that decrements the optop register by 3 words. On an Intel system you might write this as:

```
addl ebx, -12
```

Similarly, you can look for sequences like:

```
...
bipush 100
iadd
```

and replace this with code that directly adds 100 to the top item on the stack, saving one push instruction.

Another improvement is to use some of the hardware registers in your processor for local variables. You might place local variables 0 to 3 in registers, so that an:

```
iinc 0, 1
```

would become, say, the single instruction:

```
addl edx, 1
```

Where to Go from Here

This chapter has covered some of the important aspects of Java Virtual Machine implementation. We only touched briefly on a few topics, but you should now have a better picture of the scale of work required to implement a runtime system. Fortunately, several groups have already created good implementations of the JVM, so there are reference implementations to work with.

If you want more information, look at the Jasmin home page on the Web, *http://cat.nyu.edu/meyer/jasmin*. We will try to maintain an up-to-date list of pointers to relevant documentation and online material on the JVM.

In this chapter:
- *Stack Manipulation*
- *Local Variables*
- *Arrays*
- *Objects*

Data Operations

This chapter contains an overview of the instructions in the JVM for managing data. These instructions, which we've grouped under the heading "Data Operations," utilize the stack, local variables, arrays and objects to store data and move data from one part of a program to another. This chapter contains a listing of all the instructions related to data management, along with examples and additional notes. For more detail on any given instruction, consult the reference section in Chapter 13, *Instruction Reference.*

Stack Manipulation

Each method invocation has its own private *operand stack*, which is used to pass arguments to methods and to collect return results. Methods declare how large an operand stack they need. In Jasmin, you do this using the ".limit" directive:

```
.method example()V
    .limit stack 20 ; can push up to twenty single-word items onto the stack
    ...
.end method
```

We've already seen the operand stack in action in Chapter 2, *Quick Tour*. Let's now look at the set of support instructions that work with the stack.

Pushing Constants onto the Stack

A set of instructions are provided simply to push constant numbers and strings onto the stack (see Table 7-1).

Table 7–1: Instructions for pushing constants

Name	Description
bipush	push one-byte signed integer
sipush	push two-byte signed integer
ldc	push single-word constant onto stack
ldc_w	push single-word constant onto stack (wide index)
ldc2_w	push two-word constant onto stack
aconst_null	push null
iconst_m1	push the integer constant –1
iconst_<n>	push the integer constant 0, 1, 2, 3, 4 or 5
lconst_<l>	push the long integer 0 or 1
fconst_<f>	push the single float 0.0, 1.0 or 2.0
dconst_<d>	push the double 0.0 or 1.0

For example, to push the integer –1, use:

```
iconst_m1 ; push -1 onto the stack
```

to push an integer in the range 0-255, use bipush:

```
bipush 100    ; push 100 onto the stack
```

ldc, ldc_w and ldc2_w are slightly special. These are used to retrieve values from the *constant pool.* For example:

```
ldc "Hello"    ; push the string "Hello"
ldc2_w 10.0    ; push the double 10.0 onto the stack
```

Table 7-2 shows which instruction to use for each constant type.

Table 7–2: Constant pool types and ldc

Constant Type	Instruction(s)
CONSTANT_Integer	ldc or ldc_w
CONSTANT_Float	ldc or ldc_w
CONSTANT_String	ldc or ldc_w
CONSTANT_Long	ldc2_w
CONSTANT_Double	ldc2_w

The "_w" suffix on ldc_w and ldc2_w indicates a "wide" instruction. Wide instructions can address any of the 65535 entries in the constant pool, whereas their non-wide counterparts can only address the first 255 entries. (ldc_w is stored in bytecode along with a 2-byte index, whereas ldc is stored with only a 1-byte index). Jasmin users don't have to worry about which one to use, since the Jasmin assembler automatically selects the appropriate instruction for you.

Strings pushed using ldc are "interned," using the String.intern() method. See "Constant Pool Resolution" in Chapter 4, *Classes*, for more details.

Stack Manipulation

If you already have some items on the stack, but you want them in a different order, the JVM provides a set of instructions to do that (see Table 7-3).

Table 7–3: Stack manipulation instructions

Name	Description
nop	do nothing
pop	discard top word on stack
pop2	discard top two words on stack
dup	duplicate top single-word item on the stack
dup2	duplicate top two stack words
dup_x1	duplicate top stack word and insert beneath second word
dup2_x1	duplicate two words and insert beneath third word
dup_x2	duplicate top stack word and insert beneath third word
dup2_x2	duplicate two words and insert beneath fourth word
swap	swap top two stack words

For example, to swap the top two items on the stack:

```
bipush 10
bipush 20
; stack now contains 10, 20

swap
; stack now contains 20, 10

pop
; stack now contains 20

dup
; stack now contains 20, 20

pop2
; stack is now empty
```

It's important to remember that longs and doubles occupy two entries on the stack. To pop a long or double from the stack, you must use pop2. You can't instead use two pop instructions, or otherwise try to treat two-word values as two single-word values.

Local Variables

Each method invocation has its own set of local variables. Local variables are used to store partial results and state information. When a method returns, any values in its local variables are discarded. Methods declare how many local variables they use.

In Jasmin you use the ".limit" directive to do this, such as:

```
.method example()V
    .limit locals 100 ; can use up to 100 local variables
.end method
```

Local variables are numbered. Local variable 0 is the lowest numbered local variable—for non-static methods, local variable 0 holds this—the object that the method is being applied to. Each method can use up to 65535 local variables.

There are really only two things you can do with local variables—you can store values in them ("pushing"), and you can retrieve values from them ("popping").

Pushing Local Variables onto the Stack

The instructions in Table 7-4 push the values of local variables onto the stack.

Table 7-4: Retrieving values from local variables

Name	Description
iload	retrieve integer from local variable
iload_<n>	retrieve integer from local variable <n>
lload	retrieve long from local variable
lload_<n>	retrieve long integer from local variables <n> and <n> + 1
fload	retrieve float from local variable
fload_<n>	retrieve float from local variable <n>
dload	retrieve double from local variable
dload_<n>	retrieve double from local variables <n> and <n> + 1
aload	retrieve object reference from local variable
aload_<n>	retrieve object reference from local variable <n>

Popping Stack Values into Local Variables

The instructions in Table 7-5 pop the top item off the stack and store it in a local variable.

Table 7–5: Storing values in local variables

Name	Description
istore	store integer in local variable
istore_<n>	store integer in local variable <n>
lstore	store long integer in local variable
lstore_<n>	store long in local variables <n> and <n> + 1
fstore	store float in local variable
fstore_<n>	store float in local variable <n>
dstore	store double in local variable
dstore_<n>	store double in local variables <n> and <n> + 1
astore	store object reference in local variable
astore_<n>	store object reference in local variable <n>

For example:

```
; store the null object reference in local variable 1
aconst_null
astore_1

; push 20 onto the stack and store it in local variable 5
bipush 20
istore 5

iload 5
; stack now contains 20
```

Doubles and longs take two consecutive local variables apiece. So when you do:

```
dconst_0
dstore 5
```

to store 0.0 in local variable 5, one word of the two-word value is stored in local variable 5, and the other is stored in local variable 6.

Miscellaneous Local Variable Instructions

OK, so we exaggerated when we said that there are only two things you can do with local variables. There are also a few additional instructions relevant to local variables, as shown in Table 7-6.

Table 7–6: The wide and iinc instructions

Name	Description
iinc	increment integer in local variable
wide	next instruction uses 16-bit index

iinc is used to increment an integer value stored in a local variable. For example:

```
iinc 1 2
```

increments the int value in local variable 1 by 2. This is shorthand for writing:

```
iload_1     ; push int in local variable 1 onto the stack
iconst_2    ; push the int 2 onto the stack
iadd        ; add them
istore_1    ; store the result in local variable 1
```

The wide modifier is used to extend the number of local variables you can reach. It is used as a modifier to the other local variable instructions. Without wide, each local variable instruction can only address up to 256 local variables. Using the wide modifier, you can access local variables in the range 0-65535. For example:

```
wide
iload 300   ; retrieve the int value in local variable 300.
```

Jasmin automatically inserts "wide' opcodes when you reference a local variable number greater than 255.

Arrays

In the JVM, arrays are actually represented as objects. As with objects, array instances belong to a specific class. You can invoke methods on arrays—for example, you can use the clone() method to make a copy of an array, or the getClass() method to get the class that an array instance belongs to. The major differences between objects and arrays are:

• The contents of arrays are accessed using an array index rather than a field name.

• Arrays are heterogeneous—every component in an array is the same type.

• Array instances can be different lengths.

• The JVM generates class records for arrays automatically, rather than reading them from a class file.

Every array has a class associated with it. The JVM constructs these classes for arrays automatically, whenever they are needed. So when you make an instance of a two-dimensional int array, with the type descriptor "[[I", then the JVM also constructs a class called "[[I" representing that type of array (it does this only once for each array type). Array classes all inherit from java.lang.Object, so methods that apply to Object also apply to arrays. Arrays also implement the same interfaces as objects— for example, arrays implement Cloneable. The class hierarchy for arrays is illustrated in Figure 7-1.

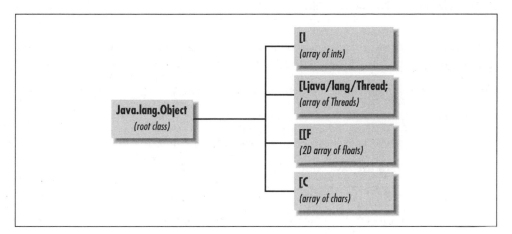

Figure 7–1: Some array classes

JVM instructions that work with objects also, as a general rule, work with arrays. For example, you can use instanceof to test for arrays of specific types:

```
aload_1              ; push object reference in local variable 1 onto the stack
instanceof [I        ; test if it's an int array
; stack now contains 1 if local variable 1 holds an int array, or 0 otherwise.
```

The JVM also provides instructions specifically for use with arrays. These instructions are used to create arrays, store values in arrays and retrieve values from arrays (more on this later).

Note that although you can create byte, char, short and boolean arrays (using newarray), when you retrieve values from these arrays, the JVM automatically promotes the values to ints.

Similarly, to store a value in a byte, char, short or boolean array, you pass the JVM an int, and it truncates the int into the relevant size before storing it in the array.

Creating Arrays

There are three instructions for creating arrays, shown in Table 7-7.

Table 7–7: Instructions for creating arrays

Name	Description
newarray	allocate new array for numbers or booleans
anewarray	allocate new arrray for objects
multianewarray	allocate multi-dimensional array

newarray is used to create arrays of ints, floats, chars, and other primitive types. The entries in the array are initialized to zero.

For example, to create a five-element array of ints, use:

```
bipush 5          ; push 5 onto the stack
newarray int      ; make an array of 5 ints
astore_1          ; store the array in local variable 1
```

This is equivalent to the Java code:

```
int x[] = new int[5];
```

anewarray is used to create arrays of references (i.e., arrays holding references to other objects and arrays). For example, to create an array for holding five threads, use:

```
bipush 5
anewarray java/lang/Thread
astore_1
```

This is equivalent to the Java code:

```
Thread x[] = new Thread[5];
```

Note that initially, all the elements of the array will be null.

multianewarray is the most complex of the array creation instructions. It is used to create multidimensional arrays. For example, to create an array like:

```
float matrix[][] = new float[4][4];
```

you would use:

```
bipush 4
bipush 4
multianewarray [[F 2   ; make array of array of floats. Allocate both dimensions
astore_1
```

See the multianewarray reference page for more details on how multidimensional arrays are managed in Java.

Retrieving Values from Arrays

The instructions in Table 7-8 are provided for retrieving values from arrays.

Table 7–8: Retrieving values from arrays

Name	Description
iaload	retrieve integer from array
laload	retrieve long integer from array
faload	retrieve float from array
daload	retrieve double-precision float from array
aaload	retrieve object reference from array
baload	retrieve byte/boolean from array
caload	retrieve character from array
saload	retrieve short from array

For example, when you write Java code like:

```
arr[5]
```

then, assuming arr is an array of ints, this is compiled into JVM code like:

```
aload 1      ; push array reference in local variable 1 (i.e., arr) onto stack
bipush 5     ; push the int 5 onto the stack
iaload       ; pops arr and 5 off the stack, pushes arr[5] onto the stack
```

For other array types, replace iaload with the appropriate instruction mnemonic (e.g., aaload if the array is an array of object references, laload for arrays of longs, etc.).

Storing Values in Arrays

The instructions in Table 7-9 are provided for storing values in arrays.

Table 7–9: Storing values in arrays

Name	Description
iastore	store in integer array
lastore	store in long integer array
fastore	store in single-precision float array
dastore	store in double-precision float array
aastore	store object reference in array
bastore	store in byte/boolean array

Table 7–9: Storing values in arrays (continued)

Name	Description
castore	store in character array
sastore	store in short array

For example, if local variable 1 is a reference to an int array, you can set the fifth element of the array to the value 3 by using:

```
aload_1                 ; load int array in local variable 1 onto stack
bipush 5
bipush 3

iastore                 ; array[5] := 3
```

Miscellaneous Array Instructions

The single array instruction we haven't mentioned is also one of the most useful: the instruction `arraylength` gets the length of an array.

For example:

```
.method public static main([Ljava/lang/String;)V
    aload_0
    arraylength
    ; stack now contains the number of strings in the array passed to main...
    ...
.end method
```

Objects

The JVM provides instructions to create new objects, manipulate object fields, recognize objects, and invoke methods on objects. Method invocation is described in Chapter 9, *Flow Control*. In this chapter, we will look at how to create objects, work with fields, and check for specific kinds of objects.

Creating Objects

Use the instruction new to create new objects. Note that new by itself is not enough to create usable object instances. After using new to create an object, you must initialize it by calling one of its <init> methods—illustrated by the following example:

```
new java/lang/StringBuffer   ; allocate memory for a StringBuffer
; now initialize it. To do this, we make an extra copy of the
; object reference using dup, and then call the object's <init> method.
dup
invokespecial java/lang/StringBuffer/<init>()V
; the object is now on the stack, ready for use.
```

```
; Store the new object in local variable 1.
astore_1
```

Java's verifier mandates that objects cannot be stored in local variables (or fields) until they have been initialized. Similarly, you cannot perform a backwards jump while there is an uninitialized object on the operand stack.

Manipulating Fields

Each object in Java consists of a collection of fields. Fields are either defined locally in a class, or they can be inherited from a superclass. You cannot override inherited fields, although you can *shadow* them. For example, if you have the two class definitions:

```
class Foo {
    int myField;
}
class Foo2 extends Foo {
    float myField;
}
```

the two fields, myField in Foo and myField in Foo2, appear to conflict. In fact, the JVM treats these as two separate fields. If you were to look at the instance data block for an instance of Foo2 it would contain:

*   (fields inherited from java.lang.Object)

*   int Foo.myField;

*   float Foo2.myField;

The Foo2's myField is said to shadow Foo's myfield. At the JVM level, there is no ambiguity over which field is intended, since instructions for retrieving or setting the value of a field explicitly name the class that introduced the field (as we will see below).

As well as per-object fields, the JVM supports per-class fields, called *static fields*. The storage for a static field is contained in the class record, rather than in an instance—so you don't need to create an object instance in order to set or get static fields.

In Jasmin, you add new fields using the ".field" directive. For example, in the class called HelloWeb from Chapter 2, you saw:

```
.field private HelloWeb/font Ljava/awt/Font;
```

This declares a private instance field called font, associated with the class HelloWeb, which holds a reference to a Font object.

The four instructions in Table 7-10 are used to retrieve and set the values of fields.

Table 7–10: Field instructions

Name	Description
putfield	set value of object field
getfield	get value of object field
putstatic	set value of static field
getstatic	get value of static field

Each of these instructions takes the same parameters: the name of a class, the name of a field in that class, and the type descriptor for a field. For example:

```
; get the PrintStream object in java.lang.System.out
getstatic java/lang/System/out Ljava/io/PrintStream;

; stack now holds a reference to a PrintStream object

; get this.font, assuming -this- is an instance of HelloWeb
aload_0    ; push -this-
getfield HelloWeb/font Ljava/awt/Font;    ; get this.font
; stack now holds a reference to a Font object
```

See the instruction reference pages for more details and examples.

Miscellaneous Object Operations

The two instructions in Table 7-11 are used to test for instances of particular types.

Table 7–11: The checkcast and instanceof instructions

Name	Description
checkcast	ensure object or array belongs to type
instanceof	test if object or array belongs to type

For example:

```
; check for an object type:
aload_0
instanceof java/lang/Thread
; the stack now holds the int 1 if local variable 0 refers to a Thread
; (or one of its subclasses), or 0 otherwise.

; check for an array type
aload_0
instanceof [I
; the stack now holds the int 1 if local variable 0 refers to an int[]
; array, or 0 otherwise.
```

```
; check for an interface
aload_0
checkcast java/lang/Throwable
; if local variable 0 holds an object which implements the Throwable interface,
; that object is left on the stack and execution proceeds at the next instruction.
; If it doesn't, a ClassCastException is thrown.
```

Assignment Compatibility

The checkcast and instanceof instructions use a concept of "compatibility." Two types are said to be compatible if one implements all of the operations defined by the other.

For objects, the following pseudo-code illustrates how Java determines whether a given object (whose type is myType) is compatible with a particular class (called requiredType):

```
boolean compatible(Class myType, Class requiredType) {
    if (requiredType.isInterface()) {// comparing against an interface
        // return true if I implement the interface
        return (myType.implements(requiredType));
    } else if (requiredType.isClass()) { // comparing against another class
        // Test if my type is the same as requiredType,
        if (myType == requiredType) return true;
        // or if requiredType one of my superclasses
        while (myType != java.lang.Object) {
            if (myType == requiredType)
                return true;
            myType = myType.getSuperClass();
        }
    }
    return false; // I'm not compatible with requiredType
}
```

For arrays, a slightly more involved definition is required, since you have to examine the types of the data elements stored in the arrays. In the simplified pseudo-code shown below, myType is the type of the array object, and requiredType is the type you are testing for:

```
boolean compatible(Class myType, Class requiredType) {
    if (requiredType.isInterface()) {
        // arrays implement the interfaces of java.lang.Object
        return(java.lang.Object.implements(requiredType));
    } else if (requiredType.isClass()) {
        // superclass of an array type is java.lang.Object, so:
        return (requiredType == myType || requiredType == java.lang.Object);
    } else {
        // I'm an array and requiredType is an array type. Get the types
        // of the data stored in the arrays:
        Class type1 = myType.getComponentType();
        Class type2 = requiredType.getComponentType();
```

```
        // now recursively test these types:
        return (type1 == type2 || compatible(type1, type2));
    }
}
```

Given these two primitives, you can think of instanceof and checkcast as being like the functions:

```
boolean instanceof(Type t) {
    return compatible(this.getClass(), t);
}
void checkcast(Type t) {
    if (!compatible(this.getClass(), t)) {
        throw new ClassCastException();
    }
}
```

The concept of compatibility is also used during assignment operations—when you assign an object to a field, or store it in an array (using aastore), the JVM checks that the type of the object is compatible with the destination location you are assigning the object to, and throws an exception if the type of the object is not compatible with the type of the location.

In this chapter:
- *Arithmetic Operators*
- *Bitwise Operators*
- *Conversion Operators*
- *Arithmetic Exceptions*

8

Arithmetic

All of the mathematical operators in the Java language are provided as instructions in the Java Virtual Machine. This chapter contains an overview of those instructions and also describes how to convert values from one numeric type to another. The instructions are described in more detail in the reference section of this book.

Arithmetic Operators

The binary operators in Table 8-1 are provided by the JVM to do basic arithmetic.

Table 8–1: Binary operators

Name	Description
iadd	add two integers
ladd	add two long integers
fadd	add two floats
dadd	add two doubles
isub	subtract two integers
lsub	subtract two longs
fsub	subtract two floats
dsub	subtract two doubles
imul	multiply two integers
lmul	multiply two longs
fmul	multiply two floats
dmul	multiply two doubles
idiv	divide two integers

Table 8–1: Binary operators (continued)

Name	Description
ldiv	divide a long integer
fdiv	divide two floats
ddiv	divide two doubles
irem	remainder of two integers
lrem	modulus of two longs
frem	remainder of two floats
drem	remainder of two doubles

All of these operators take two operands off the operand stack, perform a computation, and push the result of the computation back on the stack. For example, you add two numbers using:

```
bipush 10
bipush 20
iadd
; stack now contains 30
```

There are also unary operators, as shown in Table 8-2.

Table 8–2: Unary operators

Name	Description
ineg	negate an integer
lneg	negate a long
fneg	negate a float
dneg	negate a double

These operators take a single value off the stack, negate it, and push the negated value back on the stack. For example:

```
bipush 20
ineg
; stack now contains -20
```

Bitwise Operators

The instructions in Table 8-3 operate on the bit level of integers and long integers.

Table 8–3: Bitwise operators

Name	Description
ishl	integer shift left
ishr	integer arithmetic shift right
iushr	integer logical shift right
lshl	long integer shift left
lshr	long integer arithmetic shift right
lushr	long integer logical shift right
iand	integer bitwise and
land	long integer bitwise and
ior	integer bitwise or
lor	long integer bitwise or
ixor	integer bitwise exclusive or
lxor	long integer bitwise exclusive or

These instructions are all binary operators—they pop two values off the stack, perform a bitwise computation, and push the result back onto the stack. For example, to shift an int left by 1 (i.e., multiply it by two) use:

```
bipush 10
iconst_1
ishl
; stack now contains 20
```

Note that the lushr and iushr instructions are used by Java's >>> operator, which performs an unsigned shift right.

Conversion Operators

Unlike the Java language, which automatically converts numbers in expressions to the appropriate types (for example, converting ints to floats, if the desired result is a float), at the JVM level you must always explicitly convert numbers to the appropriate representation type.

The unary operators in Table 8-4 convert numbers from one numeric representation to another.

Table 8–4: Conversion operators

Name	Description
i2l	convert integer to long integer
i2f	convert integer to float
i2d	convert integer to double
l2i	long to integer conversion
l2f	convert long to float
l2d	convert long to double
f2i	convert long to integer
f2l	convert float to long integer
f2d	convert float to double
d2I	convert double to integer
d2l	covert double to long integer
d2f	convert double to float
i2b	convert integer to byte
i2c	convert integer to character
i2s	convert integer to short integer

For example, to add a float and an int, producing a float result, use something like:

```
ldc 1.5          ; push the float 1.5 onto the stack
iload_1          ; push the int in local variable 1 onto the stack
i2f              ; convert the integer on top of the stack to a float
fadd             ; add the two floats
```

When converting a floating-point type to an integral type, the mantissa is ignored. This is generally referred to as "rounding toward zero." So, the floating-point number 9.6 is converted to the integer 9. When converting from an integral type to a floating-point type, the closest floating-point value to the integral value will be used:

```
ldc 1.7          ; push the float 1.7 onto the stack
f2i              ; convert to an integer. The integer value
                 ; 1 is now on top of the stack
iconst_1         ; push the integer constant 1 onto the stack
i2d              ; the double-precision floating point value
                 ; 1.0 is now on the stack
```

Note that i2b, i2c and i2s are slightly special—these three operators all return an int result, rather than a byte, char, or short result as you might expect. The int result is truncated so that it only contains 8 significant bits (for a byte) or 16 significant bits (for a char or short). For example, if local variables 1 and 2 are declared as a byte and a short respectively, and you want to add them and produce a short result in local variable 1, use:

```
iload_1
iload_2
iadd
i2s      ; truncate to a 16-bit signed result
istore_1
```

Arithmetic Exceptions

Operations on integral types can throw only one exception: in the case of division by zero, an ArithmeticException is thrown. There are no exceptions generated by underflow or overflow as the result of operations on integral types. An underflow (or overflow) will just wrap around and give the wrong value. Unfortunately, there is currently no mechanism in the JVM to detect overflow or underflow, so programmers must manually check for these conditions, or use a class which supports arbitrary precision arithmetic (such a class is available in the JDK 1.1).

No exceptions are generated by operations on floating point values. For floating point underflow, the result is either positive or negative zero. For overflow, the result is positive or negative infinity. In the case of an undefined operation such as 0.0/0.0, the result will be the IEEE 754 representation of "Not a Number" or NaN. This value is defined in the Java class libraries in java/lang/Float/NaN and java/lang/Double/NaN.

9

Flow Control

The JVM contains a wide assortment of branch instructions, including a set of conditional and non-conditional branch instructions, subroutines, and table jumping instructions. In addition, the JVM handles method invocation and return (described at the end of this chapter), and exceptions (which are covered in Chapter 10, *Exceptions*).

Branches and Subroutines

Within a method, JVM programs have a wide range of branch instructions at their disposal. In bytecode, all of these branch instructions are encoded as a single-byte opcode (e.g., goto), followed by an integer which is a *relative* offset from the current bytecode address. Some branch instructions use one-byte offsets. Others (usually those with a "_w" suffix) use a two-byte offset. Addresses are measured in bytes, from the start of the method's bytecode. For example, the code:

```
int test(int i) {
    if (i < 10) {
        return i;
    }
    return 10;
}
```

is compiled into the code shown in Table 9-1.

Calculating these bytecode offsets manually would be very tedious. Jasmin provides labels as an convenient way of indicating bytecode addresses. The Jasmin assembler automatically determines the correct offset to use for a given label.

Table 9–1: Bytecode addressing

Bytecode Address	Code
0	iload_1
1	bipush 10
3	if_cmpge +5 ; if local var 1 >= 10, goto location 8
6	iload_1
7	ireturn ; return I
8	bipush 10
10	ireturn ; return 10

An Example Loop

Conditional branches are often used in loops. Consider the Java code:

```
int c=10;
while(c>0) c--;
```

(This not a very useful loop! In fact, most optimizing compilers would eliminate the loop entirely, replacing it with a single assignment. But it serves our purposes.)

In Jasmin, you could write this loop as:

```
        bipush 10
        istore_1          ; initialize local variable 1 to 10
        goto End          ; jump to the end point of the loop
Start:
        iinc 1 -1         ; decrement the local variable

End:
        iload_1           ; push local variable 1 onto the stack
        ifgt Start        ; and branch to the Start point of the loop if
                          ; the int on the stack is greater than zero
        ; otherwise, carry on from here
```

This code seems a bit contrived—why use a goto to jump to the end of the loop, only to almost immediately jump backward to the start of the loop? But consider the alternative version:

```
        bipush 10
        istore_1          ; initialize local variable 1 to 10
Loop:
        iload_1           ; push local variable 1 onto the stack
        ifle Done         ; jump out of the loop if the int on the stack
                          ; is less than or equal to zero
```

```
    iinc 1 -1
    goto Loop          ; jump back to the start of the loop

Done:
  ; carry on from here
```

This seems more intuitive—and is probably how most programmers would write the loop. But notice that in the second version, the body of the loop contains two branch instructions for each iteration—one at the start of the loop (to break out when the condition is met) and the other at the end of the loop to go back to the start of the loop. The first version we saw, on the other hand, only has one branch instruction for each iteration around the loop (the `ifgt` at the end of the loop). In cases where the loop body is performed many times (which is, after all, the point of most loops), the first version is more efficient.

This illustrates an important point: writing efficient control flow statements by hand in the JVM is tricky. It's a task probably best left to an optimizing compiler.

Conditional Branches

The first eight branch instructions listed in Table 9-2 all pop a single item off the stack, examine it, and branch accordingly. The last six (those starting with "if_") pop two items off the stack, compare the two items, and branch accordingly.

Table 9–2: Conditional branch instructions

Name	Description
ifeq	jump if zero
ifnull	jump if null
iflt	jump if less than zero
ifle	jump if less than zero or equal to zero
ifne	jump in nonzero
ifnonnull	jump if non-null
ifgt	jump if greater than zero
ifge	jump if greater than zero or equal to zero
if_icmpeq	jump if two integers are equal
if_icmpne	jump if two integers are not equal
if_icmplt	jump if one integer is less than another
if_icmpgt	jump if one integer is greater than another
if_icmple	jump if one integer is less than or equal to another
if_icmpge	jump if one integer is greater than or equal to another

For example:

```
    bipush 2        ; push the integer 2 onto the stack
    iload_1         ; push the integer value of local variable 1 onto the stack
    if_icmpeq Label ; if the value of local variable 1 equals 2, jump to Label
    return          ; return if not equal
Label:
    ; execution continues here if local variable 1 equals 2...
```

See the instruction reference pages for details on each branch instruction.

Comparisons

In addition to the compare-and-jump instructions above, the JVM includes a set of instructions that just compare two values (see Table 9-3). The result of the comparision is either the int 0 (for false) or the int 1 (for true).

Table 9–3: Comparison instructions

Name	Description
lcmp	long integer comparison
fcmpl	single-precision float comparison (–1 on NaN)
fcmpg	single-precision float comparison (1 on NaN)
dcmpl	compare two doubles (–1 on NaN)
dcmpg	compare two doubles (1 on NaN)

For example:

```
    dload_1         ; push the double in local variable 1
    dconst_0        ; push the double 0.0 onto the stack
    dcmpl           ; compare the two numbers

    ; The integer result on the stack is:
    ;     0 if local variable 1 equals 0.0
    ;     -1 if local variable 1 is less than 0.0
    ;     1 if local variable 1 is greater than 0.0
```

The instructions dcmpl and dcmpg (or fcmpl and fcmpg) are identical except for their treatment of NaN. If you want a comparison to produce –1 when either number is NaN, use dcmpl (or fcmpl). Otherwise use dcmpg (fcmpg)—which produces 1 if either number is NaN. The appropriate comparison to use depends on the condition you are trying to trap. For example, consider the statement:

```
if (val > 3.14) {
    return;
}
```

You probably don't want the method to return if val is NaN (since that's not greater than 3.14), so you would write this as:

```
    dload_1            ; push val onto the stack
    ldc2_w 3.14        ; push 3.14 onto the stack
    dcmpl
    ; Stack contains:
    ; -1 if val < 3.14, or is NaN
    ; 1 if val > 3.14
    ; 0 if val == 3.14
    ifle Continue      ; skip to Continue of stack is <= 0
    return             ; return from the method if val > 3.14, but not NaN
Continue:
    ; continue from here if val is NaN or <= 3.14
```

Unconditional Branches and Subroutines

You already saw the goto instruction in the first example we showed. The JVM provides several other unconditional branch instructions, as shown in Table 9-4.

Table 9–4: Unconditional branch instructions

Name	Description
goto	branch to address
goto_w	branch to address using wide offset
jsr	jump to subroutine
jsr_w	jump to subroutine using wide offset
ret	return from subroutine
ret_w	return from subroutine using wide offset

The instructions with the "_w" suffix are "wide" forms of the instruction—they let you branch to an address that is further away (they are encoded in bytecode using a 16-bit branch offset, rather than an 8-bit branch offset). If you are using Jasmin, you'll find it automatically decides which variant to use, based on the distance to the label you want to jump to.

Subroutines

jsr and ret (and their cousins jsr_w and ret_w) are used to implement subroutines. A subroutine is like a lightweight method. You jump to a subroutine using the jsr instruction, and return from it using the ret instruction. Below is an example of a subroutine, PrintMe, that prints a string:

```
.method messages()V
    .limit stack 2
    .limit locals 1

    ldc "Hello"        ; push a string onto the stack
    jsr PrintInt       ; call the subroutine to print it out
```

```
    ldc "Goodbye"      ; push another string onto the stack
    jsr PrintInt       ; call the subroutine a second time to print it

    return

PrintInt:                ; the PrintInt subroutine definition
    ; when a subroutine is called, the return address
    ; is left on the stack. Store it in a local variable:
    astore_1

    ; The string to print is now on the top of the stack. Print it...

    getstatic java/lang/System/out Ljava/io/PrintStream;
    swap
    invokevirtual java/io/PrintStream/println(Ljava/lang/String;)

    ; now return to the address in local variable 1:
    ret 1

.end method
```

Notice that the first action the subroutine performs is to store the top item on the stack in a local variable. When a subroutine is called, jsr places the return address (the address of the instruction immediately following the jsr) on the operand stack. ret, on the other hand, is given a local variable number and returns to the address stored in that local variable; programmers must manually store the return address in a local variable, for use with ret. The asymmetry between these instructions is intentional, since it makes verification of subroutines possible.

Table Jumping

Two instructions are used to implement computed jumps and switch statements (see Table 9-5).

Table 9–5: Jump instructions

Name	Description
lookupswitch	match key in table and jump
tableswitch	perform computed jump

For example, the switch statement:

```
int i;
...
switch (i) {
case 1:
    return 1;
case 10:
    return 2;
```

```
case 100:
    return 3;
default:
    return 0;
}
```

is compiled into:

```
        iload_1                 ; push i onto the stack
        lookupswitch
            1      : R1         ; jump to R1 if it equals 1
           10      : R2         ; jump to R2 if it equals 10
          100      : R3         ; jump to R3 if it equals 100
         default: R4            ; otherwise jump to R4
R1:
        iconst_1
        ireturn
R2:
        iconst_2
        ireturn
R3:
        iconst_3
        ireturn
R4:
        iconst_0
        ireturn
```

For cases where the range of values being tested is contiguous, tableswitch is more efficient. For example, the switch statement:

```
int i;
...
switch (i) {
case 1:
    return 1;
case 2:
    return 2;
case 3:
    return 3;
default:
    return 0;
}
```

is compiled into the following code:

```
        iload_1         ; push i onto the stack
        tableswitch 1 3
                 R1      ; jump to R1 if i == 1
                 R2      ; jump to R2 if i == 2
                 R3      ; jump to R3 if i == 3
          default: R4    ; otherwise jump to R4
R1:
        iconst_1
        ireturn
```

```
R2:
    iconst_2
    ireturn
R3:
    iconst_3
    ireturn
R4:
    iconst_0
    ireturn
```

See the reference pages in Chapter 13, *Instruction Reference*, for lookupswitch and tableswitch for more details.

Method Invocation and Return

Java programs call methods frequently, so method invocation must be efficient. In this section, we look at the four styles of method invocation, and at how you return from methods. Then we examine how methods are dispatched by the JVM.

Method Invocation

There are four instructions for invoking methods, as shown in Table 9-6.

Table 9–6: Method invocation instructions

Name	Description
invokevirtual	call an instance method
invokespecial	invoke method belonging to a specific class
invokestatic	invoke a class (static) method
invokeinterface	invoke an interface method

invokevirtual, invokespecial, and invokeinterface all follow a basic form, which looks like:

- push object whose method you want to call

- push argument 1

- push argument 2

- ...

- push last argument

- invoke method

- stack now contains the method result, if any

invokestatic is the same, except that you don't push an object at the start of the process—static methods are standalone methods; they aren't applied to objects.

invokevirtual

invokevirtual is used to invoke "normal" Java methods. That is, when you write a class like:

```
class Point {
    float x, y;
    float length() {return sqrt(x*x + y*y); }
}
```

the length() method is a "normal" instance method. To invoke this method, assuming you have a Point instance in local variable 1, you use code like:

```
aload_1 ; Push a Point object onto the stack. This is the object whose method we
        ; are calling.

        ; Now call the length() method - this takes no arguments
        ; and returns a float
invokevirtual Point/length()F

; the stack now contains a single float - the result of calling length().
```

The "Point/length()F" token after invokevirtual is a Jasmin method specification. "Point" is the name of the class containing the method. "length" is the name of the method you want to call. The "()F" is a method type descriptor—telling the JVM that the method takes no arguments and returns a float result. Chapter 4, *Classes*, describes type descriptors. The reference section describes method specifications in more detail.

invokestatic

Where invokevirtual is used to call instance methods, invokestatic is used to invoke "static" methods—methods defined for a class rather than an instance. For example, to call System.exit(0), you would use:

```
iconst_0    ; push the argument 0 onto the stack
invokestatic java/lang/System/exit(I)V
```

In this case, the "(I)V" descriptor indicates that exit takes an integer argument (the 0 we pushed onto the stack) and returns no result.

invokeinterface

As you probably guessed, invokeinterface is used to call a method which is defined by an interface. For example, consider the code:

```
void printVector(Vector vec) {
    for (Enumeration enum = vec.elements(); enum.hasMoreElements(); ) {
        System.out.println(enum.nextElement());
    }
}
```

This is, in Jasmin:

```
; printVector takes a Vector, and returns no result
.method printVector(Ljava/util/Vector;)V
    .limit stack 2
    .limit vars 3

    ; first get vec.elements() and store it in local variable 2 (enum)
    aload_1
    invokevirtual java/util/Vector/elements()Ljava/util/Enumeration;
    astore_2

    goto Label2    ; jump to the end of the loop

Label1:

    getstatic java/lang/System/out Ljava/io/PrintStream;
    ; call enum.nextElement() - which returns an object
    aload_2
    invokeinterface java/util/Enumeration/nextElement()Ljava/lang/Object; 1

    ; print out the object - this uses the System/out object we retrieved and
    ; also the object on the stack that we got by calling nextElement()
    invokevirtual java/io/PrintStream/println(Ljava/lang/Object;)V

Label2:
    ; call enum.hasMoreElements(), which returns a boolean result:
    aload_2
    invokeinterface java/util/Enumeration/hasMoreElements()Z 1

    ifne Label1    ; jump back to Label1 if there are more elements

    return   ; done
.end method
```

Notice that, for historical reasons, invokeinterface takes one more parameter than the other invoke instructions. So looking at:

```
invokeinterface java/util/Enumeration/hasMoreElements()Z 1
```

you can see a trailing 1 at the end of the line—this number is the number of arguments taken by the method plus one.

invokespecial

The last method invocation instruction is invokespecial. This is used in the following situations:

- to call an instance initialization method, <init>
- to call a method belonging to this

- to call private methods
- to call a method in a superclass of this

We've already seen invokespecial used for the first of these reasons—to initialize an object. The other three cases are for handling Java's super() keyword, and for supporting private methods. For example, consider the classes:

```
class Teacher {
    private int actualAge() {return(50); }

    public int getAge() {
        return(actualAge() / 2);
    }
}
```

The call to actualAge() is handled by invokespecial:

```
aload_0    ; push -this- onto the stack
invokespecial Teacher/actualAge()I    ; get my actual age
```

Similarly, for the class:

```
class Professor extends Teacher {
    void printAge() {
        System.out.println(super.getAge());
    }
}
```

the super.getAge() is compiled into:

```
aload_0    ; push -this- onto the stack
invokespecial Teacher/getAge()I    ; get my reported age
```

Method Return

To return from a method, use one of the instructions listed in Table 9-7.

Table 9–7: Method return instructions

Name	Description
ireturn	return from method with integer result
lreturn	return from method with long result
freturn	return from method with float result
dreturn	return from method with double result
areturn	return from method with object reference result
return	return from method (no result)

For example:

```
; trivial method that takes no arguments and returns an int result:
.method getHeight()I
    bipush 100
    ireturn                    ; return the result 100
.end method
```

Notice that, unlike in the Java language, it is illegal to "fall off" the end of a method. So you cannot write things like:

```
.method botch()V
    bipush 100
.end method
```

Method Dispatch

An important consideration in Java programs is the efficiency of method dispatch. To give you an idea of what the JVM does to invoke a method, we've implemented a small piece of a hypothetical Java Virtual Machine interpreter in C, illustrating how method dispatch is done.

Dispatching invokevirtual, invokespecial, or invokestatic

For the invokevirtual, invokespecial, and invokestatic, the following pseudo-code illustrates what the heart of the JVM interpreter does:

```
switch (opcode) {
  // (many other cases deleted...)
  case invokevirtual:
  case invokespecial:
  case invokestatic:
      // after the opcode, in bytecode, there is a 2 byte index which
      // references a CONSTANT_Methodref in the constant pool. Get that entry:
      int index = pc[1] * 256 + pc[2];                 // get index from
                                                       // bytecode
      CP_Method *entry = (CP_Method*)constant_pool[index];  // get cp entry

      // test if the entry needs to be resolved:
      if (entry->first_time) {   // first time this CP entry is used
         entry->first_time = FALSE;

         // resolve the class name into a pointer to the address
         // of a Class record in the current Java runtime system:
         entry->its_class = GetClassFromName(entry->classname);

         // locate the method with the given methodname and
         // type descriptor. This will return an integer index that indicates
         // where the method appears in the list of methods of the class
         entry->method_offset = LookupMethodInClass(entry->its_class,
                                           entry->name, entry->type);
      }
```

```
        // Now we have the method_offset to use, we can do the
        // invokevirtual/invokevirtual/invokestatic part:

        Object *object; // pointer to object whose method is being run
        Method *method; // pointer to method to call

        if (opcode == invokevirtual) {
            object = (Object*)Pop();      // get object off operand stack

            // gets method based on the runtime type of -object-:
            method = object->its_class->method_table[entry->method_offset];
        } else if (opcode == invokespecial) {
            object = (Object*)Pop();      // get object off operand stack

            // gets method based on class given in -entry-
            method = entry->its_class->method_table[entry->method_offset];
        } else if (opcode == invokestatic) {
            object = NULL; // no object involved in static methods

            // gets method based on class given in -entry-
            method = entry->its_class->method_table[entry->method_offset];
        }

        // now the method is located, call it
        CallMethod(object, method);

        // done
```

Of course, this example is simplified in a number of ways:

- It doesn't check for the public/private/protected access flags of the method.

- It doesn't properly handle arguments to the method.

- It is not fully implementing the semantics of each method invocation type.

- It isn't optimal code.

However, you can see from the code that most method invocations really turn into looking up a method in an array. Because Java only supports single inheritance, JVM implementations can arrange to represent the method table of a class as an array. Each method table contains a copy of all the entries in the superclass's method table, with some entries replaced (for overridden methods), or appended to the end (for new methods). The important point is that a given method is at the same index in the array for every class that has that method. For example, consider the two classes:

```
class A {
    int foo();
    int baz();
    int ding();
}
```

```
class B extends A {
    int baz(); // overrides A's baz()
    int bob(); // new method
}
```

Inside the JVM, these classes have method tables like those shown in Table 9-8.

Table 9–8: Method tables

	Class A Method Table	Class B extends A Method Table
1	int foo();	int foo(); // A's foo
2	int baz();	int baz(); // overrides A's baz()
3	int ding();	int ding(); // A's ding
4		int bob(); // new method

For instances of either A or B the JVM knows that the first method in the table is foo(), the second is baz(), and the third is ding(). So to call foo() for either class (or for any class that inherits from A, for that matter), the JVM simply retrieves the first method in the method table and calls that.

Dispatching invokeinterface

Whereas invoking static, special or virtual methods can be handled by using a simple array access, handling interface methods is more involved.

Methods defined in an interface can be inherited by any class that implements that interface—so there isn't a neat orderly procession of classes that inherit everything from a single parent interface and extend the parent's method table by adding more methods to the end. Instead, classes anywhere in the hierarchy can implement the interface.

To dispatch interface methods, the JVM needs to use the equivalent of a hash table. The hash table must map from a specific class to a structure containing that class's implementation of a specific interface. In implementation terms, there are a number of ways you could arrange this—for example, each interface method could maintain its own hash table, or you could have a hash table per class, or per interface, etc.

Sun's implementation makes use of the space available after the invokeinterface opcode in bytecode to store a "hint" byte that aids in the lookup of interface methods. So that if you apply an interface method to the same object several times in a row, method lookup is faster.

10

Exceptions

Managing exceptions is an integral part of programming in Java. In this chapter, you will learn what exceptions are, how to throw, catch, and declare exceptions using the JVM and Jasmin, and you will see how these mechanisms work in the VM.

Overview

Exceptions are Java's way of signaling to an application that something out-of-the-ordinary has happened—for example, when Java runs out of memory, an OutOfMemoryError exception is generated. (see *Java in a Nutshell* for a description of Java exceptions). Exceptions also get used for more mundane purposes, such as signaling that the end of a file has been reached.

Exceptions usually get generated (or "thrown") by the system—for example, when an application tries to open a file that doesn't exist, the system generates and throws a FileNotFoundException exception.

Java methods can also throw exceptions using the throw statement, which is implemented at the JVM level using the athrow instruction. Being able to throw exceptions is especially useful when you are developing a Java library and want to use the same error-reporting mechanisms the Java system uses.

All exceptions in Java are instances of the java.lang.Throwable class, or one of its subclasses. Throwable has two subclasses: java.lang.Error and java.lang.Exception. Subclasses of java.lang.Error are used to indicate an unrecoverable situation such as running out of memory. Subclasses of java.lang.Exception are used for conditions that can be trapped and recovered from, such as java.io.EOFException which signals that the end of a file has been reached.

When an exception is generated, the Java runtime system searches for a handler for that exception. The search starts within the method the exception occurred within, and then propagates up through the methods on the call stack. If a handler is found, it "catches" the exception, and the code associated with the handler is executed. The handler is responsible for deciding what to do next. It might:

- use a goto instruction to continue executing the method

- use return to exit from the method

- use athrow to throw a different exception

If no handler for an exception is found, the system handler is run. This typically prints out an error message and exits.

Generating Exceptions

The athrow instruction is used to generate exceptions. athrow takes one item off the stack and signals the exception identified by that item. The item must be a reference to an object which is a subclass of Throwable. For example, to throw an IndexOutOfBoundsException, you could write:

```
; construct the Exception, duplicate it and call its initializer
new java/lang/IndexOutOfBoundsException
dup
invokenonvirtual java/lang/IndexOutOfBoundsException/<init>()V

; use athrow to throw the Exception on the stack
athrow
```

This example is equivalent to the Java code:

```
throw new java.lang.IndexOutOfBoundsException();
```

Declaring Exceptions

Methods written in the Java language are required to declare any "normal exceptions" they throw but don't also catch. This includes any exceptions that are thrown as a side effect of calling some other method. You declare exceptions using the throws keyword. For example:

```
public void myMethod() throws IOException {
    // some code that can cause an IOException to be generated
}
```

Normal exceptions are any subclass of Throwable that is not a subclass or java.lang.Error or java.lang.RuntimeException. (Errors and RuntimeExceptions need not be declared since nearly all methods could conceivably generate them.)

In Jasmin, the .throws directive is used to declare that a method can throw an exception. For example:

```
.method public example()V
    .throws java/io/IOException
    .throws java/io/FileNotFoundException

    ...
.end method
```

The .throws directive takes a class name and adds it to an "Exceptions" attribute, which is then attached to the "Code" attribute for the method when the method is written out into a class file. Chapter 12, *Class File Reference*, describes the details of the exceptions and code attributes. See also Chapter 4, *Classes*, for a general description of attributes in class files.

Note that exception declaration is only a formality. The runtime system doesn't actually require that exceptions be declared before they can be thrown (at least, existing implementations of the runtime system don't use or check for declarations). Exception declaration is required by the Java compiler to encourage good coding practices. Nevertheless, it is a good idea to declare your exceptions, at least for the benefit of programmers using the Java language.

Catching Exceptions

Consider the Java example:

```
import java.io.*;

class FileReadable {
    public static void main(String args[]) {
        try {
            try {
                String filename = args[0];
                FileInputStream stream = new FileInputStream(filename);
                // if we get here, the file could be opened, so...
                System.out.println("file exists and is readable");
            } catch (FileNotFoundException e) {
                // handler for the FileNotFoundException
                System.out.println("file doesn't exist or is unreadable");
            }
        } catch (ArrayIndexOutOfBoundsException e) {
            // if args[] is empty, then the statement args[0]
            // will throw an ArrayIndexOutOfBoundsException.
            System.out.println("usage: java FileReadable <filename>");
        }
    }
};
```

Save this example in a file "FileReadable.java" and then compile it using:

```
% javac FileReadable.java
```

Running FileReadable with a filename that exists prints "file exists and is readable". Running it with a file that doesn't exist prints "file doesn't exist or is unreadable". Running it with no arguments prints a usage message. For example:

```
% java FileReadable FileReadable.java
file exists and is readable

% java FileReadable footle
file doesn't exist or is unreadable

% java FileReadable
usage: java FileReadable <filename>
```

The example code is a little contrived, but is a good illustration of using exceptions as a form of flow control. Now let's look at how this Java code is translated into Java VM statements, using javap:

```
% javap -c FileReadable
Compiled from FileReadable.java
class FileReadable extends java.lang.Object {
    public static void main(java.lang.String []);
    FileReadable();

Method void main(java.lang.String [])
   0 aload_0
   1 iconst_0
   2 aaload
   3 astore_1
   4 new #7 <Class java.io.FileInputStream>
   7 aload_1
   8 invokenonvirtual #14
       <Method java.io.FileInputStream.<init>(Ljava/lang/String;)V>
  11 getstatic #13 <Field java.lang.System.out Ljava/io/PrintStream;>
  14 ldc #1 <String "file exists and is readable>
  16 invokevirtual #12 <Method java.io.PrintStream.println(Ljava/lang/String;)V>
  19 return
  20 pop
  21 getstatic #13 <Field java.lang.System.out Ljava/io/PrintStream;>
  24 ldc #3 <String "file doesn't exist or is unreadable>
  26 invokevirtual #12 <Method java.io.PrintStream.println(Ljava/lang/String;)V>
  29 return
  30 pop
  31 getstatic #13 <Field java.lang.System.out Ljava/io/PrintStream;>
  34 ldc #2 <String "usage: java FileReadable <filename>>
  36 invokevirtual #12 <Method java.io.PrintStream.println(Ljava/lang/String;)V>
  39 return
```

```
Exception table:
   from   to   target  type
     0    19     20    <Class java.io.FileNotFoundException>
     0    30     30    <Class java.lang.ArrayIndexOutOfBoundsException>

Method FileReadable()
  0 aload_0
  1 invokenonvirtual #11 <Method java.lang.Object.<init>()V>
  4 return


}
```

You can see that try and catch do not appear as VM instructions. Instead, the method contains an "exception table", which is printed out at the end of the main() method. Every Java method has an exception table, although in most cases the table is empty. When an exception is raised, this table is searched for a handler (more on the search algorithm later). In this case, the main() method has two entries in the table.

The exception table is an array of handlers, each of which would, if written in Java, look something like:

```
class Handler {
    int from_pc;      // start of range of bytecode where handler is active
    int to_pc;        // end of range of bytecode where handler is active
    int handler_pc;   // address in bytecode to jump to when handler is invoked
    Class catch_type; // class of Exception this handler recognizes
}
```

(The exact data format is described in Chapter 12.)

from_pc and to_pc define the range of code that the exception handler is active— i.e., the code that is "protected" by the handler. handler_pc is the starting address of the code that handles the exception. catch_type is the class of exceptions that the handler is used for.

The javac compiler follows a number of rules when generating the exception handlers table:

- Handlers are placed outside the range of code that is being protected.

- The range of code protected by two different exception handlers never partially overlap—they are either completely disjoint or one is a subrange of the other.

- Handlers are not reachable except through an exception—so methods do not "fall through" or "goto" code that is in a handler.

These restrictions may not be enforced by the Virtual Machine implementation. However, it is a good idea to follow them since some implementations of the Virtual Machine may assume that code is always as well-behaved as this.

Searching for a Handler

When an exception is thrown, the runtime system searches for a handler for that exception. First it searches the active method. If no handler is found, the current method's frame is discarded, and the invoker's frame is reinstated. Then the exception is immediately rethrown. If a handler is found, the runtime system clears the operand stack, pushes the exception object onto the stack, and then continues execution from the address of the handler.

The following pseudo-code illustrates this process:

```
void gotoHandler(Frame f, Throwable exception) {
    while (f != null) {
        int pc = f.getPC(); // get the PC register
        // get Exceptions table for the current method
        Handler handlers[] = f.method.getExceptionTable();
        for (i = 0; i < handlers.length; i++) {
            Handler h = handlers[i];
            if (pc >= h.from_pc && pc < h.to_pc &&
                        exception instanceof h.catch_type) {
                // found a handler
                clearStack();
                push(exception);
                f.setPC(h.catch_pc);
                return;
            }
        }
        // move up the call chain
        Frame caller = f.getCaller();
        removeFromCallstack(f);
        f = caller;
    }
    // no handler found - invoke top-level exception handler
    topLevelHandler(exception);
    System.exit(-1);
}
```

Catching Exceptions in Jasmin

In Jasmin you use the .catch directive to declare exception handlers. For example:

```
.catch java/io/IOException from Label1 to Label2 using Handler
```

creates an exception handler which is active in the region of code between the labels Label1 and Label2. If an IOException (or a subclass) occurs while the runtime system is executing the code between Label1 and Label2, then the runtime system jumps to the code starting at the label called Handler.

The .catch directive creates an entry in the "handler table" in the "Code" attribute for the method (see Chapter 12). In the case we saw above, the catch clause is creating an entry in the hander table whose from_pc is the address of Label1, to_pc is the address of Label2, target_pc is the address of the Handler label, and catch_type is the class java.io.IOException.

An Example

To tie all of these ideas together, the following is the Jasmin code for Catcher—an example program that throws an exception and then catches it, printing out the message "Exception Caught".

By now, most of the code in the example should be familiar to you, so we won't go over the code step by step. You can look up unfamiliar instructions in the back of the book.

```
.class public Catcher
.super java/lang/Object

; standard initializer for the Catch class
.method public <init>()V
    aload 0
    invokenonvirtual java/lang/Object.<init>()V
    return
.end method

; Entry point
.method static main([Ljava/lang/String;)V

    .limit locals 3
    .limit stack 3

    ; catch java.lang.Exception exceptions in the region of code
    ; from Label1 to Label2 by jumping to the code at Handler:

    .catch java/lang/Exception from Label1 to Label2 using Handler

Label1:  ; Start of protected block of code

    ; Make a new instance of Exception
    new java/lang/Exception
    dup
    invokenonvirtual java/lang/Exception.<init>()V

    ; Throw the exception
    athrow

Label2:  ; End of protected block of code
```

```
    ; This is the address of the handler for the exception
Handler:

    ; The handler is passed the Exception that was raised. We
    ; use pop to remove the Exception from the stack.
    pop

    ; Get the object in java.lang.System.out
    ; then push a message onto the stack and call println to print it
    getstatic java/lang/System/out Ljava/io/PrintStream;
    ldc "Exception caught"
    invokevirtual java/io/PrintStream/println(Ljava/lang/String;)V

    ; done
    return

.end method
```

Try/Finally

So far we have discussed try/catch clauses. The Java language also provides a feature called finally, which you see illustrated below:

```
try {
    //
    // perform something that may cause an exception
    //
} catch (SomeException e1) {
    // handle an exception object e1 of type SomeException
    // (or a subclass)
} catch (AnotherException e2) {
    // handle an exception object e2 of type  AnotherException
    // (or a subclass)
} finally {
    // Always execute this code when leaving the try construct.
}
```

The code after the finally keyword is guaranteed to be run and is generally used to clean up (close files, release resources, etc.) after activities performed by the code following the try keyword

The Virtual Machine doesn't provide any nice mechanism for implementing the finally feature. Instead, it's up to the compiler to produce code which traps the four routes out of the try clause:

1.   normal exit from the bottom of the protected code

2.   exit because of a break, continue, or return statement

3. after an exception that is handled explicitly with a catch

4. after an exception that isn't handled

To do this, the Java compiler places the `finally` code block in a "subroutine", and then arranges in all four of these cases for that subroutine to be called. More on subroutines in a moment.

For a normal exit, the compiler simply has to add a `jsr` to the `finally` subroutine at the end of the block of protected code. Similary, for break and continue, a `jsr` is inserted before the goto that leaves the block of protected code. For a return statement, the compiler generates code to:

*   save the return value (if any) in a local variable

*   `jsr` to the finally subroutine

*   push the return value back onto the stack and return

The same safeguards work for catch clauses: a `jsr` is inserted before the end of the block of catch code and also before any jumps/returns out of the block.

To deal with exceptions that aren't caught explicitly with a catch clause, one more twist is needed. The compiler registers an exception handler at the end of the exception handlers' table whose protected range of code is all the code within the try and catch clauses, and which responds to all Throwable classes. This handler:

*   saves the exception object left on the stack in a local variable

*   uses `jsr` to call the finally subroutine

*   uses `athrow` to re-throw the exception

Consider the following Java method:

```
public void test() {
    FileInputStream x;
    try {
        try {
            // try to open a file "myfile"
            x = new FileInputStream("myfile");
        } catch (java.io.FileNotFoundException e1) {
            // file doesn't exist
            System.out.println("no such file");
        }
    } catch (Exception IOException) {
        // some other kind of IO exception was raised
        System.out.println("IO exception");
    } finally {
        // this code is guaranteed to run, even if an exception was raised
        System.out.println("done");
    }
}
```

At the JVM level, how is this encoded? The following code shows the same method written in Jasmin:

```
.method public test()V
    .limit stack 3
    .limit vars 4

    ; set up the exceptions table

    ; if a FileNotFoundException occurs between Start and End1, jump to NotFound
    .catch java/io/FileNotFoundException from Start to End1 using NotFound

    ; if an IOException occurs between Start and End2, jump to IOE:
    .catch java/lang/IOException from Start to End2 using IOE

    ; if any other kind of exception is raised between Start and Done, jump
    ; to the Other_Exception
    .catch all from Start to Done using Other_Exception

Start:
    ; x = new FileInputStream("myfile");
    new java/io/FileInputStream
    dup
    ldc "myfile"
    invokenonvirtual java/io/FileInputStream/<init>(Ljava/lang/String;)V
    astore_1
End1:
    ; finished my work - return from the method
    goto Done

NotFound:    ; a FileNotFound exception was raised

    pop        ; pop the exception off the stack

    ; print out a message
    getstatic java/lang/System/out Ljava/io/PrintStream;
    ldc "not such file"
    invokevirtual java/io/PrintStream/println(Ljava/lang/String;)V

    ; finished - return from the method
    goto Done
End2:

IOE:          ; an IOException was raised

    pop        ; pop the exception off the stack

    ; print out a message
    getstatic java/lang/System/out Ljava/io/PrintStream;
    ldc "IO exception"
    invokevirtual java/io/PrintStream/println(Ljava/lang/String;)V

    ; finished - return from the method
    goto Done
```

```
Done:
    ; to return from the method, use:

    jsr FinalSub    ; call the finally code
    return          ; return from the method

Other_Exception:  ; some other exception occurs during the above code:
    astore_2        ; store the exception in a local variable

    jsr FinalSub    ; call the finally code

    aload_2         ; now rethrow the exception
    athrow

FinalSub:
    ; this contains the code in the finally clause:

    astore_3    ; store the return address in local variable 3

    ; print a message
    getstatic java/lang/System/out Ljava/io/PrintStream;
    ldc "done"
    invokevirtual java/io/PrintStream/println(Ljava/lang/String;)V

    ret 3       ; return to the address in local variable 3
.end method
```

You can see that the method contains two exception handlers, NotFound and IOE. It also contains a handler for any other kind of exception, called Other_Exception. All of these routes out of the method call the FinalSub first before leaving the method.

11

Threads

Overview

Java supports multithreaded applications. In Java runtime systems, threads are either simulated in software, or they can be implemented using native calls to the underlying operating system—so in computers with more than one processor, threads can be run concurrently.

This section contains a brief discussion of the API to threads. We do not have space in this book for an extended discussion on the topic of threads—readers should consult the Java Language Specification or Java Virtual Machine Specification for detailed rules on the semantics of threads in Java. You could consider also reading *Java Threads* by Scott Oaks and Henry Wong (published by O'Reilly & Associates, Inc.).

At the JVM level, there are three ways that Java programs interact with threads:

- calling methods associated with java.lang.Thread

- using monitorenter and monitorexit to synchronize a block of code

- calling methods which are marked synchronized

Java API to Threads

Java programs create instances of the Thread class to make new threads, and instances of ThreadGroup to manage collections of threads. The Thread class contains methods to start thread execution or stop thread execution, as well as suspend or resume thread execution.

For example:

```
Thread.yield();
```

tells the current thread to give up its control of a processor and let another thread execute. Similarly:

```
Thread.sleep(10);
```

causes the current thread to suspend itself for 10 milliseconds.

In addition to the Thread and ThreadGroup, the Object.wait(), Object.notify(), and Object.notifyAll() methods interact with the thread mechanism.

See *Java in a Nutshell* for a discussion of the Java API to threads.

Monitors

In the JVM, monitor instructions are used to synchronize object access across multiple threads (see Table 11-1).

Table 11–1: Monitor instructions

Name	Description
monitorenter	enter synchronized region of code
monitorexit	leave synchronized region of code

For example, when you write the Java code:

```
void myMethod(Object obj) {
    synchronized (obj) {
        // some statements
    }
}
```

the statements inside the synchronized block are guarded with a monitorenter/monitorexit. In Jasmin this is written as:

```
.method myMethod(Ljava/lang/Object;)V
    aload_1           ; push -obj- onto the stack
    monitorenter      ; enter a monitor for obj
    ; some statements ...
    aload_1           ; push obj onto the stack
    monitorexit       ; exit the monitor for obj
.end method
```

Only one thread at a time can own a monitor on an object—though that thread can own multiple monitors on the same object. See the reference pages for monitorenter/monitorexit in Chapter 13, *Instruction Reference*, for more details.

Note that it is up to the programmer to make sure that monitorenters and monitorexits are balanced correctly—this becomes more tricky when you start taking exceptions into account. See Chapter 10, *Exceptions*, for a discussion of exceptions.

Synchronized Methods

Methods can be marked as synchronized. For example, if this is in the Java class:

```
class SyncExample {
    synchronized void s() {
        // some statements
    }
}
```

then when you call s(), the JVM implicitly calls monitorenter on this at the start of the method, and monitorexit on this when the method returns. In Jasmin, the above class translates to:

```
.class SyncExample
.super java/lang/Object

.method synchronized s()V
    ; some statements
.end method
```

12

Class File Reference

This chapter contains a byte-by-byte description of the format of Java class files. For an overview of class files, see Chapter 4, *Classes.*

Organization and Data Format

Class files are organized as a series of nested tables and arrays. All data entries in the tables are one-byte, two-byte, or four-byte unsigned integers, unless otherwise noted in the text. For example, in the following table:

Size	Name
4	magic
2	minor_version
2	constant_pool_count
N/A	constant pool

magic is a four-byte unsigned integer, *minor_version* and *constant_pool_count* are two-byte unsigned integers, and *constant_pool* is a sub-table which is described separately. No padding is inserted between these items in the file.

Remember that data in class files is stored in network order. So to reconstruct a two-byte unsigned value (byte1, byte2), where byte1 appears first in the file, and byte2 appears after byte1, use:

```
(byte1 << 8) + byte2
```

A four-byte value is reconstructed using:

```
(byte1 << 24) + (byte2 << 16) + (byte3 << 8) + byte4
```

Signed values (and floating-point values) are stored using the same representation as is implemented by the java.io.DataInput and java.io.DataOutput classes.

The Top-Level Table

The topmost table in a class file contains information relating to the class itself. It has this form:

Size	Name
4	magic
2	minor_version
2	major_version
2	constant_pool_count
N/A	constant pool
2	access_flags
2	this_class
2	super_class
2	interfaces_count
N/A	interfaces
2	fields_count
N/A	fields
2	methods_count
N/A	methods
2	attributes_count
N/A	attributes

magic
> The unsigned integer 0xCAFEBABE. Class file readers use the first four bytes in a file to identify the file as a Java class file.

minor_version
major_version
> These version numbers indicate what level of Java VM specification this class file is using. Currently, the Java compiler uses a major version number of 45 and a minor version of 3. Java VM implementations may reject files with version numbers greater than or less than this.

constant_pool_count

The size of this class's (or interface's) constant pool.

constant_pool

A table constituting the constant pool of this class. Each entry in the table starts with a tag byte indicating the type of the entry. The tag byte is followed by a variable number of bytes, depending on the type of entry.

Notice that only (*constant_pool_count*–1) items are written in the class file. The first given item in the class file will be given the constant pool index 1, the second will be index 2, and so on. The entry at index 0 of a constant pool does not appear in class files—in fact, JVM classes should not refer to the *zero*th entry of a constant pool (though the runtime system may use this index).

Also, constants representing Doubles and Longs are considered to take two entries each—see the following sections for more details.

access_flags

A short integer whose bits specify the access mode for the class. The flags in the following table can be specified for classes.

Name	Value	Description
ACC_PUBLIC	0x0001	Class is visible to everyone
ACC_FINAL	0x0010	No further subclassing allowed
ACC_SUPER	0x0020	Use new invokespecial semantics
ACC_INTERFACE	0x0200 File	Contains an interface
ACC_ABSTRACT	0x0400	Class cannot be instanced

NOTE   The ACC_SUPER flag exists for backwards compatibility. In early versions of the JVM, the invokespecial instruction was called invokenonvirtual and had more relaxed semantics. When the specification was released, Sun tightened the semantics of invokenonvirtual, and renamed it invokespecial. All modern compilers should set the ACC_SUPER bit in class files to indicate that they follow the new semantics. Runtime systems should also use the newer semantics— see the reference page for invokespecial.

this_class

The index of an entry in the constant pool. The entry must be tagged as a CONSTANT_Class entry. It defines the name of this class or interface.

super_class

> The index of an entry in the constant pool. The entry must be tagged as a CONSTANT_Class entry. It names the superclass of this class. For java.lang.Object, super_class is zero. For interfaces, super_class is often (but not necessarily) the class java.lang.Object.

interfaces_count

> The number of interfaces this class implements.

interfaces

> A table listing the interfaces that this class implements. Each entry in the table is a two-byte unsigned short. The number of items in the table is given by interfaces_count. Each unsigned short in this table is an index of an entry in the constant pool. The corresponding constant pool entry must be tagged as a CONSTANT_Class, and identifies a Java interface this class implements.

field_count

> The number of items in the fields table.

fields

> A table listing the new fields introduced by this class. The number of fields in the table is given by fields_count. We will come back to field definitions later in this chapter.

methods_count

> The number of methods defined in the class.

methods

> A table listing the methods declared by this class. The number of methods in the table is given by methods_count. We will come back to method definitions later in this chapter.

attributes_count

> The number of items in the attributes table.

attributes

> An array of attribute structures. Currently the "SourceFile" attribute is the only recognized top-level attribute (see the following section).

Top-Level Attributes

Attributes give optional or additional information. Each attribute is named and has the general form:

Size	Name
2	attribute_name_index
4	bytes_count
N/A	bytes

attribute_name_index

> The index of an entry in the constant pool which is tagged as a CON-STANT_Utf8 entry, and which gives the name of the attribute.

bytes_count

> The number of bytes of data used by the attribute.

bytes

> An array of bytes containing attribute data. The interpretation of the data depends on the type of attribute.

Class file readers are expected to ignore attributes whose names they don't recognize.

The "SourceFile" attribute is the only attribute that is defined in the specification for top-level class file structures. "SourceFile" attributes are laid out as follows:

Size	Name
2	attribute_name_index
4	bytes_count
2	source_file_index

attribute_name_index

> The index of an entry in the constant pool which is tagged as a CON-STANT_Utf8 entry, and which contains the name "SourceFile".

bytes_count

> This contains the value 0x02.

source_file_index

> This is the index of an entry in the constant pool which is tagged a CON-STANT_Utf8 entry, and which gives the name of the source file that this class file was derived from.

The "SourceFile" attribute is optional. If it is present, interpreters may use this for debugging purposes—e.g., to locate the source file on a local disk and show it in an editor window.

Type Descriptors

Type descriptors are used to describe the types of fields and local variables. They are also used to indicate the types of arguments to methods, and the type of the return result of a method.

Type descriptors are encoded using ASCII strings. The following grammar rules are used to construct a type descriptor for a single field:

```
<field_type> ::= <base_type> | <object_type> | <array_type>
<base_type> ::= B|C|D|F|I|J|S|Z
<object_type> ::= L<fullclassname>;
<array_type> ::= [<data_type>
```

where the base types are:

Size	Name
B	byte
C	char
D	double
F	float
I	int
J	long
S	short
Z	boolean

Methods use a more elaborate type descriptor:

```
<method_type_descriptor> ::= ( <argument_types> ) <return_type>
<argument_types> ::= <field_type>*
<return_type> ::= <field_type> | V
```

for example:

```
(ILjava/lang/String;)Z
```

is the type descriptor of a method that takes two arguments (an int and a String) and returns a boolean result.

The Constant Pool Table

The constant pool table in a class file is structured as an ordered sequence of items. Each item starts with a one-byte tag indicating the type of the item. The tags' bytes are defined in Table 12-1.

Table 12–1: Constant pool tags

Tag Name	Value
CONSTANT_Utf8	1
CONSTANT_Integer	3
CONSTANT_Float	4
CONSTANT_Long	5
CONSTANT_Double	6
CONSTANT_Class	7
CONSTANT_String	8
CONSTANT_Fieldref	9
CONSTANT_Methodref	10
CONSTANT_InterfaceMethodref	11
CONSTANT_NameAndType	12

Entries in the constant pool are referenced using an index number. The first constant in a class file is given an index of 1, the second is 2, and so on.

NOTE   For obscure reasons, when an entry tagged CONSTANT_Long or CONSTANT_Double appears in the constant pool, the JVM considers this as taking up two entries. For example, if a CONSTANT_Long appears at index 3 in the constant pool, then the next constant in the class file will be given an index number of 5. Index 4 is treated as an invalid index, and must not be referred to by the class file.

CONSTANT_Utf8

An entry tagged as CONSTANT_Utf8 holds a string. These have the structure:

Size	Name
1	tag
2	length
N/A	bytes

tag
    The tag byte CONSTANT_Utf8 (1).
length
    The number of bytes in the string. The string need not be NULL-terminated.

bytes

> The array of bytes that make up the string. The number of bytes is given by the length field (see the previous section).

The bytes that make up the string are encoded using a modified form of the UTF-8 format. In UTF-8, ASCII characters are represented using just their ASCII code, with a 0 in the top-end bit, i.e.:

```
    Byte 0
 7 6 5 4 3 2 1 0
 0 -  7 bits   -
```

Non-ASCII characters in the range 0x0080 to 0x007ff, as well as the NULL character, are represented using two bytes:

```
    Byte 0              Byte 1
 7 6 5 4 3 2 1 0    7 6 5 4 3 2 1 0
 1 1 0 - 5 bits-    1 0 - 6 bits  -
```

Characters in the range 0x0800 to 0xFFFF take three bytes:

```
    Byte 0              Byte 1              Byte 3
 7 6 5 4 3 2 1 0    7 6 5 4 3 2 1 0    7 6 5 4 3 2 1 0
 1 1 1 0 4 bits     1 0 - 6 bits  -    1 0 - 6 bits  -
```

UTF-8 also defines longer formats, but these are not recognized by Java. Another difference between Java's Utf8 format and the official UTF-8 format is that Java does not encode the NULL character using 0, so that embedded NULLS do not occur in a string; instead, a NULL is encoded as the two bytes 0xC0, 0x80.

All literal strings in Java class files (class names, descriptors, method names, etc.) are encoded in Utf8.

CONSTANT_Integer

An entry tagged as a CONSTANT_Integer holds a 32-bit integer. The entry is stored in the class file using the structure:

Size	Name
1	tag
4	value

tag

> The tag byte CONSTANT_Integer (3).

value

> The four bytes holding the 32-bit signed integer value. The bytes are stored in network (most significant byte first) order.

CONSTANT_Float

An entry tagged as a CONSTANT_Float holds a 32-bit float. Its structure is:

Size	Name
1	tag
4	value

tag

> The tag byte CONSTANT_Float (4).

value

> The four bytes holding the float value. The bytes are stored in network (most significant byte first) order, and are in the IEEE 754 standard single-format representation for floating-point values.

CONSTANT_Long

An entry tagged as a CONSTANT_Long holds a 64-bit long. Its structure is:

Size	Name
1	tag
8	value

tag

> The tag byte CONSTANT_Long (5).

value

> The eight bytes holding the long integer value. The bytes are stored in network (most significant byte first) order.

CONSTANT_Double

A double-precision float is stored in the constant pool using an entry tagged as CONSTANT_Double. Its structure is:

Size	Name
1	tag
8	value

tag

> The tag byte CONSTANT_Double (6).

value

The eight bytes holding the double-precision floating-point value. The bytes are stored in network (most significant byte first) order, and use the the IEEE 754 standard single-format representation for double-precision floating-point numbers.

CONSTANT_Class

An entry tagged as CONSTANT_Class represents a reference to a Java class. The reference is symbolic—i.e., the entry gives the name of the Java class. Class references use the form:

Size	Name
1	tag
2	name_index

tag

The tag byte CONSTANT_Class (7).

name_index

The index of an entry in the constant pool which is tagged a CON-STANT_Utf8, and which is a string that gives the full name of the class.

In these Class entries, the name_index points to a Utf8 string that is either:

• the name of a class, e.g., "java/lang/String", or

• a type descriptor for an array, e.g., "[I" for an array of ints.

CONSTANT_String

Entries tagged CONSTANT_String are used to represent instances of java.lang.String objects in the constant pool. They are used in conjunction with the ldc and ldc_w instructions to push literal strings onto the operand stack. They have the structure:

Size	Name
1	tag
2	string_index

tag

The integer value CONSTANT_String (8).

string_index
> The index of an entry in the constant pool which is tagged a CON-STANT_Utf8, and which gives the contents of the string.

CONSTANT_Fieldref

Entries tagged as CONSTANT_Fieldref give the name, type descriptor, and class of a Java field. These constants are used by instructions like getfield and putfield, and have the structure:

Size	Name
1	tag
2	class_index
2	name_and_type_index

tag
> The tag byte CONSTANT_Fieldref (9).

class_index
> The index of an entry in the constant pool tagged as a CONSTANT_Class entry, which specifies the class that the field belongs to.

name_and_type_index
> The index of an entry in the constant pool which is tagged a CON-STANT_NameAndType entry. This gives the name and type descriptor for the field.

CONSTANT_Methodref

A method is referenced in the class file using a constant pool entry which is tagged CONSTANT_Methodref. It has the form:

Size	Name
1	tag
2	class_index
2	name_and_type_index

tag
> The tag byte CONSTANT_Methodref (10).

class_index

> The index of an entry in the constant pool tagged as a CONSTANT_Class entry, which specifies the class that the method belongs to.

name_and_type_index

> The index of an entry in the constant pool which is tagged a CONSTANT_NameAndType entry. This gives the name and type descriptor of the method. Type descriptors for methods encode both the types of the arguments to the method, and the types of the return results.

CONSTANT_InterfaceMethodref

This is used to reference a method defined by an interface (see `invokeinterface`). Its structure is similar to CONSTANT_Methodref:

Size	Name
1	tag
2	class_index
2	name_and_type_index

tag

> The tag byte CONSTANT_InterfaceMethodref (11).

class_index

> The index of an entry in the constant pool tagged as a CONSTANT_Class entry, which specifies the class that the method belongs to.

name_and_type_index

> The index of an entry in the constant pool which is tagged a CONSTANT_NameAndType entry. This gives the name and type descriptor of the method. Type descriptors for methods encode both the types of the arguments to the method, and the types of the return results.

CONSTANT_NameAndType

Used to give name and type information for fields and methods. Entries tagged as CONSTANT_NameAndType have the structure:

Size	Name
1	tag
2	name_index
2	type_index

tag
>   The tag byte CONSTANT_NameAndType (12).

name_index
>   The index of an entry in the constant pool which is tagged CONSTANT_Utf8, and which defines the name of the field or method.

type_index
>   The index of an entry in the constant pool which is tagged CONSTANT_Utf8, which gives the type descriptor for the field.

Fields

After the constant pool, the next table in a class file gives the fields that the class defines. Each entry in this table uses a structure with the form:

Size	Name
2	access_flags
2	name_index
2	type_index
2	attributes_count
N/A	attributes

access_flags
>   a bitwise-or of the flags in the following table.
>
>   At most, one of ACC_PUBLIC, ACC_PRIVATE and ACC_PROTECTED can be set for each field.

Name	Value	Meaning
ACC_PUBLIC	0x0001	Visible to everyone
ACC_PRIVATE	0x0002	Visible only to the defining class
ACC_PROTECTED	0x0004	Visible to this class and subclasses
ACC_STATIC	0x0008	A static field
ACC_FINAL	0x0010	No further assignment after initialization
ACC_VOLATILE	0x0040	Can't cache value
ACC_TRANSIENT	0x0080	Not to be written or read by persistent object manager

name_index
>   The index of a CONSTANT_Utf8 entry in the constant pool indicating the name of the field.

type_index
> The index of a CONSTANT_Utf8 string entry in the constant pool giving the type descriptor of field.

attribute_count
> The number of items in the attribute table.

attributes
> A list of field attributes. Currently, only the "ConstantValue" attribute has a defined meaning for fields—see the next section.

Field Attributes

Only one field attribute is currently recognized: the "ConstantValue" attribute. This gives the initial value of a static field. It uses a structure of the form:

Size	Name
2	attribute_name_index
4	bytes_count
2	constant_value_index

attribute_name_index
> The index of an entry in the constant pool which is tagged CONSTANT_Utf8, and which contains the string "ConstantValue".

bytes_count
> This must be the integer 2.

constant_value_index
> The index of an entry in the constant pool that gives the initial value for this field. The tag byte of the constant pool entry and the type of the field must be consistent, as shown in the following table.

Field Type	Constant Type
int	CONSTANT_Integer
short	CONSTANT_Integer
char	CONSTANT_Integer
byte	CONSTANT_Integer
boolean	CONSTANT_Integer
long	CONSTANT_Long
float	CONSTANT_Float
double	CONSTANT_Double
string	CONSTANT_String

Methods

After the fields table, the next table in the class file defines all of the methods in the class. Each method in this table uses a structure of the form:

Size	Name
2	access_flags
2	name_index
2	type_index
2	attributes_count
N/A	attributes

access_flags

> A bitwise-or of the flags in the following table.

Name	Value	Meaning
ACC_PUBLIC	0x0001	Visible to everyone
ACC_PRIVATE	0x0002	Visible only to the defining class
ACC_PROTECTED	0x0004	Visible to this class and subclasses
ACC_STATIC	0x0008	A static field
ACC_FINAL	0x0010	No further overriding
ACC_SYNCHRONIZED	0x0020	Use monitor lock when method is invoked
ACC_NATIVE	0x0100	Implemented using "native" code (e.g., "C")
ACC_ABSTRACT	0x0400	No body—no "Code" attribute provided

At most, one of ACC_PUBLIC, ACC_PRIVATE, and ACC_PROTECTED can be set for each method.

name_index

> The index of an entry in the constant pool which is tagged CONSTANT_Utf8, and which gives the name of the method.

type_index

> The index of an entry in the constant pool which is tagged CONSTANT_Utf8, and which gives the type descriptor of the method.

attributes_count

> The number of entries in the attributes table.

attributes

> An array of attributes. Currently, only the "Code" and "Exceptions" attributes are recognized (see the following section).

Method Attributes

Two method attributes are recognized: "Exceptions" and "Code".

Exceptions

The "Exceptions" attribute is used to specify which exceptions a method can throw. It uses the format:

Size	Name
2	attribute_name_index
4	bytes_count
2	throws_count
N/A	throws

attribute_name_index

> The index of a constant pool entry which has the tag CONSTANT_Utf8, and which contains the string "Exceptions".

bytes_count

> This is (throws_count * 2) + 2.

throws_count

> The number of entries in the throws array.

throws

> An array of two-byte unsigned integers. Each entry in the array is an index into the constant pool. The constant at that index must be tagged as a CONSTANT_Class, and names a Throwable class that this method is declared to throw.

Code

The "Code" attribute uses the format:

Size	Name
2	attribute_name_index
4	bytes_count
2	max_stack

Size	Name
2	max_locals
4	code_count
N/A	code
2	handlers_count
N/A	handlers
2	attributes_count
N/A	attributes

attribute_name_index
> The index of an entry in the constant pool tagged CONSTANT_Utf8 that contains the string "Code".

bytes_count
> The total length of the "Code" attribute, excluding the initial six bytes.

max_stack
> The maximum number of items placed on the operand stack by this method.

max_locals
> The number of local variables used by this method.

code_count
> The number of bytes in the code array.

code
> The bytecode for this method. This array of bytes contains the virtual machine instructions used to execute the method. The format of the bytecode in this array is described in the instruction reference.

handlers_count
> The number of entries in the exception handlers table.

handlers
> An array of exception handlers for this method. See below.

attributes_count
> The number of attributes in the attribute table.

attributes
> A table of attributes. Currently the "LineNumberTable" and "LocalVariableTable" attributes are defined. See below.

The handlers table in a "Code" attribute specifies the exception handlers that catch exceptions generated during the execution of the method. Each entry in the handlers table uses a structure of the following form.

Size	Name
2	start_pc
2	end_pc
2	handler_pc
2	catch_type_index

start_pc
> The index in the bytecode where this handler becomes active.

end_pc
> The index in bytecode where this handler becomes inactive. The code in the range code[start_pc] to code[end_pc–1] is the range of code managed by this handler.

handler_pc
> The index in the bytecode where the handler starts.

catch_type_index
> If this is zero, the handler is activated for any exception. Otherwise, catch_type_index is the index of CONSTANT_Class entry in the constant pool specifying which class of exceptions this handler is used for.

Code Attributes

The "Code" attribute itself can have attributes. These are used to include debugging information about the code. Two code attributes are defined: "LineNumberTable" and "LocalVariableTable".

LineNumberTable

The "LineNumberTable" attribute provides a mapping between bytecode addresses and line numbers in the source file.[*] It has the structure:

Size	Name
2	attribute_name_index
4	bytes_count
2	lines_count
N/A	lines

---

* Note the Sun's javac compiler can generate more than one LineNumberTable attribute per method.

attribute_name_index
> The index of an entry in the constant pool tagged CONSTANT_Utf8 and containing the string "LineNumberTable".

bytes_count
> The value (4 * lines_count) + 2

lines_count
> The number of entries in the lines table.

lines
> An array of structures containing the starting offsets and line numbers for the code. See below.

Each line in the lines array is represented using a structure of the form:

Size	Name
2	start_pc
2	line_number

start_pc
> The index in bytecode where a new line of source begins.

line_number
> The line number in the source file for the corresponding start_pc.

LocalVariableTable

The "LocalVariableTable" attribute is used to give details on local variable usage by the method, so that debuggers know the types and names of local variables. This attribute has the structure:

Size	Name
2	attribute_name_index
4	bytes_count
2	local_variables_count
N/A	local_variables

attribute_name_index
> The index of an entry in the constant pool tagged CONSTANT_Utf8 and containing the string "LocalVariableTable".

bytes_count
> The value (10 * local_variables_count) + 2

local_variables_count
> The number of entries in the local_variables array.

local_variables
> An array of structures containing the names and types of local variables. See below.

Each local variable in the local_variables array is a structure of the form:

Size	Name
2	start_pc
2	length
2	name_index
2	type_index
2	slot

start_pc
> The index in the code where this local variable becomes active.

length
> The number of bytes in the bytecode that utilize this local variable.

name_index
> The index of a Utf8 string in the local pool giving the name of the local variable.

type_index
> The index of a Utf8 string in the local pool specifying the type descriptor of the local variable.

slot
> The local variable number being used for this local variable (i.e., the number given to iload, istore, etc., to access or set this local variable).

13

Instruction Reference

---

example an example of an instruction entry

Jasmin Syntax

```
example <param1> <param2> ...
```

Stack

Before	After
item1	item2
item2	item1
...	...

Description

Explains the format for instruction reference pages.

The first line on a reference page lists the name of an instruction and gives a brief synopsis of the instruction.

The *Jasmin Syntax* section indicates the Jasmin assembler syntax for the instruction. In the example above, the instruction is shown with two *parameters*, one called <param1> and the other called <param2>. The *Jasmin Syntax* also includes additional notes for Jasmin users.

The *Stack* section describes the effect that the instruction has on the operand stack. It shows a symbolic representation of the stack state before and after the execution of the instruction. Each row in the tables represents a one-word entry on the stack. The first row represents the top of the stack. In the example above, it's clear that the order of the top two words on the stack is reversed by the instruction.

The section you are reading is the *Description* section, which gives details of how the instruction works and what its side effects are.

Example

```
; This section often contains examples illustrating how
; an instruction is used.

; Examples are written using the Jasmin assembler syntax.
```

Exceptions

This section lists any exceptions generated by the instruction at runtime, and it explains what causes each exception.

Bytecode

This section gives details on how the instruction is laid out in the bytecode of a class file. It shows a table listing the opcode for the instruction, as well as any additional parameters that follow the opcode in bytecode.

Type	Description
u1	This line usually shows the opcode for the instruction
u1	A "u1" field is an unsigned 1-byte integer field
u2	A "u2" field is an unsigned 2-byte integer field
u4	A "u4" field is an unsigned 4-byte integer field
s1	A "s1" field is a signed 1-byte integer field
s2	A "s2" field is a signed 2-byte integer field
s4	A "s4" field is a signed 4-byte integer field

See Also

This section lists related instructions that you should read.

Notes

This section gives additional details that you should be aware of.

aaload retrieve object reference from array

Jasmin Syntax

```
aaload
```

Stack

Before	After
index	value
arrayref	...
...	

Description

Retrieves an object reference from an array of objects and places it on the stack. *arrayref* is a reference to an array of objects. *index* is an int. The *arrayref* and *index* are removed from the stack, and the object reference at the given *index* in the array is pushed onto the stack.

Example

```
; This is like the Java code:
;     Object x = arr[0];
; where x is local variable 2 and arr is an array of objects in local variable 1

aload_1      ; load local variable 1 onto the stack
iconst_0     ; push the integer 0 onto the stack
aaload       ; retrieve the entry
astore_2     ; store the entry in local variable 2
```

Exceptions

- NullPointerException—*arrayref* is null
- ArrayIndexOutOfBoundsException—*index* is < 0 or >= *arrayref.length*

Bytecode

Type	Description
u1	aaload opcode = 0x32 (50)

See Also

iaload, faload, daload, laload, baload, caload, saload, iastore, lastore, fastore, dastore, aastore, bastore, castore, sastore

aastore store object reference in array

Jasmin Syntax

```
aastore
```

Stack

Before	After
value	...
index	
arrayref	
...	

Description

Stores an object reference in an array of objects. *arrayref* is a reference to an array of object references. *index* is an int. *value* is the object reference to be stored in the array. *arrayref, index,* and *value* are removed from the stack, and *value* is stored in the array at the given *index*.

The runtime type of *value* must be assignment-compatible with the type of the array. For example, if the array is declared as an array of Threads, then *value* must either be null or an instance of Thread or one of its subclasses. An ArrayStoreException is generated if you attempt to store an incompatible type of object in an array. Assignment compatibility is described in more detail in Chapter 7, *Data Operations.*

Exceptions

* ArrayIndexOutOfBoundsException—*index* is < 0 or $>= arrayref.length$
* ArrayStoreException—*value* is not compatible with the type of the array
* NullPointerException—*arrayref* is null

Bytecode

Type	Description
u1	aastore opcode = 0x53 (83)

See Also

iastore, lastore, fastore, dastore, bastore, castore, sastore, iaload, laload, faload, daload, aaload, baload, caload, saload

---

aconst_null push null

Jasmin Syntax

```
aconst_null
```

Stack

Before	After
...	null
	...

Description

Pushes the special null object reference onto the stack. null is a reference to no object and has no type (null can be cast to any reference type). null conventionally represents an invalid or uncreated object. Fields, variables, and the elements of object reference arrays have null as their initial value.

Bytecode

Type	Description
u1	aconst_null opcode = 0x01 (1)

See Also

bipush, sipush, ldc, ldc_w, ldc2_w, iconst_m1, iconst_<n>, lconst_<l>, fconst_<f>, dconst_<d>

aload   retrieve object reference from local variable

Jasmin Syntax

```
     aload <varnum>
  or
     wide
     aload <varnum>
```

In the first form, <varnum> is an unsigned integer in the range 0 to 0xFF. In the second (wide) form, <varnum> is an unsigned integer in the range 0 to 0xFFFF.

Stack

Before	After
...	objectref
	...

Description

Retrieves an object reference from a local variable and pushes it onto the operand stack. The aload instruction takes a single parameter, <varnum>, an unsigned integer which indicates which local variable to retrieve. The object reference in that local variable is retrieved and placed on the stack. <varnum> must be a valid local variable number in the current frame.

Example

```
  aload 1          ; push object reference in local variable 1 onto the stack
```

Bytecode

To access local variables in the range 0–255, use:

Type	Description
u1	aload opcode = 0x19 (25)
u1	<varnum>

There is also a wide format for this instruction, which supports access to all local variables from 0 to 65535:

Type	Description
u1	wide opcode = 0xC4 (196)
u1	aload opcode = 0x19 (25)
u2	<varnum>

See Also

fload, iload, lload, dload, wide

Notes

If you use `astore` to store a returnAddress in a local variable, you cannot then use `aload` to retrieve the value of that local variable. Instead, if a local variable holds a returnAddress, your only choices are to use `ret` to return to that address or to use one of the store instructions to store some other value in the local variable.

aload_<n> retrieve object reference from local variable <n>

Jasmin Syntax

```
    aload_0
or
    aload_1
or
    aload_2
or
    aload_3
```

Stack

Before	After
...	objectref
	...

Description

Represents the series of opcodes `aload_0`, `aload_1`, `aload_2`, and `aload_3` that retrieve an object reference held in local variables 0, 1, 2, or 3 and push it onto the stack. <n> must be a valid local variable number in the current frame.

'aload_<n>' is functionally equivalent to 'aload <n>', although it is typically more efficient and also takes fewer bytes in the bytecode.

Example

```
aload_0          ;push object in local variable 0
aload_1          ;push object in local variable 1
aload_2          ;push object in local variable 2
aload_3          ;push object in local variable 3
```

Bytecode

Type	Description
u1	aload_0 opcode = 0x2A (42)
u1	aload_1 opcode = 0x2B (43)
u1	aload_2 opcode = 0x2C (44)
u1	aload_3 opcode = 0x2D (45)

See Also

fload, iload, lload, dload

Notes

If you use astore to store a returnAddress in a local variable, you cannot then use aload_<n> to retrieve the value of that local variable. Instead, if a local variable holds a returnAddress, your only choices are to either use ret to return to that address or use one of the store instructions to store some other value in the local variable.

---

anewarray   allocate new array for objects

Jasmin Syntax

```
anewarray <type>
```

<type> is either the name of a class or interface, e.g., java/lang/String, or to create the first dimension of a multidimensional array, <type> can be an array type descriptor, e.g., [Ljava/lang/String;

Stack

Before	After
size	arrayref
...	...

Description

Allocates a new array for holding object references. It pops an int, *size*, off the stack and constructs a new array capable of holding *size* object references of the type indicated by <*type*>.

<*type*> indicates what types of object references are to be stored in the array (see aastore). It is the name of a class or an interface, or an array type descriptor. If it is java/lang/Object, for example, then any type of object reference can be stored in the array. <*type*> is resolved at runtime to a Java class, interface or array. See Chapter 4, *Classes*, for a discussion of how classes are resolved.

A reference to the new array is pushed onto the stack. Entries in the new array are initially set to null.

Example

```
; Allocate a 10-element array for holding references to
; Threads. This is like the Java code:
;        Thread x[] = new Thread[10];

bipush 10
anewarray java/lang/Thread
astore_1     ; store the new array in local variable 1

; Allocate a multi-dimensional array like:
;        new String[2][5]

; using anewarray. First, allocate new 2-element array for holding
; arrays of strings and store it in local variable 1.
iconst_2
anewarray [Ljava/lang/String;      ; type descriptor for array-of-String
astore_1

; next, allocate first array of String[5] and store it in index 0
aload_1
iconst_0
bipush 5
anewarray java/lang/String
aastore

; finally, allocate second array of String[5] and store it in index 1
aload_1
iconst_1
bipush 5
anewarray java/lang/String
aastore
```

Exceptions

* NegativeArraySizeException—*size* is less than zero

Bytecode

In bytecode, immediately after the `anewarray` opcode there is a 16-bit unsigned integer *index*. This is the index of an entry in the constant pool that is tagged as a CONSTANT_Class entry. The name field of this entry is given by `<type>` parameter in Jasmin.

Type	Description
u1	anewarray opcode = 0xBD (189)
u2	index

See Also

newarray, multianewarray, new

Notes

It is more efficient to use `multianewarray` to allocate multi-dimensional arrays.

---

areturn return from method with object reference result

Jasmin Syntax

```
areturn
```

Stack

Before	After
objectref	n/a
...	

Description

Refers to an object. It must be *assignment compatible* with the return type of the current method (see Chapter 7 for details of assignment compatibility). `areturn` pops objectref off the stack and pushes it onto the operand stack of the invoker (i.e., the method which used `invokevirtual`, `invokespecial`, `invokestatic` or `invoke-interface` to call the currently executing method). All other items on the current method's operand stack are discarded. If the current method is marked as synchronized, then an implicit monitorexit instruction is executed. Then the current method's frame is discarded, the invoker's frame is reinstated, and control returns to the invoker.

Example

```
.class Example
.super java/lang/Object

; This method takes an integer parameter n, and returns a new array of ints
; of length n.
.method public static makeIntArray(I)[I
    aload_0          ; push the array size (i.e., n) parameter onto the stack
    newarray int     ; make the array
    areturn          ; return the array
.endmethod

    ; an example of calling makeIntArray to make a 10 element array of ints:
    bipush 10
    invokestatic Example/makeIntArray(I)[I
    astore_1 ; store array in local variable 1
```

Bytecode

Type	Description
u1	areturn opcode = 0xB0 (176)

See Also

lreturn, freturn, dreturn, ireturn, return, invokevirtual, invokespecial, invokestatic, invokeinterface

arraylength get length of array

Jasmin Syntax

```
arraylength
```

Stack

Before	After
arrayref	length
...	...

Description

Removes *arrayref* (a reference to an array) from the stack and replaces it with the length of the array (an int). For multi-dimensional arrays, the length of the first dimension is returned.

Exceptions

- NullPointerException—*arrayref* is null

Bytecode

Type	Description
u1	arraylength opcode = 0xBE(190)

---

astore   store object reference in local variable

Jasmin Syntax

```
    astore <varnum>
or
    wide
    astore <varnum>
```

In the first form, <*varnum*> is an unsigned integer in the range 0 to 0xFF. In the second (wide) form, <*varnum*> is an unsigned integer in the range 0 to 0xFFFF.

Stack

Before	After
objectref	...
...	

Description

Pops *objectref* (a reference to an object or array) off the stack and stores it in local variable <*varnum*>. The astore instruction takes a single parameter, <*varnum*>, an unsigned integer which indicates which local variable is used. <*varnum*> must be a valid local variable number in the current frame.

Example

```
aload 1     ; Push object reference in local variable 1 onto stack
astore 3    ; and store it in local variable 3
```

Bytecode

For local variable numbers in the range 0–255, use:

Type	Description
u1	astore opcode = 0x3A (58)
u1	<varnum>

There is also a wide format for this instruction, which supports access to all local variables from 0 to 65535:

Type	Description
u1	wide opcode = 0xC4 (196)
u1	astore opcode = 0x3A (58)
u2	<varnum>

See Also

lstore, istore, dstore, fstore, wide

Notes

astore can also be used to store a returnAddress in a local variable. See the jsr instruction for more details.

astore_<n> store object reference in local variable <n>

Jasmin Syntax

```
    astore_0
or
    astore_1
or
    astore_2
or
    astore_3
```

Stack

Before	After
objectref	...
...	

Description

Pops objectref (a reference to an object or array) off the stack and stores it in local variable <n>, where <n> is 0, 1, 2 or 3. <n> must be a valid local variable number in the current frame.

"astore_<n>" is functionally equivalent to "astore <n>", although it is typically more efficient and also takes fewer bytes in the bytecode.

Example

```
astore_0        ; store reference in local variable 0
astore_1        ; store reference in local variable 1
astore_2        ; store reference in local variable 2
astore_3        ; store reference in local variable 3
```

Bytecode

Type	Description
u1	astore_0 opcode = 0x4B (75)
u1	astore_1 opcode = 0x4C (76)
u1	astore_2 opcode = 0x4D (77)
u1	astore_3 opcode = 0x4E (78)

See Also

astore, istore, fstore, dstore, lstore, aload, iload, fload, dload, lload

Notes

astore can also be used to store a returnAddress in a local variable. See the jsr instruction for more details.

athrow throw an exception or error

Jasmin Syntax

```
athrow
```

Stack

Before	After
objectref	n/a
...	

Description

Removes *objectref* (a reference to an object) from the operand stack, and "throws" the exception represented by that object. *objectref* is an instance of Throwable or one of its subclasses.

To throw an exception, the system searches for a handler for *objectref*'s class in the exception table of the currently active method.

If no handler is found, the current method's frame is discarded, its invoker's frame is reinstated, and the exception is immediately rethrown. This process is repeated until a handler is found or until there are no more procedures on the callstack (at which point, the current thread dies, typically printing out an error message).

If a handler is found, the operand stack of the active method is cleared, *objectref* is pushed on the operand stack of the current method, and execution continues at the first instruction of the handler.

See Chapter 10, *Exceptions*, for a full description of exceptions in the JVM.

Example

```
; Throw an IOException. This is equivalent to the Java code:
;
;    throw new java.io.IOException();
;
new java/io/IOException          ; 1) create and initialize an IOException instance
dup
invokespecial java/io/IOException/<init>()V
athrow                           ; 2) throw the IOException instance on the stack
```

Exceptions

- NullPointerException—the *objectref* on the stack is null

Bytecode

Type	Description
u1	athrow opcode = 0xBF (191)

baload retrieve byte/boolean from array

Jasmin Syntax

```
baload
```

Stack

Before	After
index	value
arrayref	...
...	...

Description

Retrieves a byte from a byte array, expands it to an integer and places it on the operand stack. *arrayref* is a reference to an array of bytes. *index* is an int. The *arrayref* and *index* are removed from the stack, and the 8-bit signed byte at the given *index* in the array is retrieved, sign-extended to a 32-bit int, and pushed onto the stack.

baload is also used to retrieve values from boolean arrays. In this case, *arrayref* is a reference to an array of booleans (see the newarray instruction). If the entry at the given *index* is true, then the int 1 is pushed onto the stack, otherwise the int 0 is pushed onto the stack. In Sun's implementation, boolean arrays are actually stored as byte arrays, using one byte per boolean value. Other implementations might use packed arrays—or even int arrays—this is invisible to programs running on the JVM, which always use baload and bastore to access and store values in boolean arrays.

Example

```
; This is like the Java code:
;     byte x = arr[0];
; where x is local variable 2 and arr is a byte array in local variable 1
aload_1          ; load local variable 1 onto the stack
iconst_0         ; push the integer 0 onto the stack
baload           ; retrieve the entry
istore_2         ; store the entry in local variable 2
```

Exceptions

- NullPointerException—*arrayref* is null
- ArrayIndexOutOfBoundsException—*index* is < *0 or* >= *arrayref.length*

Bytecode

Type	Description
u1	baload opcode = 0x33 (51)

See Also

iaload, laload, faload, daload, aaload, caload, saload, iastore, lastore, fastore, dastore, aastore, bastore, castore, sastore, newarray

---

bastore store in byte/boolean array

Jasmin Syntax

```
bastore
```

Stack

Before	After
value	...
index	
arrayref	
...	

Description

Takes a 32-bit int from the stack, truncates it to an 8-bit signed byte, and stores it in an array of bytes. *arrayref* is a reference to an array of bytes. *index* is an int. *value* is the int value to be stored in the array. *arrayref, index* and *value* are removed from the stack, and *value* is truncated to 8 bits and stored in the array at the given *index*.

bastore is also used to store values in boolean arrays. In this case, *arrayref* is a reference to an array of booleans (see the newarray instruction). If value is zero, false is stored at the given index in the array, otherwise true is stored at the given index. In Sun's implementation, boolean arrays are actually stored as byte arrays, using one byte per boolean value. Other implementations might use packed arrays—or even int arrays—this is invisible to programs running on the JVM, which always use baload and bastore to access and store values in boolean arrays.

Exceptions

- NullPointerException—*arrayref* is null
- ArrayIndexOutOfBoundsException—*index* is < 0 or >= *arrayref.length*

Bytecode

Type	Description
u1	bastore opcode = 0x54 (84)

See Also

iastore, lastore, fastore, dastore, aastore, castore, sastore, iaload, laload, faload, daload, aaload, baload, caload, saload, newarray

---

bipush push one-byte signed integer

Jasmin Syntax

```
bipush <n>
```

<n> is an integer >= –128 and <= 127 that is pushed onto the stack.

Stack

Before	After
...	<n>
...	...

Description

Takes a single parameter, <n> (an 8-bit signed integer), sign extends it to a 32-bit int, and pushes the resulting int value onto the operand stack.

bipush is typically more efficient than ldc. It also occupies fewer bytes in the class file.

Example

```
bipush    0x10    ; push the value 0x10 (16) onto the operand stack
```

Bytecode

The bipush opcode is followed in the bytecode by an 8-bit signed byte specifying the integer value to push.

Type	Description
u1	bipush opcode – 0x10 (16)
s1	<n>

See Also

sipush, ldc, ldc_w, ldc2_w, aconst_null, iconst_m1, iconst_<n>, lconst_<l>, fconst_<f>, dconst_<d>

breakpoint reserved opcode

Jasmin Syntax

```
n/a
```

Stack

Before	After
...	...

Description

Opcode 0xCA (202) is a reserved opcode with the mnemonic breakpoint. This opcode is reserved for internal use by a Java implementation, and must not appear in any class file—methods containing a breakpoint will fail verification.

In Sun's implementation, the breakpoint opcode is used internally as a place-holder indicating a point in a method where control should pass to the Java debugger (jdb).

Bytecode

Type	Description
u1	breakpoint opcode = 0xCA (202)

See Also

impdep1, impdep2

---

caload retrieve character from array

Jasmin Syntax

```
caload
```

Stack

Before	After
index	value
arrayref	...
...	...

Description

Retrieves a character from an array of characters and pushes it on the operand stack. *arrayref* is a reference to an array of chars. *index* is an int. The *arrayref* and *index* are removed from the stack, and the 16-bit unsigned Unicode character at the given *index* in the array is retrieved, zero extended to a 32-bit int, and pushed onto the stack.

Example

```
; This is like the Java code:
;     char x = arr[0];
; where x is local variable 2 and arr is a
; char array in local variable 1
aload_1        ; load local variable 1 onto the stack
iconst_0       ; push the integer 0 onto the stack
caload         ; retrieve the entry
istore_2       ; store the entry in local variable 2
```

Exceptions

- NullPointerException—*arrayref* is null
- ArrayIndexOutOfBoundsException—*index* is < 0 or >= *arrayref.length*

Bytecode

Type	Description
u1	caload opcode = 0x34 (52)

See Also

iaload, laload, faload, daload, aaload, baload, saload, iastore, lastore, fastore, dastore, aastore, bastore, castore, sastore

castore   store in character array

Jasmin Syntax

```
castore
```

Stack

Before	After
value	...
index	
arrayref	
...	

Description

Pops a 32-bit integer from the stack, truncates it to a 16-bit unsigned value, and stores it in an array of characters. *arrayref* is a reference to an array of 16-bit Unicode characters. *index* is an int. *value* is the int value to be stored in the array. *arrayref, index* and *value* are removed from the stack, and *value* is stored in the array at the given *index*.

Exceptions

- NullPointerException—*arrayref* is null
- ArrayIndexOutOfBoundsException—*index* is < 0 or >= *arrayref.length*

Bytecode

Type	Description
u1	castore opcode = 0x55 (85)

See Also

iastore, lastore, fastore, dastore, aastore, bastore, sastore, iaload, laload, faload, daload, aaload, baload, caload, saload

---

checkcast   ensure object or array belongs to type

Jasmin Syntax

```
checkcast <type>
```

<type> is the name of a Java class or interface (e.g., java/lang/String), or the type descriptor of an array (e.g., [[Ljava/lang/String;).

Stack

Before	After
objectref	objectref
...	...

Description

Checks that the top item on the operand stack (a reference to an object or array) can be cast to a given type. For example, if you write in Java:

```
return ((String)obj);
```

then the Java compiler will generate something like:

```
aload_1                      ; push -obj- onto the stack
checkcast java/lang/String   ; check it's a String
areturn                      ; return it
```

checkcast is actually a shortand for writing Java code like:

```
if (! (obj == null  ||  obj instanceof <class>)) {
    throw new ClassCastException();
}
// if this point is reached, then object is either null, or an instance of
// <class> or one of its superclasses.
```

In Jasmin, checkcast takes a single parameter, *<type>*. *<type>* is either the name of a Java class or interface, or it is the type descriptor of an array. At runtime, the symbolic name given by *<type>* is resolved to a Java class (see Chapter 4 for a description of how classes are resolved). Next, checkcast examines the top item on the stack. If objectref belongs to *<type>* (or one of its subclasses), or if it is null, the objectref is left on the stack and execution continues at the subsequent instruction. If not, a ClassCastException is thrown.

Example

```
; push object in local variable 1 onto stack
aload_1

; check if it is an instance of Throwable or one of its subclasses.
checkcast java/lang/Throwable

; if execution reaches here, the object in local variable 1
; is still on the stack, and is either null or a Throwable object.

; ---
; Note that checkcast can also be used to check that an array belongs to a given type,
; e.g., to check that local variable 1 contains an array of Strings, use:

aload_1
checkcast [Ljava/lang/String;

; if execution reaches here, the  object on the stack
; is an array of Strings, or it is null.
```

Exceptions

*   ClassCastException—the object on the stack is not an instance of the specified class

Bytecode

In bytecode, immediately following the checkcast opcode is a 16-bit unsigned short integer. It is the index of an entry in the constant pool of the current class. The entry is tagged a CONSTANT_Class entry. The name field of the CONSTANT_Class entry is the same as the string given by *<type>* parameter in Jasmin.

Type	Description
u1	checkcast opcode = 0xC0 (192)
u2	index

See Also
instanceof

---

d2f convert double to float

Jasmin Syntax
    d2f

Stack

Before	After
double-word1	float-result
double-word2	...
...	

Description

Pops a two-word double precision floating-point number off of the operand stack, casts it into a single precision float, and pushes the resulting float back onto the stack. There is a loss of precision and range in the result.

This conversion is done in accordance with IEEE 754 specifications, with rounding using IEEE 754 round-to-nearest mode.

The sign of the value if preserved. A value which is too small to be represented as a float is converted to positive or negative zero. A value that is too large to be represented as a float is converted to positive infinity or negative infinity. If the value was NaN, the result is NaN.

Bytecode

Type	Description
u1	d2f opcode = 0x90 (144)

See Also
d2i, d2l

d2i convert double to integer

Jasmin Syntax

```
d2i
```

Stack

Before	After
double-word1	integer-result
double-word2	...
...	

Description

Pops a two-word double precision floating point number off of the operand stack, casts it into a 32-bit int, and pushes the resulting int onto the stack.

Rounding is done using IEEE 754 round-to-nearest mode. The fractional part is lost by rounding towards zero, so (int)–3.14 becomes –3.

If the original double value is NaN, the result is 0. If the value is too large to be represented as an integer, or if it is positive infinity, the result is the largest possible integer 0x7FFFFFFF. If the value is too small (i.e., a negative value of large magnitude, or negative infinity) then the result is the most negative integer 0x80000000.

Bytecode

Type	Description
u1	d2i opcode = 0x8E (142)

See Also

d2l, d2f

---

d2l convert double to long integer

Jasmin Syntax

```
d2l
```

Stack

Before	After
double-word1	long-word1
double-word2	long-word2
...	...

Description

Pops a two-word double precision floating point number off of the operand stack, converts it into a 64-bit long integer, and pushes the resulting two-word long onto the stack.

Rounding is done using IEEE 754 round-to-nearest mode. The fractional part is lost by rounding towards zero, so (long)–3.14 becomes –3.

If the original double value is NaN, the result is 0. If the value is too large to be represented as an integer, or if it is positive infinity, the result is the largest possible long integer Long.MAX_VALUE. If the value is too small (i.e., a negative value of large magnitude, or negative infinity) then the result is the most negative long integer Long.MIN_VALUE.

In some implementations, this may be coded using the C casting mechanism, e.g.,

```
void d2l(double d, int &l_high, int &l_low)
{
    l_low = (unsigned int)d;

    l_high = (unsigned int)(d / 2**32);
}
```

where l_low and l_high are respectively the least significant and most significant 32-bit words of the long.

Bytecode

Type	Description
u1	d2l opcode = 0x8F (143)

See Also

d2i, d2f

dadd   add two doubles

Jasmin Syntax

```
dadd
```

Stack

Before	After
value1-word1	result-word1
value1-word2	result-word2
value2-word1	...
value2-word2	
...	

Description

Takes the two top double-precision floating point numbers off of the operand stack, adds them, and pushes the result back onto the stack.

Bytecode

Type	Description
u1	dadd opcode = 0x63 (99)

See Also

iadd, fadd, ladd

Notes

The addition is computed using IEEE 754 round-to-nearest mode and gradual underflow. Standard IEEE arithmetic rules are used for the special NaN, infinity, and zero values.

---

daload   retrieve double-precision float from array

Jasmin Syntax

```
daload
```

Stack

Before	After
index	value-word1
arrayref	value-word2
...	...

Description

Retrieves an entry from a double precision float array and places it on the stack. *arrayref* is a reference to an array of double-precision floating point numbers. *index* is an int. The *arrayref* and *index* are removed from the stack, and the two-word value at the given *index* in the array is pushed onto the stack.

Example

```
; This is like the Java code:
;     double x = arr[0];
; where x is local variable 2 and arr is a double array in local variable 1
aload_1        ; load local variable 1 onto the stack
iconst_0       ; push the integer 0 onto the stack
daload         ; retrieve the entry
dstore_2       ; store the entry in local variable 2
```

Exceptions

- NullPointerException—*arrayref* is null
- ArrayIndexOutOfBoundsException—*index* is < 0 or is >= *arrayref.length*

Bytecode

Type	Description
u1	daload opcode = 0x31 (49)

See Also

iaload, faload, laload, aaload, baload, caload, saload, iastore, lastore, fastore, dastore, aastore, bastore, castore, sastore

dastore store in double-precision float array

Jasmin Syntax

```
dastore
```

Stack

Before	After
value-word1	...
value-word2	
index	
arrayref	
...	

Description

Pops a two-word double precision floating point number from the stack and stores it in an array of doubles. *arrayref* is a reference to an array of doubles. *index* is an int. *value* is the double to be stored in the array. *arrayref*, *index* and *value* are removed from the stack, and *value* is stored in the array at the given *index*.

Exceptions

* NullPointerException—*arrayref* is null
* ArrayIndexOutOfBoundsException—*index* is < 0 or is >= *arrayref.length*

Bytecode

Type	Description
u1	dastore opcode = 0x52 (82)

See Also

iastore, lastore, fastore, aastore, bastore, castore, sastore, iaload, laload, faload, daload, aaload, baload, caload, saload

dcmpg compare two doubles (1 on NaN)

Jasmin Syntax

```
dcmpg
```

Stack

Before	After
value1-word1	int-result
value1-word2	...
value2-word1	
value2-word2	
...	

Description

Takes two double-precision floating point numbers off the operand stack and compares them, using IEEE 754 rules.

If the two numbers are the same, the int 0 is pushed onto the stack. If *value2* is greater than *value1*, the int 1 is pushed onto the stack. If *value1* is greater than *value2*, −1 is pushed onto the stack. If either numbers is NaN, the int 1 is pushed onto the stack. +0.0 and −0.0 are treated as equal.

Example

```
dload_1      ; push the double in local variable 1
dconst_0     ; push the double 0.0 onto the stack
dcmpg        ; compare the two numbers

; The integer result on the stack is:
;     0 if local variable 1 equals 0
;     -1 if local variable 1 is less than 0
;     1 if local variable 1 is greater than 0
```

Bytecode

Type	Description
u1	dcmpg opcode = 0x98 (152)

See Also

lcmp, fcmpl, fcmpg, dcmpl

Notes

This instruction is identical to dcmpl except for the treatment of NaN.

---

dcmpl compare two doubles (–1 on NaN)

Jasmin Syntax

```
dcmpl
```

Stack

Before	After
value1-word1	int-result
value1-word2	...
value2-word1	
value2-word2	
...	

Description

Takes two double-precision floating-point numbers off the operand stack and compares them, using IEEE 754 rules.

If the two numbers are the same, the 32-bit integer 0 is pushed onto the stack. If *value2* is greater than *value1*, the integer 1 is pushed onto the stack. If *value1* is greater than *value2*, –1 is pushed onto the stack. If either numbers is NaN, the integer 1 is pushed onto the stack. +0.0 and –0.0 are treated as equal.

Example

```
dload_1      ; push the double in local variable 1
dconst_0     ; push the double 0.0 onto the stack
dcmpl        ; compare the two numbers

; The integer result on the stack is:
;     0 if local variable 1 equals 0
;     -1 if local variable 1 is less than 0
;     1 if local variable 1 is greater than 0
```

Bytecode

Type	Description
u1	dcmpl opcode = 0x97 (151)

See Also

lcmp, fcmpl, fcmpg, dcmpg

Notes

This instruction is identical to dcmpg except for the treatment of NaN.

---

dconst_<d> push the double 0.0 or 1.0

Jasmin Syntax

```
    dconst_0
 or
    dconst_1
```

Stack

Before	After
...	<d>-word1
	<d>-word2
	...

Description

Pushes the constant double precision floating point number <d> onto the stack, where <d> is either 0 or 1. For example, to push the double precision float 0.0 onto the stack, use:

```
  dconst_0 ; push the double 0.0 onto the stack
```

Note that you could also use:

```
  ldc2_w 0.0    ; push the double 0.0 onto the stack
```

although this instruction takes more space in the class file and is typically less efficient.

Example

```
dconst_0    ; push the double 0.0 onto the stack
dconst_1    ; push the double 1.0 onto the stack
```

Bytecode

Type	Description
u1	dconst_0 opcode = 0x0E (14)
u1	dconst_1 opcode = 0x0F (15)

See Also

bipush, sipush, ldc, ldc_w, ldc2_w, aconst_null, iconst_m1, iconst_<n>, lconst_<l>, fconst_<f>

---

ddiv divides two doubles

Jasmin Syntax

```
ddiv
```

Stack

Before	After
value1-word1	result-word1
value1-word2	result-word2
value2-word1	...
value2-word2	
...	

Description

Pops the top two double-precision floating-point numbers off of the stack, divides by the top number (i.e., computes *value2/value1*), and pushes the double precision quotient result back onto the stack.

Division by zero will result in an infinity result. The division is computed using IEEE 754 round-to-nearest mode and gradual underflow. Standard IEEE arithmetic rules are used for the special NaN, infinity, and zero values.

Bytecode

Type	Description
u1	ddiv opcode = 0x6F (111)

See Also

idiv, ldiv, fdiv

---

dload   retrieve double from local variable

Jasmin Syntax

```
    dload <varnum>
 or
    wide
    dload <varnum>
```

In the first form, <*varnum*> is an unsigned integer in the range 0 to 0xFF. In the second (wide) form, <*varnum*> is an unsigned integer in the range 0 to 0xFFFE.

Stack

Before	After
...	result-word1
	result-word2
	...

Description

Retrieves a double-precision floating-point number held in local variable and pushes it onto the operand stack.

Since double-precision floats are 64-bits wide, and each local variable only holds up to 32 bits, Java uses two consecutive local variables, <*varnum*> and <*varnum*> + 1 to store a double. So dload <*varnum*> actually places the values of both <*varnum*> and <*varnum*> + 1 onto the operand stack.

Both <*varnum*> and <*varnum*> + 1 must be valid local variable numbers in the current frame, and together they must be holding a double.

Example

```
dload 2          ; push the double held in local variables 2 and 3 onto the stack
```

Bytecode

For local variable numbers in the range 0-255, use:

Type	Description
u1	dload opcode = 0x18 (24)
u1	<varnum>

There is also a `wide` format for this instruction, which supports access to all local variables from 0 to 65534:

Type	Description
u1	wide opcode = 0xC4 (196)
u1	dload opcode = 0x18 (24)
u2	<varnum>

See Also

fload, iload, aload, lload, wide

---

dload_<n> retrieve double from local variables <n> and <n> + 1

Jasmin Syntax

```
      dload_0
  or
      dload_1
  or
      dload_2
  or
      dload_3
```

Stack

Before	After
...	result-word1
	result-word2
	...

Description

Retrieves the double-precision float stored in local variables <n> and <n> + 1 and pushes it onto the operand stack. Both <n> and <n> + 1 must be valid local variable numbers in the current frame, and together they must be holding a double. See dload's description for more on how doubles are retrieved from local variables.

'dload_<n>' is functionally equivalent to 'dload <n>', although it is typically more efficient and also takes fewer bytes in the bytecode.

Example

```
dload_0          ; push double in local variables 0 and 1 onto stack
dload_1          ; push double in local variables 1 and 2 onto stack
dload_2          ; push double in local variables 2 and 3 onto stack
dload_3          ; push double in local variables 3 and 4 onto stack
```

Bytecode

Type	Description
u1	dload_0 opcode = 0x26 (38)
u1	dload_1 opcode = 0x27 (39)
u1	dload_2 opcode = 0x28 (40)
u1	dload_3 opcode = 0x29 (41)

See Also

dload, fload, aload, iload, lload

dmul multiply two doubles

Jasmin Syntax

```
dmul
```

Stack

Before	After
value1-word1	result-word1
value1-word2	result-word1
value1-word1	...
value2-word2	
...	

Description

Pops the top two double-precision floating point numbers off the stack, multiplies them, and pushes the double-precision result back onto the stack.

Multiplication is performed using standard IEEE rules for double precision floating point arithmetic.

Bytecode

Type	Description
u1	dmul opcode = 0x6B (107)

See Also

imul, lmul, fmul

---

dneg negate a double

Jasmin Syntax

```
dneg
```

Stack

Before	After
value-word1	result-word1
value-word2	result-word2
...	...

Description

Removes the top double-precision float from the operand stack, negates it (i.e., inverts its sign), and pushes the negated result back onto the stack.

Note that, in IEEE double precision floating point arithmetic, negation is not quite the same as subtracting from 0. IEEE has two zeros, +0.0 and -0.0, and dneg applied to +0.0 is -0.0, whereas (+0.0 minus +0.0) is +0.0.

Bytecode

Type	Description
u1	dneg opcode = 0x77 (119)

See Also

ineg, fneg, lneg

drem remainder of two doubles

Jasmin Syntax

```
drem
```

Stack

Before	After
value1-word1	result-word1
value1-word2	result-word2
value2-word1	...
value2-word2	
...	

Description

Pops two double-precision numbers off the operand stack, divides by the top double, computes the remainder and pushes the double-precision result back onto the stack. This is like the C function fmod. The remainder is computed using:

remainder = *value2* − (intof(*value2/value1*) * *value1*)

where intof () rounds towards the nearest integer, or towards the nearest even integer if the number is half way between two integers.

Bytecode

Type	Description
u1	drem opcode = 0x73 (115)

See Also

irem, frem, lrem

Notes

1. Dividing by zero will result in NaN being pushed onto the stack as the result.
2. This operation is not the same as the IEEE-defined remainder operation, which uses slightly different rules for rounding. Use the Java library routine Math.IEEEremainder if you want the IEEE behavior.

dreturn return from method with double result

Jasmin Syntax

```
dreturn
```

Stack

Before	After
return-value-word1	n/a
return-value-word2	
...	

Description

Pops the two-word double off the stack and pushes it onto the operand stack of the invoker (i.e., the method which used `invokevirtual`, `invokespecial`, `invokestatic` or `invokeinterface` to call the currently executing method). All other items on the current method's operand stack are discarded. If the current method is marked as synchronized, then an implicit monitorexit instruction is executed. Then the current method's frame is discarded, the invoker's frame is reinstated, and control returns to the invoker. This instruction can only be used in methods whose return type is double.

Bytecode

Type	Description
u1	dreturn opcode = 0xAF (175)

See Also

areturn, lreturn, freturn, ireturn, return, invokevirtual, invokespecial, invokestatic, invokeinterface

---

dstore   store double in local variable

Jasmin Syntax

```
        dstore <varnum>
    or
        wide
        dstore <varnum>
```

In the first form, `<varnum>` is an unsigned integer in the range 0 to 0xFF. In the second (wide) form, `<varnum>` is an unsigned integer in the range 0 to 0xFFFE.

Stack

Before	After
doube-word1	...
double-word2	
...	

Description

Pops a two-word double-precision float off the operand stack and stores it in a local variable. It takes a single parameter, `<varnum>`, an unsigned integer indicating which local variable to use.

Since double-precision floats are 64-bits wide, and each local variable can only hold up to 32 bits, Java uses two consecutive local variables, `<varnum>` and `<varnum>` + 1 to store a double. So dstore `<varnum>` actually modifies the values of both `<varnum>` (which is set to double-*word1*) and `<varnum>` + 1 (which is set to *double-word2)*.

Both `<varnum>` and `<varnum>` + 1 must be valid local variable numbers in the current frame.

Example

```
    ldc2_w 10.0    ; push the double 10.0 onto the stack
    dstore 3       ; pop 10.0 off of the stack and store it in local variables 3 and 4
```

Bytecode

For local variables in the range 0-255, use:

Type	Description
u1	dstore opcode = 0x39 (57)
u1	<varnum>

There is also a `wide` format for this instruction, which supports access to all local variables from 0 to 65534:

Type	Description
u1	wide opcode = 0xC4 (196)
u1	dstore opcode = 0x39 (57)
u2	<varnum>

See Also

lstore, fstore, istore, astore, wide

---

dstore_<n> store double in local variables <n> and <n> + 1

Jasmin Syntax

```
    dstore_0
or
    dstore_1
or
    dstore_2
or
    dstore_3
```

Stack

Before	After
value-word1	...
value-word2	
...	

Description

Pops a double-precision float off of the operand stack and stores it in the local variables <n> and <n> + 1. Both <n> and <n> + 1 must be valid local variable numbers in the current frame. See the description of dstore for more information on how doubles are stored in local variables.

"dstore_<n>" is functionally equivalent to "dstore <n>", although it is typically more efficient and also takes fewer bytes in the bytecode.

Example

```
dstore_0        ;store double in local variable 0 and 1
dstore_1        ;store double in local variable 1 and 2
dstore_2        ;store double in local variable 2 and 3
dstore_3        ;store double in local variable 3 and 4
```

Bytecode

Type	Description
u1	dstore_0 opcode = 0x47 (71)
u1	dstore_1 opcode = 0x48 (72)
u1	dstore_2 opcode = 0x49 (73)
u1	dstore_3 opcode = 0x4A (74)

See Also

astore, dstore, istore, fstore, lstore

---

dsub subtract two doubles

Jasmin Syntax

```
dsub
```

Stack

Before	After
value1-word1	result-word1
value1-word2	result-word2
value2-word1	...
value2-word2	
...	

Description

Takes the top two double-precision floating point numbers from the stack, subtracts the top one from the second (i.e., computes *value2 – value1*), and pushes the double-precision result back onto the stack. Subtraction is done according to IEEE 754 rules for double precision floating point numbers.

Bytecode

Type	Description
u1	dsub opcode = 0x67 (103)

See Also

isub, lsub, fsub

---

dup   duplicate top single-word item on the stack

Jasmin Syntax

```
dup
```

Stack

Before	After
item	item
...	item
	...

Description

Pops the top single-word value off the operand stack, and then pushes that value twice—i.e., it makes an extra copy of the top item on the stack.

This instruction cannot be used to duplicate two-word items (longs or doubles) —use dup2 instead.

Example

```
; This is like the java expression:
;
;    StringBuffer x = new StringBuffer();
;
```

```
; Make a new StringBuffer object and leave a reference to it on the stack:
new java/lang/StringBuffer

; [ Stack now contains: objectref ]

; Duplicate the object reference:
dup

; [ Stack now contains: objectref objectref ]

; Invoke the object's initializer:
invokespecial java/lang/StringBuffer/<init>()V

; [ Stack now contains: objectref ]

; Store the objectref in local variable 1.
astore_1

; [ Stack is now empty. ]
```

Bytecode

Type	Description
u1	dup opcode = 0x59 (89)

See Also

dup2, dup_x1, dup2_x1, dup2_x2

dup2   duplicate top two stack words

Jasmin Syntax

```
dup2
```

Stack

Before	After
word1	word1
word2	word2
...	word1
	word2
	...

Description

Duplicates the top two words on the stack and pushes the duplicates onto the stack in the same order. You can use this to duplicate two single-word items (e.g., two integers, or an integer and an object reference) or one two-word item (i.e., a double or a long).

Bytecode

Type	Description
u1	dup2 opcode = 0x5C (92)

See Also

dup, dup_x1, dup2_x1, dup2_x2

---

dup2_x1 duplicate two words and insert beneath third word

Jasmin Syntax

    dup2_x1

Stack

Before	After
word1	word1
word2	word2
word3	word3
...	word1
	word2
	...

Description

Duplicates the top two-word item on the stack and inserts the duplicate before the previous (single-word) item on the stack. Alternatively, this instruction could also be used to duplicate two single-word items and insert them before the third single-word item on the stack.

Example

```
bipush 100
dconst_0
; stack now contains:
;      0.0 | double-word1
;      0.0 | double-word2
;      100   integer-word1

dup2_x1
; stack now contains:
;      0.0 | double-word1
;      0.0 | double-word2
;      100   integer-word1
;      0.0 | double-word1
;      0.0 | double-word2
```

Bytecode

Type	Description
u1	dup2_x1 = 0x5D (93)

See Also

dup, dup2, dup_x1, dup2_x2

dup2_x2 duplicate two words and insert beneath fourth word

Jasmin Syntax

```
dup2_x2
```

Stack

Before	After
word1	word1
word2	word2
word3	word3
word4	word4
...	word1
	word2
	...

Description

Duplicates the top two-word item on the stack and inserts the duplicate before the previous (two-word) item on the stack. Alternatively, this instruction could be used to duplicate two single-word items and insert them before the before the third two-word (or fourth single-word) item on the stack.

Example

```
bipush 100
bipush 200
dconst_0
; stack now contains:
;      0.0 | double-word1
;      0.0 | double-word2
;      200   integer2-word1
;      100   integer1-word1

dup2_x2
; stack now contains:
;      0.0 | double-word1
;      0.0 | double-word2
;      200   integer2-word1
;      100   integer1-word1
;      0.0 | double-word1
;      0.0 | double-word2
```

Bytecode

Type	Description
u1	dup2_x2 opcode = 0x5E (94)

See Also

dup, dup2, dup_x1, dup2_x1

---

dup_x1 duplicate top stack word and insert beneath second word

Jasmin Syntax

```
dup_x1
```

Stack

Before	After
word1	word1
word2	word2
...	word1

Description

Duplicates the top item on the stack and inserts the duplicate below the second-from-top item. Both items must be single-word items.

Bytecode

Type	Description
u1	dup_x1 = 0x5A (90)

See Also

dup, dup2, dup2_x1, dup2_x2

Notes

This can't be used if either item1 or item2 are two-word items. To duplicate a two-word item (a long or a double) you must use dup2, dup2_x1 or dup2_x2.

---

dup_x2   duplicate top stack word and insert beneath third word

Jasmin Syntax

```
dup_x2
```

Stack

Before	After
word1	word1
word2	word2
word3	word3
...	word1
	...

Description

Duplicates the top single-word stack item inserts the duplicate three words down.

Example

```
dconst_0
bipush 100
; stack now contains:
;      0.0 | double-word1
;      0.0 | double-word2
;      100   integer
dup_x2
; stack now contains:
;      100   integer1
;      0.0 | double-word1
;      0.0 | double-word2
;      100   integer1
```

Bytecode

Type	Description
u1	dup_x2 = 0x5B (91)

See Also

dup, dup2, dup_x1, dup2_x2

Notes

This instruction cannot be used if the top item on the stack is a two-word item (i.e., a long or a double-precision float). Use dup2, dup2_x1 or dup2_x2 instead.

---

f2d convert float to double

Jasmin Syntax

```
f2d
```

Stack

Before	After
float	double-word1
...	double-word2
	...

Description

Pops a single precision float off of the stack, casts it to a double, and pushes the double-precision floating point number back onto the stack. This conversion is done in accordance with IEEE 754 specifications. Note that nothing is lost in this conversion. If the original value is NaN, the result will be NaN. Similarly, if the original value is an infinity, the result will be the same infinity.

Bytecode

Type	Description
u1	f2d opcode = 0x8D (141)

See Also

f2i, f2l

---

f2i convert float to integer

Jasmin Syntax

```
f2i
```

Stack

Before	After
float	integer
...	...

Description

Pops a single-precision float off of the stack, casts it to a 32-bit int, and pushes the int value back onto the stack.

Rounding is done using IEEE 754 round-to-nearest mode. The fractional part is lost by rounding towards zero, so (int)−3.14 becomes −3.

If the original float value is NaN, the result is 0. If the value is too large to be represented as an integer, or if it is positive infinity, the result is the largest possible integer 0x7FFFFFFF. If the value is too small (i.e., a negative value of large magnitude, or negative infinity) then the result is the most negative integer 0x80000000.

Bytecode

Type	Description
u1	f2i opcode = 0x8B (139)

See Also

f2l, f2d

f2l convert float to long integer

Jasmin Syntax

```
f2l
```

Stack

Before	After
float	long-word1
...	long-word2
	...

Description

Casts a single-precision float value into a 64-bit long integer value. f2l removes a float from the stack, converts it to a long integer, and pushes the two-word long integer back onto the stack. Rounding is done using IEEE 754 round-to-nearest mode. The fractional part is lost by rounding towards zero, so (long)−3.14 becomes −3.

If the original value is NaN, the result is 0. If the value is too large to be represented as an integer, or if it is positive infinity, the result is the largest possible long integer Long.MAX_VALUE. If the value is too small (i.e., a negative value of large magnitude, or negative infinity) then the result is the most negative long integer Long.MIN_VALUE.

Bytecode

Type	Description
u1	f2l opcode = 0x8C (140)

See Also

f2i, f2d

---

fadd add two floats

Jasmin Syntax

```
fadd
```

Stack

Before	After
value1	result
value2	...
...	

Description

Pops two single-precision floating point numbers off the operand stack, adds them, and pushes the result back onto the stack. Floating point addition follows IEEE rules.

Bytecode

Type	Description
u1	fadd opcode = 0x62 (98)

See Also

dadd, iadd, ladd

---

faload retrieve float from array

Jasmin Syntax

```
faload
```

Stack

Before	After
index	value
arrayref	...
...	

Description

Retrieves an entry from a float array and places it on the stack. *arrayref* is a reference to an array of single-precision floats. *index* is an int. The *arrayref* and *index* are removed from the stack, and the single-precision float entry at the given *index* in the array is pushed onto the stack.

Example

```
; This is like the Java code:
;     float x = arr[0];
; where x is local variable 2 and arr is a float
; array in local variable 1
aload_1        ; load local variable 1 onto the stack
iconst_0       ; push the integer 0 onto the stack
faload         ; retrieve the entry
fstore_2       ; store the entry in local variable 2
```

Exceptions

- NullPointerException—*arrayref* is null
- ArrayIndexOutOfBoundsException—*index* is < 0 or >= *arrayref.length*

Bytecode

Type	Description
u1	faload opcode = 0x30 (48)

See Also

iaload, laload, daload, aaload, baload, caload, saload, iastore, lastore, fastore, dastore, aastore, bastore, castore, sastore

fastore   store in single-precision float array

Jasmin Syntax

```
fastore
```

Stack

Before	After
value	...
index	
arrayref	
...	

Description

Takes a single-precision float from the stack and stores it in an array of floats. *arrayref* is a reference to an array of single-precision floats. *index* is an int. *value* is the single-precision float *value* to be stored in the array. *arrayref, index* and *value* are removed from the stack, and *value* is stored in the array at the given *index*.

Exceptions

* NullPointerException — *arrayref* is null
* ArrayIndexOutOfBoundsException — *index* is < 0 or >= *arrayref.length*

Bytecode

Type	Description
u1	fastore opcode = 0x51 (81)

See Also

iastore, lastore, dastore, aastore, bastore, castore, sastore, iaload, laload, faload, daload, aaload, baload, caload, saload

fcmpg single-precision float comparison (1 on NaN)

Jasmin Syntax

```
fcmpg
```

Stack

Before	After
value1	int-result
value2	...
...	

Description

Takes two single-precision floating-point numbers off the stack and compares them, using IEEE 754 rules.

If the two numbers are the same, the integer 0 is pushed onto the stack. If *value2* is greater than *value1*, the integer 1 is pushed onto the stack. If *value1* is greater than *value2*, the integer –1 is pushed onto the stack. If either number is NaN, the integer 1 is pushed onto the stack. +0.0 and –0.0 are treated as equal.

Example

```
fload_1         ; push the float in local variable 1
fconst_0        ; push the float 0 onto the stack
fcmpl           ; compare the two numbers

; The integer result on the stack is:
;     0 if local variable 1 equals 0
;     -1 if local variable 1 is less than 0
;     1 if local variable 1 is greater than 0
```

Bytecode

Type	Description
u1	fcmpg opcode = 0x96 (150)

See Also

lcmp, fcmpl, dcmpl, dcmpg

Notes

This instruction is identical to `fcmpl` except for the treatment of NaN.

---

fcmpl single-precision float comparison (–1 on NaN)

Jasmin Syntax

```
fcmpl
```

Stack

Before	After
value1	result
value2	...
...	

Description

Takes two single-precision floating-point numbers off the stack and compares them, using IEEE 754 rules.

If the two numbers are the same, the integer 0 is pushed onto the stack. If *value2* is greater than *value1*, the integer 1 is pushed onto the stack. If *value1* is greater than *value2*, the integer –1 is pushed onto the stack. If either number is NaN, the integer 1 is pushed onto the stack. +0.0 and –0.0 are treated as equal.

Example

```
fload_1        ; push the float in local variable 1
fconst_0       ; push the float 0 onto the stack
fcmpl          ; compare the two numbers

; The integer result on the stack is:
;     0 if local variable 1 equals 0
;     -1 if local variable 1 is less than 0
;     1 if local variable 1 is greater than 0
```

Bytecode

Type	Description
u1	fcmpl opcode = 0x95 (149)

See Also

lcmp, fcmpg, dcmpl, dcmpg

Notes

This instruction is identical to fcmpg except for the treatment of NaN.

---

fconst_<f> push the single float 0.0, 1.0 or 2.0

Jasmin Syntax

```
    fconst_0
or
    fconst_1
or
    fconst_2
```

Stack

Before	After
...	<f>
	...

Description

Represents the series of opcodes fconst_0, fconst_1, and fconst_2 that are used to push the constant single-precision floats 0.0, 1.0 and 2.0 onto the stack.

For example, to push the single-precision float zero onto the stack, use:

```
fconst_0 ; push single-precision float 0 onto the stack
```

Note that you could also use:

```
ldc 0.0  ; push the float 0.0 onto the stack
```

although this instruction takes more space in the class file and is also less efficient.

Example

```
fconst_0    ; push the float 0.0 onto the stack
fconst_1    ; push the float 1.0 onto the stack
fconst_2    ; push the float 2.0 onto the stack
```

Bytecode

Type	Description
u1	fconst_0 opcode = 0x0B (11)
u1	fconst_1 opcode = 0x0C (12)
u1	fconst_2 opcode = 0x0D (13)

See Also

bipush, sipush, ldc, ldc_w, ldc2_w, aconst_null, iconst_m1, lconst_<l>, iconst_<n>, dconst_<d>

fdiv divide two floats

Jasmin Syntax

```
fdiv
```

Stack

Before	After
value1	result
value2	...
...	

Description

Pops two single-precision floats from the stack, divide by the top float, and push the single-precision quotient result back onto the stack (i.e., computes *value2/value1*). Division is carried out using IEEE 754 rules.

Bytecode

Type	Description
u1	fdiv opcode = 0x6E (110)

See Also

idiv, ldiv, ddiv

Notes

Divide by zero results in the value NaN to be pushed onto the stack.

---

fload retrieve float from local variable

Jasmin Syntax

```
    fload <varnum>
or
    wide
    fload <varnum>
```

In the first form, <varnum> is an unsigned integer in the range 0 to 0xFF. In the second (wide) form, <varnum> is an unsigned integer in the range 0 to 0xFFFF.

Stack

Before	After
...	float-value
	...

Description

Pushes the float value held in a local variable onto the operand stack. The `fload` instruction takes a single parameter, <varnum>, an unsigned integer which indicates which local variable to retrieve. The single-word float held in that local variable is retrieved and placed on the stack. <varnum> must be a valid local variable number in the current frame.

Example

```
fconst_2        ; push 2.0 onto the stack
fstore 1        ; pop 2.0 off of the stack and store in local variable 1
fload 1         ; push the value from local variable 1 (the value 2.0)
                ; back onto the stack
```

Bytecode

For local variable numbers in the range 0–255, use:

Type	Description
u1	fload opcode = 0x17 (23)
u1	<varnum>

There is also a **wide** format for this instruction, which supports access to all local variables from 0 to 65535:

Type	Description
u1	wide opcode = 0xC4 (196)
u1	fload opcode = 0x17 (23)
u2	<varnum>

See Also

iload, lload, aload, dload, wide

---

fload_<n> retrieve float from local variable <n>

Jasmin Syntax

```
    fload_0
or
    fload_1
or
    fload_2
or
    fload_3
```

Stack

Before	After
...	float-value
	...

Description

Represents the series of opcodes fload_0, fload_1, fload_2, and fload_3 that retrieve a single-precision float in local variables 0, 1, 2 or 3 and push it onto the stack. <n> must be a valid local variable number in the current frame.

"fload_<n>" is functionally equivalent to "fload <n>", although "fload_<n>", although it is typically more efficient and also takes fewer bytes in the bytecode.

Example

```
fload_0        ;push float in local variable 0
fload_1        ;push float in local variable 1
fload_2        ;push float in local variable 2
fload_3        ;push float in local variable 3
```

Bytecode

Type	Description
u1	fload_0 opcode = 0x22 (34)
u1	fload_1 opcode = 0x23 (35)
u1	fload_2 opcode = 0x24 (36)
u1	fload_3 opcode = 0x25 (37)

See Also

aload, iload, lload, dload, fload

fmul multiply two floats

Jasmin Syntax

```
fmul
```

Stack

Before	After
value1	result
value2	...
...	

Description

Pops two single-precision floating-point numbers off of the stack, multiplies them, and pushes the single precision result back onto the stack. IEEE 754 rules for floating point arithmetic are used.

Bytecode

Type	Description
u1	fmul opcode = 0x6A (106)

See Also

imul, lmul, dmul

---

fneg negate a float

Jasmin Syntax

fneg

Stack

Before	After
value	value
...	...

Description

Removes the top single-precision float from the operand stack, negates it (i.e., inverts its sign), and pushes the negated result back onto the stack.

Note that, in IEEE floating-point arithmetic, negation is not quite the same as subtracting from 0. IEEE has two zeros, +0.0 and –0.0. fneg applied to +0.0 is –0.0, whereas (+0.0 minus +0.0) is +0.0.

Bytecode

Type	Description
u1	fneg opcode = 0x76 (118)

See Also

ineg, lneg, dneg

---

frem remainder of two floats

Jasmin Syntax

```
frem
```

Stack

Before	After
value1	result
value2	...
...	

Description

Pops two single-precision numbers off the operand stack, divides by the top float, computes the remainder and pushes the single-precision result back onto the stack. This is like the C function fmod. The remainder is computed using the equation:

remainder = *value2* − (intof(*value2/value1*) * *value1*)

where intof () rounds towards the nearest integer, or towards the nearest even integer if the number is half way between two integers.

Bytecode

Type	Description
u1	frem opcode = 0x72 (114)

See Also

irem, lrem, drem

Notes

1. Dividing by zero will result in NaN being pushed onto the stack as the result.
2. This operation is not the same as the IEEE-defined remainder operation, which uses slightly different rules for rounding. Use the Java library routine Math.IEEEremainder if you want the IEEE behavior.

freturn return from method with float result

Jasmin Syntax

```
freturn
```

Stack

Before	After
return-value	n/a
...	

Description

Pops a float from the top of the stack and pushes it onto the operand stack of the invoker (i.e., the method which used invokevirtual, invokespecial, invokestatic or invokeinterface to call the currently executing method). All other items on the current method's operand stack are discarded. If the current method is marked as synchronized, then an implicit monitorexit instruction is executed. Then the current method's frame is discarded, the invoker's frame is reinstated, and control returns to the invoker. This instruction can only be used in methods whose return type is float.

Bytecode

Type	Description
u1	freturn opcode = 0xAE (174)

See Also

lreturn, ireturn, dreturn, areturn, return

---

fstore store float in local variable

Jasmin Syntax

```
    fstore <varnum>
or
    wide
    fstore <varnum>
```

In the first form, <varnum> is an unsigned integer in the range 0 to 0xFF. In the second (wide) form, <varnum> is an unsigned integer in the range 0 to 0xFFFF.

Stack

Before	After
value	...
...	

Description

Pops a single-precision float off the stack and stores it in local variable *<varnum>*. The fstore instruction takes a single parameter, *<varnum>*, an unsigned integer which indicates which local variable is used. *<varnum>* must be a valid local variable number in the current frame.

Example

```
fconst_2        ; push 2.0 onto the stack
fstore 3        ; pop 2.0 off of the stack and store it in local variable 3
```

Bytecode

For local variable numbers in the range 0–255, use:

Type	Description
u1	fstore opcode = 0x38 (56)
u1	<varnum>

There is also a wide format for this instruction, which supports access to all local variables from 0 to 65535:

Type	Description
u1	wide opcode = 0xC4 (196)
u1	fstore opcode = 0x38 (56)
u2	<varnum>

See Also

lstore, istore, dstore, astore, wide

fstore_<n> store float in local variable <n>

Jasmin Syntax

```
        fstore_0
  or
        fstore_1
  or
        fstore_2
  or
        fstore_3
```

Stack

Before	After
value	...
...	

Description

Pops a single-precision floating-point number off the stack and stores it in local variable <*n*>, where <*n*> is 0, 1, 2 or 3. <*n*> must be a valid local variable number in the current frame.

"fstore_<*n*>" is functionally equivalent to "fstore <*n*>", although it is typically more efficient and also takes fewer bytes in the bytecode.

Example

```
    fstore_0        ;store float in local variable 0
    fstore_1        ;store float in local variable 1
    fstore_2        ;store float in local variable 2
    fstore_3        ;store float in local variable 3
```

Bytecode

Type	Description
u1	fstore_0 opcode = 0x43 (67)
u1	fstore_1 opcode = 0x44 (68)
u1	fstore_2 opcode = 0x45 (69)
u1	fstore_3 opcode = 0x46 (70)

See Also

istore, fstore, astore, dstore, lstore

---

fsub subtract two floats

Jasmin Syntax

```
fsub
```

Stack

Before	After
value1	result
value2	...
...	

Description

Pops two single-precision floating-point numbers off the operand stack, subtracts the top one from the second (i.e., computes *value2 – value1*), and pushes the single-precision result back onto the stack. Subtraction is done according to IEEE 754 rules for single precision floating point numbers.

Bytecode

Type	Description
u1	fsub opcode = 0x66 (102)

See Also

isub, lsub, dsub

---

getfield get value of object field

Jasmin Syntax

```
getfield <field-spec> <descriptor>
e.g.,
getfield java/lang/System/out Ljava/io/PrintStream;
```

`<field-spec>` is composed of two parts, a *classname* and a *fieldname*. The *classname* is all of the characters in the `<field-spec>` up to the last "/" character, and the *fieldname* is the rest of the characters after the last "/". For example:

```
foo/baz/AnotherClass/aVeryLongFieldName
-- classname -------/-- fieldname -----
```

`<descriptor>` is the Java type descriptor for the field, for example `Ljava/io/PrintStream;`

In Jasmin, the `.field` directive is used to add a field to a class. See Appendix C, *Jasmin User Guide*, for a description of this and other Jasmin directives.

Stack

Before	After
objectref	value
...	...

or, for fields that hold doubles or longs:

Before	After
objectref	value-word1
...	value-word2
	...

Description

Pops *objectref* (a reference to an object) from the stack, retrieves the value of the field identified by `<field-spec>` from *objectref*, and pushes the one-word or two-word value onto the operand stack.

For example, if you have the class:

```
package xyz;
class Point {
    public int xCoord, yCoord;
};
```

Then, assuming p is an instance of the class Point, writing the Java expression:

```
int x = p.xCoord;
```

generates a call to getfield like:

```
aload_1                        ; push object in local varable 1 (i.e., p)
                               ; onto the stack
getfield xyz/Point/xCoord I    ; get the value of p.xCoord, which is an int
istore_2                       ; store the int value in local variable 2 (x)
```

In Jasmin, getfield takes two parameters, `<field-spec>` and `<descriptor>`. `<field-spec>` gives *classname*, the name of the class that defines the field, as well as *fieldname*, as the name of the field itself. In the example above, the `<field-spec>` is "xyz/Point/xCoord", indicating that the *classname* is "xyz/Point" and the *fieldname* is "xCoord". `<descriptor>` describes the type of data held in the field, and is a standard Java type descriptor (see Chapter 4 for a full description of type descriptors). In the example above, `<descriptor>` is "I", since the field holds an integer.

getfield first resolves *classname* to a Java class. Then it locates the *fieldname* in that class, determining the *width* of the field (in bytes) and its *offset* (in bytes) from the base of the object data. The type of the field must match `<descriptor>`. See Chapter 4 for more on how fields are resolved

To retrieve the value for the field, getfield obtains the bytes starting at *offset* and extending for *width* bytes from the start of *objectref* instance data, expands it to either a 4-byte or 8-byte value, and pushes the value onto the operand stack.

Exceptions

* NullPointerException—*objectref* is null

Bytecode

In bytecode, the getstatic opcode is followed by a 16-bit unsigned integer *index*. This is the index of an entry in the constant pool of the current class. The entry is tagged a CONSTANT_Fieldref entry. It indicates a CONSTANT_Class entry that gives the name of the class containing the field (i.e., *classname*), and a CONSTANT_NameAndType entry that gives the *fieldname*, and the type `<descriptor>`.

Type	Description
u1	getfield opcode = 0xB4 (180)
u2	index

See Also

putfield, putstatic, getstatic.

Notes

Fields cannot be overriden, although they can be "shadowed."

For example, with the two classes:

```
    class A {int x; }
  and
    class B extends A {int x; }
```

instances of B will have storage for both the field "A/x" and the field "B/x". Which field is accessed is determined by the class name given in *<field-spec>*.

---

getstatic   get value of static field

Jasmin Syntax

```
  getstatic <field-spec> <descriptor>
```

<field-spec> is composed of two parts, a *classname* and a *fieldname*. The *classname* is all of the characters in the *<field-spec>* up to the last '/' character, and the *field-name* is the rest of the characters after the last '/'. For example:

```
  foo/baz/AnotherClass/aVeryLongFieldName
  -- classname -------/-- fieldname -----
```

<descriptor> is the Java type descriptor for the field, for example Ljava/io/PrintStream;

In Jasmin, the .field directive is used to add a field to a class. See Appendix C for a description of this and other Jasmin directives.

Stack

Before	After
...	value
	...

or, for static fields that hold doubles or longs:

Before	After
...	value-word1
	value-word2
	...

Description

Pops *objectref* (a reference to an object) from the stack, retrieves the value of the static field (also known as a class field) identified by `<field-spec>` from *objectref*, and pushes the one-word or two-word value onto the operand stack.

For example, when you write the Java expression:

```
PrintStream obj = java.lang.System.out;
```

this generates a call to getstatic like:

```
getstatic java/lang/System/out Ljava/io/PrintStream;
astore_1   ; store the object reference result in local variable 1
```

In Jasmin, getstatic takes two parameters, `<field-spec>` and `<descriptor>`. `<field-spec>` provides *classname*, the name of the class that defines the static field, as well *fieldname*, as the name of the field. In the example above, the `<field-spec>` is "java/lang/System/out", indicating that the *classname* is "java/lang/System" and the *fieldname* is "out". `<descriptor>` indicates the type of data held in the field, and is a standard Java type descriptor (see Chapter 4). In the example above, `<descriptor>` is "Ljava/io/PrintStream;", i.e., a reference to a PrintStream object.

getstatic first resolves *classname* into a Java class. Then it locates the *fieldname* in that class, determining the *width* of the field (in bytes) and its *offset* (in bytes) from the base of the class's static data. The type of the field must match `<descriptor>`. See Chapter 4 for more on how fields are resolved

To retrieve the value for the field, getstatic obtains the bytes starting at *offset* and extending for *width* bytes from the start of the class's static data, expands it to either a 4-byte or 8-byte value, and pushes the value onto the operand stack.

Bytecode

In bytecode, the getstatic opcode is followed by a 16-bit unsigned integer *index*. This is the index of an entry in the constant pool of the current class. The entry is tagged a CONSTANT_Fieldref entry. The fieldref entry lists a CONSTANT_Class entry in the constant pool whose name is the *classname* given in `<field-spec>`, as well as a CONSTANT_NameAndType entry in the constant pool, whose name is the *fieldname* given in `<field-spec>`, and whose descriptor is the string given by `<descriptor>`.

Type	Description
u1	getstatic opcode = 0xB2 (178)
u2	index

See Also

putfield, getfield, putstatic

Notes

Fields cannot be overriden, although they can be 'shadowed'. For example, with the two classes:

```
class A {static int x; }
```
and
```
class B extends A {static int x; }
```

then the runtime system will allocate storage for both the static field "A/x" and the static field "B/x". Which field is accessed is determined by the class name given in <field-spec>.

---

goto branch to address

Jasmin Syntax

```
goto <label>
```

<label> is a label name. To define the location of the label, use the <label> name followed by a colon:

```
<label>:
```

then becomes associated the address of the following instruction. Labels can only be assigned one location in a method. On the other hand, a single <label> can be the target of multiple branch instructions.

Stack

Before	After
...	...

Description

Causes execution to branch to the instruction at the address ($pc + branchoffset$), where pc is the address of the goto opcode in the bytecode and *branchoffset* is a 16-bit signed integer parameter that immediately follows the goto opcode in the bytecode. In Jasmin, *branchoffset* is computed for you using the address associated with <label>.

Example

```
;
; This is like the Java code:
;      while (true) {i++; }

Label:
      incr 1 1        ; Increment local variable 1 by 1
      goto Label      ; jump back to Label
```

Bytecode

Type	Description
u1	goto opcode = 0xA7 (167)
s2	*branchoffset*

See Also

goto_w, jsr, jsr_w

Notes

Addresses are measured in bytes from the start of the bytecode—i.e., address 0 is the first byte in the bytecode of the currently executing method. The maximum address in a method is 65535.

goto_w branch to address using wide offset

Jasmin Syntax

```
goto_w <label>
```

is a label name. To define the location of the label, use the <label> name followed by a colon:

```
<label>:
```

then becomes associated the address of the following instruction. Labels can only be assigned one location in a method. On the other hand, a single <label> can be the target of multiple branch instructions.

Stack

Before	After
...	...

Description

Causes execution to branch to the instruction at the address (*pc* + *branchoffset*), where *pc* is the address of the goto_w opcode in the bytecode and *branchoffset* is a 32-bit signed integer parameter that follows the goto_w opcode in the bytecode. If you are using Jasmin, *branchoffset* is determined for you from the address associated with <label>.

Bytecode

Type	Description
u1	goto_w opcode = 0xC8 (200)
s4	branchoffset

See Also

goto, jsr, jsr_w

Notes

1. goto_w is identical to goto, except that a 32-bit signed integer *branchoffset* is used instead of a 16-bit *branchoffset*.
2. In Jasmin, goto and goto_w are synonymous, since the Jasmin assembler automatically decides which version of the instruction to use, based on the address of the <label>.
3. Addresses are measured in bytes from the start of the bytecode—i.e., address 0 is the first byte in the bytecode of the currently executing method. The maximum address in a method is 65535.

---

i2b convert integer to byte

Jasmin Syntax

```
i2b
```

Stack

Before	After
value	result
...	...

Description

Converts an integer to a signed byte. A 32-bit int is popped off the stack, the top 24 bits are discarded (they are set to zero), then the resulting value is sign extended to an int. The int result is pushed back onto the stack.

i2b is used in Java where there is a cast between an int and a byte. Notice that i2b can cause a change in sign. For example, in the code:

```
int x = -134;
byte b = (byte)x;
```

The value of b is positive 122—the sign bit of x is lost in the conversion.

Bytecode

Type	Description
u1	i2b opcode = 0x91 (145)

See Also

i2c, i2s

i2c convert integer to character

Jasmin Syntax

```
i2c
```

Stack

Before	After
value	result
...	...

Description

Converts an integer to a 16-bit unsigned char. A 32-bit int is popped off the stack, the top 16 bits are set to zero and the resulting int value is pushed back onto the stack.

i2c is used in Java when there is an explicit cast between an int and a char. Notice that i2c produces an unsigned value—any sign bit for the original number is lost.

For example, in the code:

```
int x = -1;
char c = (char)x;
```

The value of c is positive 0xFFFF.

Bytecode

Type	Description
u1	i2c opcode = 0x92 (146)

See Also

i2b, i2s

i2d convert integer to double

Jasmin Syntax

```
i2d
```

Stack

Before	After
int	double-word1
...	double-word2
	...

Description

Pops an int off the operand stack, casts it into a double-precision floating-point number, and pushes the two-word double-precision result back onto the stack. This conversion is exact, since doubles have enough precision to represent all int values.

Bytecode

Type	Description
u1	i2d opcode = 0x87 (135)

See Also

i2f, i2l

i2f convert integer to float

Jasmin Syntax

```
i2f
```

Stack

Before	After
int	float
...	...

Description

Pops an int off the operand stack, casts it into a single-precision *float*, and pushes the *float* back onto the stack. Notice that there is may be a loss of precision (floats have 24 bits of significand, as compared to 32 bits for an *int*, so the least significant bits of int are lost). However, the magnitude of the result will be preserved (the range of a float is greater than the range of an int). Rounding is done using the IEEE 754 round-to-nearest mode.

Bytecode

Type	Description
u1	i2f opcode = 0x86 (134)

See Also

i2l, i2d

i2l convert integer to long integer

Jasmin Syntax

```
i2l
```

Stack

Before	After
int	long-word1
...	long-word2
	...

Description

Pops an integer off the operand stack, sign extends it into a long integer, and pushes the two-word long back onto the stack.

Bytecode

Type	Description
u1	i2l opcode = 0x85 (133)

See Also

i2f, i2d

---

i2s convert integer to short integer

Jasmin Syntax

```
i2s
```

Stack

Before	After
value	result
...	...

Description

Converts an integer to a signed short. A 32-bit int is popped off the stack, the top 16 bits are set to zero, and the resulting value is then sign extended to an int. The int result is pushed back onto the stack.

i2s is used in Java where there is an explicit case between an int and a short. Notice that i2s can cause a change in sign. For example, in the code:

```
int x = -40000;
short s = (short)x;
```

The value of s is positive 25536, since the sign bit of x is lost in the conversion.

Bytecode

Type	Description
u1	i2s opcode = 0x93 (147)

See Also

i2b, i2c

---

iadd add two integers

Jasmin Syntax

```
iadd
```

Stack

Before	After
value1	result
value2	...
...	

Description

Pops two integers from the operand stack, adds them, and pushes the integer result back onto the stack. On overflow, iadd produces a result whose low order bits are correct, but whose sign bit may be incorrect.

Example

```
bipush  5        ; push first int
bipush  4        ; push second int
iadd             ; add integers

                 ; the top of the stack now
                 ; contains the integer 9
```

Bytecode

Type	Description
u1	iadd opcode = 0x60 (96)

See Also

ladd, fadd, dadd

---

iaload retrieve integer from array

Jasmin Syntax

```
iaload
```

Stack

Before	After
index	value
arrayref	...
...	

Description

Retrieves an entry from a int array and places it on the stack. *arrayref* is a reference to an array of ints. *index* is an int. The *arrayref* and *index* are removed from the stack, and the int value at the given *index* in the array is pushed onto the stack.

Example

```
; get x[1], where x is an int array stored in local variable 1
aload_1          ; push an integer array onto the stack
iconst_1         ; push the integer 1 onto the stack
iaload           ; get the int at index 1 from the array

                 ; the top item on the stack is now x[1]
```

Exceptions

- NullPointerException—*arrayref* is null
- ArrayIndexOutOfBoundsException—*index* is < 0 or >= *arrayref.length*

Bytecode

Type	Description
u1	iaload opcode = 0x2E (46)

See Also

laload, faload, daload, aaload, baload, caload, saload, iastore, lastore, fastore, dastore, aastore, bastore, castore, sastore

---

iand integer bitwise and

Jasmin Syntax

```
iand
```

Stack

Before	After
value1	result
value2	...
...	

Description

Computes the bitwise and of *value1* and *value2* (which must be ints). The int result replaces *value1* and *value2* on the stack.

Example

```
; This is like the Java code:
;       int x;
;       x &= 2;
;
iload_1          ; push integer in local variable 1 onto stack
iconst_2         ; push the integer 2 onto the stack
iand             ; compute the bitwise and
istore_1         ; store the result in local variable 1
```

Bytecode

Type	Description
u1	iand opcode = 0x7E (126)

See Also

ishl, ishr, iushr, lshl, lshr, lushr, land, ior, lor, ixor, lxor

---

iastore store in integer array

Jasmin Syntax

```
iastore
```

Stack

Before	After
value	...
index	
arrayref	
...	

Description

Takes an int from the stack and stores it in an array of ints. *arrayref* is a reference to an array of ints. *index* is an int. *value* is the int value to be stored in the array. *arrayref*, *index* and *value* are removed from the stack, and *value* is stored in the array at the given *index*.

Exceptions

• NullPointerException—*arrayref* is null
• ArrayIndexOutOfBoundsException—*index* is < *0 or* >= *arrayref.length*

Bytecode

Type	Description
u1	iastore opcode = 0x4F (79)

See Also

lastore, fastore, dastore, aastore, bastore, castore, sastore, iaload, laload, faload, daload, aaload, baload, caload, saload

---

iconst_m1 push the integer constant −1

Jasmin Syntax

```
iconst_m1
```

Stack

Before	After
...	−1
	...

Description

Pushes the int −1 onto the operand stack.

Bytecode

Type	Description
u1	iconst_m1 opcode = 0x02 (2)

See Also

bipush, sipush, ldc, ldc_w, ldc2_w, aconst_null, iconst_<n>, lconst_<l>, fconst_<f>, dconst_<d>

Notes

You could also use bipush -1, sipush -1 or ldc -1 to achieve the same effect, although iconst_m1 is typically more efficient and uses fewer bytes in the bytecode.

iconst_<n> push the integer constant 0, 1, 2, 3, 4 or 5

Jasmin Syntax

```
        iconst_0
or
        iconst_1
or
        iconst_2
or
        iconst_3
or
        iconst_4
or
        iconst_5
```

Stack

Before	After
...	<n>
	...

Description

Represents the series of opcodes iconst_0, iconst_1, iconst_2, iconst_3, iconst_4 and iconst_5. These are used to push the constant ints 0 through 5 onto the stack. For example, to push the int zero onto the stack, use:

```
    iconst_0 ; push 0 onto the stack.
```

Note that you could also use:

```
    bipush 0 ; push 0 onto the stack
```

or

```
    sipush 0 ; push 0 onto the stack
```

or

```
    ldc 0 ; push 0 onto the stack
```

although these instructions are typically less efficient than the equivalent iconst_<n> and also take up more bytes in the class file.

Example

```
iconst_0  ; push 0 onto the stack
iconst_1  ; push 1 onto the stack
iconst_2  ; push 2 onto the stack
iconst_3  ; push 3 onto the stack
iconst_4  ; push 4 onto the stack
iconst_5  ; push 5 onto the stack
```

Bytecode

Type	Description
u1	iconst_0 opcode = 0x03 (3)
u1	iconst_1 opcode = 0x04 (4)
u1	iconst_2 opcode = 0x05 (5)
u1	iconst_3 opcode = 0x06 (6)
u1	iconst_4 opcode = 0x07 (7)
u1	iconst_5 opcode = 0x08 (8)

See Also

bipush, sipush, ldc, ldc_w, ldc2_w, aconst_null, iconst_m1, lconst_<l>, fconst_<f>, dconst_<d>

idiv divide two integers

Jasmin Syntax

```
idiv
```

Stack

Before	After
value1	result
value2	...
...	

Description

Pops the top two integers from the operand stack and divides the second-from top integer (*value2*) by the top integer (*value1*), i.e., computes (*value2* div *value1*). The quotient result is truncated to the nearest integer (with rounding going towards zero, so 1.7 becomes 1) and placed on the stack.

Exceptions

*   ArithmeticException—attempt to divide by 0 (i.e., *value1* is 0)

Bytecode

Type	Description
u1	idiv opcode = 0x6C (108)

See Also

ldiv, fdiv, ddiv

Notes

Because of the two's-complement representation used for negative numbers, dividing Integer.MIN_VALUE by −1 produces Integer.MIN_VALUE, not Integer.MAX_VALUE as you might expect.

if_acmpeq jump if two object references are equal

Jasmin Syntax

```
if_acmpeq <label>
```

<label> is a label name. To define the location of the label, use the *<label>* name followed by a colon:

```
<label>:
```

<label> then becomes associated the address of the following instruction. Labels can only be assigned one location in a method. On the other hand, a single *<label>* can be the target of multiple branch instructions.

Stack

Before	After
value1	...
value2	
...	

Description

Pops the top two object references off the stack and compares them. If the two object references are equal (i.e., if they both refer to the same object), execution branches to the address (*pc* + *branchoffset*), where *pc* is the address of the if_acmpeq opcode in the bytecode and *branchoffset* is a 16-bit signed integer parameter following the if_acmpeq opcode in the bytecode. If the object references refer to different objects, execution continues at the next instruction.

If you are using Jasmin, *branchoffset* is computed for you from the address of `<label>`.

Example

```
aload_1         ; push the object reference in local variable 1 onto stack
aload_2         ; push the object reference in local variable 2 onto stack
if_acmpeq Label ; if the two references on the stack are identical, jump to Label
return          ; return if not equal
Label:
    ; execution continues here if local variables 1 and 2 refer to the same object
```

Bytecode

Type	Description
u1	if_acmpeq opcode = 0xA5 (165)
s2	*branchoffset*

See Also

if_acmpne

Notes

Addresses are measured in bytes from the start of the bytecode (i.e., address 0 is the first byte in the bytecode of the currently executing method).

---

if_acmpne jump if two object references are not equal

Jasmin Syntax

```
if_acmpne <label>
```

`<label>` is a label name. To define the location of the label, use the `<label>` name followed by a colon:

```
<label>:
```

then becomes associated the address of the following instruction. Labels can only be assigned one location in a method. On the other hand, a single <label> can be the target of multiple branch instructions.

Stack

Before	After
value1	...
value2	
...	

Description

Pops the top two object references off the stack and compares them. If the two object references are not equal (i.e., if they refer to different objects), execution branches to the address ($pc + branchoffset$), where pc is the address of the if_acmpne opcode in the bytecode and *branchoffset* is a 16-bit signed integer parameter following the if_acmpne opcode in the bytecode. If the object references refer to the same object, execution continues at the next instruction.

If you are using Jasmin, *branchoffset* is computed for you from the address of <label>.

Example

```
aload_1         ; push the object reference in local variable 1 onto stack
aload_2         ; push the object reference in local variable 2 onto stack
if_acmpne Label ; if the two references on the stack differ, jump to Label
return          ; return if local variables 1 and 2 are the same object
Label:
; execution continues here if local variables 1 and 2
; refer to the different objects
```

Bytecode

Type	Description
u1	if_acmpne opcode = 0xA6 (166)
s2	*branchoffset*

See Also

if_icmpne, if_icmplt, if_icmpgt, if_icmple, if_icmpge

Notes

Addresses are measured in bytes from the start of the bytecode (i.e., address 0 is the first byte in the bytecode of the currently executing method).

if_icmpeq jump if two integers are equal

Jasmin Syntax

```
if_icmpeq <label>
```

`<label>` is a label name. To define the location of the label, use the `<label>` name followed by a colon:

```
<label>:
```

`<label>` then becomes associated the address of the following instruction. Labels can only be assigned one location in a method. On the other hand, a single `<label>` can be the target of multiple branch instructions.

Stack

Before	After
value1	...
value2	
...	

Description

Pops the top two ints off the stack and compares them. If the two integers are equal, execution branches to the address ($pc + branchoffset$), where pc is the address of the if_icmpeq opcode in the bytecode and *branchoffset* is a 16-bit signed integer parameter following the if_icmpeq opcode in the bytecode. If the integers are not equal, execution continues at the next instruction.

If you are using Jasmin, *branchoffset* is computed for you from the address of `<label>`.

Example

```
bipush 2         ; push the int 2 onto the stack
iload_1          ; push the int value in local variable 1 onto the stack
if_icmpeq Label  ; if the value of local variable 1 equals 2, jump to Label
return           ; return if not equal
Label:
    ; execution continues here if local variable 1 equals 2...
```

Bytecode

Type	Description
u1	if_icmpeq opcode = 0x9F (159)
s2	*branchoffset*

See Also

if_icmpne, if_icmplt, if_icmpgt, if_icmple, if_icmpge

Notes

Addresses are measured in bytes from the start of the bytecode (i.e., address 0 is the first byte in the bytecode of the currently executing method).

if_icmpge jump if one integer is greater than or equal to another

Jasmin Syntax

```
if_icmpge <label>
```

is a label name. To define the location of the label, use the <label> name followed by a colon:

```
<label>:
```

then becomes associated the address of the following instruction. Labels can only be assigned one location in a method. On the other hand, a single <label> can be the target of multiple branch instructions.

Stack

Before	After
value1	...
value2	

Description

Pops the top two ints off the stack and compares them. If *value2* is greater than or equal to *value1*, execution branches to the address (*pc* + *branchoffset*), where *pc* is the address of the if_icmpge opcode in the bytecode and *branchoffset* is a 16-bit signed integer parameter following the if_icmpge opcode in the bytecode. If *value2* is less than *value1*, execution continues at the next instruction.

If you are using Jasmin, *branchoffset* is computed for you from the address of `<label>`.

Example

```
    iload_1         ; push the int value in local variable 1 onto the stack
    bipush 2        ; push the int 2 onto the stack
    if_icmpge Label ; if the value of local variable 1 >= 2, jump to Label
    return          ; return if local variable 1 < 2
  Label:
    ; execution continues here if local variable 1 >= 2...
```

Bytecode

Type	Description
u1	if_icmpge opcode = 0xA2 (162)
s2	*branchoffset*

See Also

if_icmpeq, if_icmpne, if_icmplt, if_icmpgt, if_icmple

Notes

Addresses are measured in bytes from the start of the bytecode (i.e., address 0 is the first byte in the bytecode of the currently executing method).

if_icmpgt jump if one integer is greater than another

Jasmin Syntax

```
  if_icmpgt <label>
```

`<label>` is a label name. To define the location of the label, use the `<label>` name followed by a colon:

```
  <label>:
```

<*label*> then becomes associated the address of the following instruction. Labels can only be assigned one location in a method. On the other hand, a single <*label*> can be the target of multiple branch instructions.

Stack

Before	After
value1	...
value2	

Description

Pops the top two ints off the stack and compares them. If *value2* is greater than *value1*, execution branches to the address ($pc + branchoffset$), where pc is the address of the if_icmpgt opcode in the bytecode and *branchoffset* is a 16-bit signed integer parameter following the if_icmpgt opcode in the bytecode. If *value2* is less than or equal to *value1*, execution continues at the next instruction.

If you are using Jasmin, *branchoffset* is computed for you from the address of <*label*>.

Example

```
      iload_1        ; push the integer value of local variable 1 onto the stack
      bipush 2       ; push the integer 2 onto the stack
      if_icmpgt Label ; if the value of local variable 1 > 2, jump to Label
      return         ; return if local variable 1 <= 2
   Label:
      ; execution continues here if local variable 1 is geater than 2...
```

Bytecode

Type	Description
u1	if_icmpgt opcode = 0xA3 (163)
s2	*branchoffset*

See Also

if_icmpeq, if_icmpne, if_icmplt, if_icmple, if_icmpge

Notes

Addresses are measured in bytes from the start of the bytecode (i.e., address 0 is the first byte in the bytecode of the currently executing method).

if_icmple jump if one integer is less than or equal to another

Jasmin Syntax

```
if_icmple <label>
```

<label> is a label name. To define the location of the label, use the *<label>* name followed by a colon:

```
<label>:
```

<label> then becomes associated the address of the following instruction. Labels can only be assigned one location in a method. On the other hand, a single *<label>* can be the target of multiple branch instructions.

Stack

Before	After
value1	...
value2	

Description

Pops the top two ints off the stack and compares them. If *value2* is less than or equal to *value1*, execution branches to the address (*pc* + *branchoffset*), where *pc* is the address of the if_icmple opcode in the bytecode and *branchoffset* is a 16-bit signed integer parameter following the if_icmple opcode in the bytecode. If *value2* is greater than *value1*, execution continues at the next instruction.

If you are using Jasmin, *branchoffset* is computed for you from the address of *<label>*.

Example

```
        iload_1         ; push the int value in local variable 1 onto the stack
        bipush 2        ; push the int 2 onto the stack
        if_icmple Label ; if the value of local variable 1 is <= 2, jump to Label
        return          ; return if local variable 1 is greater than 2
Label:
    ; execution continues here if local variable 1 is less than or equal to 2...
```

Bytecode

Type	Description
u1	if_icmple opcode = 0xA4 (164)
s2	*branchoffset*

See Also

if_icmpeq, if_icmpne, if_icmplt, if_icmpgt, if_icmpge

Notes

Addresses are measured in bytes from the start of the bytecode (i.e., address 0 is the first byte in the bytecode of the currently executing method).

if_icmplt jump if one integer is less than another

Jasmin Syntax

```
if_icmplt <label>
```

<label> is a label name. To define the location of the label, use the *<label>* name followed by a colon:

```
<label>:
```

<label> then becomes associated the address of the following instruction. Labels can only be assigned one location in a method. On the other hand, a single *<label>* can be the target of multiple branch instructions.

Stack

Before	After
value1	...
value2	

Description

Pops the top two ints off the stack and compares them. If *value2* is less than *value1*, execution branches to the address (*pc* + *branchoffset*), where *pc* is the address of the if_icmplt opcode in the bytecode and *branchoffset* is a 16-bit signed integer parameter following the if_icmplt opcode in the bytecode. If *value2* is greater than or equal to *value1*, execution continues at the next instruction.

If you are using Jasmin, *branchoffset* is computed for you from the address of
`<label>`.

Example

```
    iload_1           ; push the int value in local variable 1 onto the stack
    bipush 2          ; push the int 2 onto the stack
    if_icmplt Label   ; if the value of local variable 1 is <= 2, jump to Label
    return            ; return if local variable 1 is greater than 2
  Label:
    ; execution continues here if local variable 1 is less than or equal to 2...
```

Bytecode

Type	Description
u1	if_icmplt opcode = 0xA1 (161)
s2	*branchoffset*

See Also

if_icmpeq, if_icmpne, if_icmpgt, if_icmple, if_icmpge

Notes

Addresses are measured in bytes from the start of the bytecode (i.e., address 0 is
the first byte in the bytecode of the currently executing method).

---

if_icmpne jump if two integers are not equal

Jasmin Syntax

```
    if_icmpne <label>
```

`<label>` is a label name. To define the location of the label, use the `<label>` name
followed by a colon:

```
    <label>:
```

`<label>` then becomes associated the address of the following instruction. Labels
can only be assigned one location in a method. On the other hand, a single
`<label>` can be the target of multiple branch instructions.

Stack

Before	After
value1	...
value2	
...	

Description

Pops the top two ints off the stack and compares them. If the two integers are not equal, execution branches to the address (*pc* + *branchoffset*), where *pc* is the address of the if_icmpne opcode in the bytecode and *branchoffset* is a 16-bit signed integer parameter following the if_icmpne opcode in the bytecode. If the integers are equal, execution continues at the next instruction.

If you are using Jasmin, *branchoffset* is computed for you from the address of <*label*>.

Example

```
    bipush 2       ; push the int 2 onto the stack
    iload_1        ; push the int value in local variable 1 onto the stack
    if_icmpne Label ; if the value of local variable 1 does not equal 2,
                   ; jump to Label
    return         ; return if local variable 1 equals 2
 Label:
    ; execution continues here if local variable 1 does not equals 2...
```

Bytecode

Type	Description
u1	if_icmpne opcode = 0xA0 (160)
s2	*branchoffset*

See Also

if_icmpeq, if_icmplt, if_icmpgt, if_icmple, if_icmpge

Notes

Addresses are measured in bytes from the start of the bytecode (i.e., address 0 is the first byte in the bytecode of the currently executing method).

ifeq jump if zero

Jasmin Syntax

```
ifeq <label>
```

`<label>` is a label name. To define the location of the label, use the `<label>` name followed by a colon:

```
<label>:
```

`<label>` then becomes associated the address of the following instruction. Labels can only be assigned one location in a method. On the other hand, a single `<label>` can be the target of multiple branch instructions.

Stack

Before	After
value	...
...	

Description

Pops the top int off the operand stack. If the int equals zero, execution branches to the address (*pc* + *branchoffset*), where *pc* is the address of the ifeq opcode in the bytecode and *branchoffset* is a 16-bit signed integer parameter following the ifeq opcode in the bytecode. If the int on the stack does not equal zero, execution continues at the next instruction.

If you are using Jasmin, *branchoffset* is computed for you from the address of `<label>`.

Example

```
        iload_1        ; push the int value in local variable 1 onto the stack
        ifeq Label     ; if the value of local variable 1 is zero, jump to Label
        return         ; return if local variable 1 is nonzero
    Label:
        ; execution continues here if local variable 1 equals zero...
```

Bytecode

Type	Description
u1	ifeq opcode = 0x99 (153)
s2	*branchoffset*

See Also

ifnull, iflt, ifle, ifne, ifnonnull, ifgt, ifge

Notes

Addresses are measured in bytes from the start of the bytecode (i.e., address 0 is the first byte in the bytecode of the currently executing method).

---

ifge jump if greater than or equal to zero

Jasmin Syntax

```
ifge <label>
```

is a label name. To define the location of the label, use the <label> name followed by a colon:

```
<label>:
```

then becomes associated the address of the following instruction. Labels can only be assigned one location in a method. On the other hand, a single <label> can be the target of multiple branch instructions.

Stack

Before	After
value	...
...	

Description

Pops the top int off the operand stack. If the int is greater than or equal to zero, execution branches to the address (*pc* + *branchoffset*), where *pc* is the address of the ifge opcode in the bytecode and *branchoffset* is a 16-bit signed integer parameter following the ifge opcode in the bytecode. If the int on the stack is less than zero, execution continues at the next instruction.

If you are using Jasmin, *branchoffset* is computed for you from the address of <label>.

Example

```
        iload_1          ; push the int value in local variable 1 onto the stack
        ifge Label       ; if the value on the stack is >= 0, jump to Label
        return           ; return if local variable 1 is less than zero
    Label:
        ; execution continues here if local variable 1 is greater than or equals zero...
```

Bytecode

Type	Description
u1	ifge opcode = 0x9C (156)
s2	*branchoffset*

See Also

ifnull, ifeq, iflt, ifne, ifnonnull, ifgt, ifle

Notes

Addresses are measured in bytes from the start of the bytecode (i.e., address 0 is the first byte in the bytecode of the currently executing method).

ifgt jump if greater than zero

Jasmin Syntax

```
    ifgt <label>
```

`<label>` is a label name. To define the location of the label, use the `<label>` name followed by a colon:

```
    <label>:
```

`<label>` then becomes associated the address of the following instruction. Labels can only be assigned one location in a method. On the other hand, a single `<label>` can be the target of multiple branch instructions.

Stack

Before	After
value	...
...	

Description

Pops the top int off the operand stack. If the int is greater than zero, execution branches to the address (*pc* + *branchoffset*), where *pc* is the address of the ifgt opcode in the bytecode and *branchoffset* is a 16-bit signed integer parameter following the ifgt opcode in the bytecode. If the int on the stack does is less than or equal to zero, execution continues at the next instruction.

If you are using Jasmin, *branchoffset* is computed for you from the address of `<label>`.

Example

```
    iload_1        ; push the int value in local variable 1 onto the stack
    ifgt Label     ; if the value on the stack is greater than zero, jump to Label
    return         ; return if local variable 1 is less than or equal to zero
  Label:
    ; execution continues here if local variable 1 is greater than zero...
```

Bytecode

Type	Description
u1	ifgt opcode = 0x9D (157)
s2	*branchoffset*

See Also

ifnull, ifeq, ifle, ifne, ifnonnull, iflt, ifge

Notes

Addresses are measured in bytes from the start of the bytecode (i.e., address 0 is the first byte in the bytecode of the currently executing method).

---

ifle jump if less than or equal to zero

Jasmin Syntax

```
    ifle <label>
```

`<label>` is a label name. To define the location of the label, use the `<label>` name followed by a colon:

```
    <label>:
```

`<label>` then becomes associated the address of the following instruction. Labels can only be assigned one location in a method. On the other hand, a single `<label>` can be the target of multiple branch instructions.

Stack

Before	After
value	...
...	

Description

Pops the top int off the operand stack. If the int is less than or equal to zero, execution branches to the address (*pc* + *branchoffset*), where *pc* is the address of the ifle opcode in the bytecode and *branchoffset* is a 16-bit signed integer parameter following the ifle opcode in the bytecode. If the int on the stack is greater than zero, execution continues at the next instruction.

If you are using Jasmin, *branchoffset* is computed for you from the address of <label>.

Example

```
    iload_1        ; push the int value in local variable 1 onto the stack
    ifle Label     ; if the value on the stack is <= zero, jump to Label
    return         ; return if local variable 1 is greater than zero
  Label:
    ; execution continues here if local variable 1 is less than or equal to zero...
```

Bytecode

Type	Description
u1	ifle opcode = 0x9E (158)
s2	*branchoffset*

See Also

ifnull, ifeq, iflt, ifne, ifnonnull, ifgt, ifge

Notes

Addresses are measured in bytes from the start of the bytecode (i.e., address 0 is the first byte in the bytecode of the currently executing method).

iflt jump if less than zero

Jasmin Syntax

```
iflt <label>
```

is a label name. To define the location of the label, use the <label> name followed by a colon:

```
<label>:
```

then becomes associated the address of the following instruction. Labels can only be assigned one location in a method. On the other hand, a single <label> can be the target of multiple branch instructions.

Stack

Before	After
value	...
...	

Description

Pops the top int off the operand stack. If the int is less than zero, execution branches to the address (pc + *branchoffset*), where pc is the address of the iflt opcode in the bytecode and *branchoffset* is a 16-bit signed integer parameter following the ifeq opcode in the bytecode. If the int on the stack is greater than or equal to zero, execution continues at the next instruction.

If you are using Jasmin, *branchoffset* is computed for you from the address of <label>.

Example

```
        iload_1      ; push the int value in local variable 1 onto the stack
        iflt Label   ; if the value on the stack is below zero, jump to Label
        return       ; return if local variable 1 is greater than or equal to zero
    Label:
        ; execution continues here if local variable 1 is less than zero...
```

Bytecode

Type	Description
u1	iflt opcode = 0x9B (155)
s2	*branchoffset*

See Also

ifnull, ifeq, ifle, ifne, ifnonnull, ifgt, ifge

Notes

Addresses are measured in bytes from the start of the bytecode (i.e., address 0 is the first byte in the bytecode of the currently executing method).

---

ifne jump if nonzero

Jasmin Syntax

    ifne <label>

`<label>` is a label name. To define the location of the label, use the `<label>` name followed by a colon:

    :

`<label>` then becomes associated the address of the following instruction. Labels can only be assigned one location in a method. On the other hand, a single `<label>` can be the target of multiple branch instructions.

Stack

Before	After
value	...
...	

Description

Pops the top int off the operand stack. If the int does not equal zero, execution branches to the address (*pc* + *branchoffset*), where *pc* is the address of the ifne opcode in the bytecode and *branchoffset* is a 16-bit signed integer parameter following the ifne opcode in the bytecode. If the int on the stack equals zero, execution continues at the next instruction.

If you are using Jasmin, *branchoffset* is computed for you from the address of `<label>`.

Example

```
        iload_1            ; push the int value in local variable 1 onto the stack
        ifne Label         ; if the value on the stack is nonzero, jump to Label
        return             ; return if local variable 1 is zero
   Label:
        ; execution continues here if local variable 1 does not equal zero...
```

Bytecode

Type	Description
u1	ifne opcode = 0x9A (154)
s2	*branchoffset*

See Also

ifnull, ifeq, ifle, iflt, ifnonnull, ifgt, ifge

Notes

Addresses are measured in bytes from the start of the bytecode (i.e., address 0 is the first byte in the bytecode of the currently executing method).

---

ifnonnull jump if non-null

Jasmin Syntax

```
   ifnonnull <label>
```

<label> is a label name. To define the location of the label, use the *<label>* name followed by a colon:

```
   <label>:
```

<label> then becomes associated the address of the following instruction. Labels can only be assigned one location in a method. On the other hand, a single *<label>* can be the target of multiple branch instructions.

Stack

Before	After
objectref	...
...	

Description

Pops the top object reference off the operand stack. If the object reference is not the special null reference, execution branches to the address (*pc* + *branchoffset*), where *pc* is the address of the ifnonnull opcode in the bytecode and *branchoffset* is a 16-bit signed integer parameter following the ifnonnull opcode in the bytecode. If the object reference on the stack is null, execution continues at the next instruction.

If you are using Jasmin, *branchoffset* is computed for you from the address of <*label*>.

Example

```
      aload_1           ; push the object reference in local variable 1 onto the stack
      ifnonnull Label ; if local variable isn't null, jump to Label
      return            ; return if local variable 1 is null
  Label:
      ; execution continues here if local variable 1 is something other than null ...
```

Bytecode

Type	Description
u1	ifnonnull opcode = 0xC7 (199)
s2	*branchoffset*

See Also

ifnull, ifeq, ifle, iflt, ifne, ifgt, ifge

Notes

Addresses are measured in bytes from the start of the bytecode (i.e., address 0 is the first byte in the bytecode of the currently executing method).

---

ifnull jump if null

Jasmin Syntax

```
  ifnull <label>
```

<*label*> is a label name. To define the location of the label, use the <*label*> name followed by a colon:

```
  <label>:
```

<*label*> then becomes associated the address of the following instruction. Labels can only be assigned one location in a method. On the other hand, a single <*label*> can be the target of multiple branch instructions.

Stack

Before	After
objectref	...
...	

Description

Pops the top object reference off the operand stack. If the object reference is to the special object null, execution branches to the address ($pc + branchoffset$), where pc is the address of the ifnull opcode in the bytecode and *branchoffset* is a 16-bit signed integer parameter following the ifnull opcode in the bytecode. If the object reference on the stack is not null, execution continues at the next instruction.

If you are using Jasmin, *branchoffset* is computed for you from the address of <*label*>.

Example

```
aload_1          ; push the object reference in local variable 1 onto the stack
ifnull Label     ; if local variable 1 is null, jump to Label
return           ; return if local variable 1 isn't null
Label:           ; execution continues here if local variable 1 is null...
```

Bytecode

Type	Description
u1	ifnull opcode = 0xC6 (198)
s2	branch-offset

See Also

ifeq, iflt, ifle, ifne, ifnonnull, ifgt, ifge

Notes

Addresses are measured in bytes from the start of the bytecode (i.e., address 0 is the first byte in the bytecode of the currently executing method).

iinc increment integer in local variable

Jasmin Syntax

```
    iinc <varnum> <n>
  or
    wide
    iinc <varnum> <n>
```

In the first form, *<varnum>* is an unsigned integer in the range 0 to 0xFF and *<n>* is a signed integer in the range −128 to 127. In the second (wide) form, *<varnum>* is an unsigned integer in the range 0 to 0xFFFF and *<n>* is a signed integer in the range −32768 to <= 32767.

Stack

Before	After
...	...

Description

Increments the int held in the local variable *<varnum>* by *<n>*. The iinc instruction takes two parameters: *<varnum>* is an unsigned integer which indicates which local variable should be used. *<n>* is the integer amount to increment or decrement the variable by. *<varnum>* must be a valid local variable number in the current method's frame.

Example

```
    iinc 1 10      ; increment local variable 1 by 10.
    iinc 1 -1      ; decrement local variable 1 by 1.
```

Bytecode

For local variable numbers in the range 0–255, and values of *<n>* in the range −128 to 127, use:

Type	Description
u1	iinc opcode = 0x84 (132)
u1	<varnum>
s1	<n>

There is also a `wide` format for this instruction, which supports access to all local variables from 0 to 65535, and values of <*n*> between −32768 and 32767:

Type	Description
u1	wide opcode = 0xC4 (196)
u1	iinc opcode = 0x84 (132)
u2	<varnum>
s2	<n>

See Also

wide

iload retrieve integer from local variable

Jasmin Syntax

```
    iload <varnum>
or
    wide
    iload <varnum>
```

In the first form, <*varnum*> is an unsigned integer in the range 0 to 0xFF. In the second (wide) form, <*varnum*> is an unsigned integer in the range 0 to 0xFFFF.

Stack

Before	After
...	int-value
	...

Description

Pushes the int value held in a local variable onto the operand stack. The Takes a single parameter, <*varnum*>, an unsigned integer which indicates which local variable to use. The single-word int value held in that local variable is retrieved and placed on the stack. <*varnum*> must be a valid local variable number in the current method's frame.

Example

```
bipush 5        ; push 5 onto the stack
istore 1        ; pop 5 off of the stack and store in local variable 1
iload 1         ; push the int in local variable 1 (the value 5)
                ; back onto the stack
```

Bytecode

For local variable numbers in the range 0–255, use:

Type	Description
u1	iload opcode = 0x15 (21)
u1	<varnum>

There is also a wide format for this instruction, which supports access to all local variables from 0 to 65535:

Type	Description
u1	wide opcode = 0xC4 (196)
u1	iload opcode = 0x15 (21)
u2	<varnum>

See Also

aload, fload, lload, dload, astore, fstore, lstore, dstore, istore

---

iload_<n> retrieve integer from local variable <n>

Jasmin Syntax

```
     iload_0
or
     iload_1
or
     iload_2
or
     iload_3
```

Stack

Before	After
...	int-value
	...

Description

Represents the series of opcodes iload_0, iload_1, iload_2, and iload_3 that retrieve a single precision float in local variables 0, 1, 2 or 3 and push it onto the stack. <n> must be a valid local variable number in the current frame.

"iload_<n>" is functionally equivalent to "iload <n>", although it is typically more efficient and also takes fewer bytes in the bytecode.

Example

```
iload_0        ;push integer in local variable 0 onto the stack
iload_1        ;push integer in local variable 1 onto the stack
iload_2        ;push integer in local variable 2 onto the stack
iload_3        ;push integer in local variable 3 onto the stack
```

Bytecode

Type	Description
u1	iload_0 opcode = 0x1A (26)
u1	iload_1 opcode = 0x1B (27)
u1	iload_2 opcode = 0x1C (28)
u1	iload_3 opcode = 0x1D (29)

See Also

iload, fload, lload, dload

impdep1   reserved opcode

Jasmin Syntax

```
n/a
```

Stack

Before	After
...	...

Description

Like impdep2 and breakpoint, is reserved for internal use by Java implementations, and must not appear in any class file—methods containing this opcode will fail verification.

Bytecode

Type	Description
u1	imped1 opcode = 0xFE (254)

See Also

impdep2, breakpoint

impdep2 reserved opcode

Jasmin Syntax

n/a

Stack

Before	After
...	...

Description

Like impdep1 and breakpoint, is reserved for internal use by Java implementations, and must not appear in any class file—methods containing this opcode will fail verification.

Bytecode

Type	Description
u1	imped2 opcode = 0xFF (255)

See Also

impdep1, breakpoint

---

imul multiply two integers

Jasmin Syntax

```
imul
```

Stack

Before	After
value1	result
value2	...
...	

Description

Pops the top two integers from the operand stack, multiplies them, and pushes the integer result back onto the stack. On overflow, imul produces a result whose low order bits are correct, but whose sign bit may be incorrect.

Bytecode

Type	Description
u1	imul opcode = 0x68 (104)

See Also

lmul, fmul, dmul

ineg negate an integer

Jasmin Syntax

```
ineg
```

Stack

Before	After
value	-value

Description

Pops an int off the stack, negates it, and pushes the negated integer value back onto the stack. This is the same as multiplying the integer by –1.

Bytecode

Type	Description
u1	ineg opcode = 0x74 (116)

See Also

lneg, fneg, dneg

Notes

Because of the two's-complement representation used for negative numbers, negating Integer.MIN_VALUE actually produces Integer.MIN_VALUE, not Integer.MAX_VALUE as you might expect.

---

instanceof test if object or array belongs to type

Jasmin Syntax

```
instanceof <type>
```

<type> is the name of a Java class, e.g., `java/lang/String`. Alternatively, to test for array references, *<type>* can be the type descriptor of an array, e.g., `[[Ljava/lang/String;`

Stack

Before	After
objectref	int-result
...	...

Description

Implements the Java language's `instanceof` operator, which tests whether an object reference or array belongs to a given class.

`instanceof` takes a single parameter, *<type>*. *<type>* is either the name of a Java class, or it is the type descriptor of an array.

At runtime, *<type>* is resolved (Chapter 7 describes how classes are resolved). Next, `instanceof` pops *objectref* (a reference to an object) off the top of the operand stack. If *objectref* is an instance of *<type>* or one of *<type>*'s subclasses, the int 1 is pushed onto the stack, otherwise the int 0 is pushed onto the stack. If *objectref* is null, the result is always 0. If *<type>* is an interface, int-result will be 1 if *objectref* implements that interface, and 0 if *objectref* does not implement the interface.

Example

```
; using instanceof to test for a String:
aload_1                         ; push object reference in local variable 1
                                ; onto stack
instanceof java/lang/String     ; test if item on stack is a String
ifne HaveString                 ; if so, goto HaveString
return                          ; otherwise, return
HaveString:
; if this point is reached, local variable 1 holds a string


; this example uses instanceof to test if local variable 1 holds
; an integer array
aload_1                 ; push local variable 1 onto the stack
instanceof [I           ; test if the top item on the stack is an integer array
ifne HaveIntegerArray   ; if so, jump to HaveIntegerArray
return                  ; simply return if local variable 1 is not an int array
HaveIntegerArray:
; if this point is reached, local variable 1 holds an integer array


; you can also use instanceof to test that objects implement a given interface,
; e.g.,
aload_1                         ; push local variable 1 onto the stack
instanceof java/lang/Runnable   ; test if it implements the Runnable interface
ifne HaveARunnable              ; if so, jump to HaveARunnable
return                          ; otherwise return
HaveARunnable:
```

```
; if this point is reached, local variable 1 holds a reference to an object
; that implements the Runnable interface.
```

Bytecode

In bytecode, immediately following the instanceof opcode is a 16-bit unsigned short integer. This integer is the index of an entry in the constant pool of the current class. The entry is tagged a CONSTANT_Class entry. The name field of the CONSTANT_Class entry is the same as the string given by <type> parameter in Jasmin.

Type	Description
u1	instanceof opcode = 0xC1 (193)
u2	index

See Also

- checkcast
- Chapter 7 gives a pseudo-code implementation of instanceof

invokeinterface invoke an interface method

Jasmin Syntax

```
invokeinterface <method-spec> <n>
```

<method-spec> is a method specification and <n> is an integer in the range 0-255.

The <method-spec> is a single token made up of three parts: an *interfacename*, a *methodname* and a *descriptor*. e.g.,

```
java/util/Enumeration/hasMoreElements()Z
```

is the method called "hasMoreElements" in the interface called "java.util.Enumeration", and it has the descriptor "()Z" (i.e., it takes no arguments and returns a boolean result). In Jasmin, the characters up to the "(" character in <method-spec> form the *interfacename* and *methodname* (the *interfacename* is all the characters up to the last "/" character, and the *methodname* is all the characters between the last "/" and the "(" character). The characters from "(" to the end of the string are the *descriptor*. This is illustrated in the following diagram:

```
foo/baz/MyInterface/myMethod(Ljava/lang/String;)V
-------------------        ---------------------
         |          --------          |
   interfacename        |             |
               methodname      descriptor
```

Stack

Before	After
argN	[result]
—	...
arg2	
arg1	
objectref	
...	

Description

Invokes a method declared within a Java interface. For example, if you have the Java code:

```
void test(Enumeration enum) {
    boolean x = enum.hasMoreElements();
    ...
}
```

invokeinterface will be used to call the hasMoreElements() method, since Enumeration is a Java interface, and hasMoreElements() is a method declared in that interface. In this example, the Java compiler generates code like:

```
aload_1             ; push local variable 1 (i.e., the enum object) onto the stack
; call hasMoreElements()
invokeinterface java/util/Enumeration/hasMoreElements()Z 1
istore_2            ; store the boolean result in local variable 2 (i.e., x)
```

Which particular implementation of hasMoreElements() is used will depend on the type of object held in local variable 1 at runtime.

Before performing the method invocation, the interface and the method identified by <method-spec> are resolved. See Chapter 4 for a description of how methods are resolved. See Chapter 7 for a discussion of method dispatch.

To invoke an interface method, the interpreter first pops <n> words off the operand stack, where <n> is an 8-bit unsigned integer parameter taken from the bytecode. The first of these items is *objectref*, a reference to the object whose method is being called. The rest of the items are the arguments for the method.

Then the class of the object referred to by *objectref* is retrieved. This class must implement the interface named in <method-spec>. The method table for this class is searched, and the method with the given *methodname* and *descriptor* is located.

Once the method has been located, invokeinterface calls the method. First, if the method is marked as synchronized, the monitor associated with *objectref* is entered. Next, a new stack frame is established on the callstack. Then the arguments for the method are placed in the local variable slots of the new stack frame structure. arg1 is stored in local variable 1, arg2 is stored in local variable 2 and so on. *objectref* is stored in local variable 0, the local variable used by the special Java variable this. Execution continues at the first instruction in the bytecode of the new method.

Methods marked as native are handled slightly differently. For native methods, the runtime system locates the platform-specific code for the method, loading it and linking it into the JVM if necessary. Then the native method code is executed with the arguments that were popped from the operand stack. The exact mechanism used to invoke native methods is implementation-specific.

When the method called by invokeinterface returns, any single (or double) word return result is placed on the operand stack of the current method. If the invoked method was marked as synchronized, the monitor associated with *objectref* is exited. Then execution continues at the instruction that follows invokeinterface in the bytecode.

Exceptions

* NullPointerException—*objectref* is null
* StackOverflowError—no more space in callstack for a new stack frame

Bytecode

In bytecode, after the invokeinterface opcode is a 16-bit unsigned integer *index*. This is the index of an entry in the constant pool. The entry is tagged as a CONSTANT_InterfaceMethodref entry. This entry has two fields. One field points to a CONSTANT_Class entry in the constant pool whose name is the *interfacename* from <method-spec>, and the other points to a CONSTANT_NameAndType entry in the constant pool whose name is the *methodname* from <method-spec> and whose descriptor is the type *descriptor* from <method-spec>.

invokeinterface takes an additional unsigned byte parameters in bytecode: <*n*>. <*n*> is the number of argument words the method takes plus one, (i.e., the second parameter given to the invokeinterface instruction in Jasmin). <*n*> must match the number of argument words given in the *descriptor* for the method.

After <*n*>, there follows a single byte, which must be zero (this byte location is in fact used at runtime by Sun's Java interpreter—it caches a hashing value in this byte, to speed up invokeinterface method lookup).

Type	Description
u1	invokeinterface opcode = 0xB9 (185)
u2	*index*
u1	<n>
u1	0

See Also

invokevirtual, invokespecial, invokestatic

Notes

1. Of the instructions used to invoke instance methods, invokeinterface is the most complex to implement, and typically the least efficient. See Chapter 7 for more details on this.
2. The <*n*> and 0 byte parameters in bytecode are present for historical reasons.

---

invokespecial invoke method belonging to a specific class

Jasmin Syntax

```
invokespecial <method-spec>
```

<*method-spec*> is a method specification. It is a single token made up of three parts: a *classname*, a *methodname* and a *descriptor*, for example:

```
java/lang/StringBuffer/<init>()V
```

is the method called "<*init*>" (the special name used for instance initialization methods) in the class called "java.lang.StringBuffer", and it has the descriptor "()V" (i.e., it takes no arguments and no results). In Jasmin, the characters up to the "(" character in <*method-spec*> form the *classname* and *methodname* (the *classname* is all the characters up to the last "/" character, and the *methodname* is all the characters between the last "/" and the "(" character). The characters from "(" to the end of the string are the *descriptor*. This is illustrated in the following diagram:

```
foo/baz/Myclass/myMethod(Ljava/lang/String;)V
---------------         ---------------------
       |         --------         |
       |         |                |
    classname  methodname      descriptor
```

Stack

Before	After
argN	[result]
—	
arg2	
arg1	
objectref	
...	

Description

In certain special cases, invokes a method. Specifically, invokespecial is used to invoke:

* the instance initialization method, <*init*>
* a private method of this
* a method in a superclass of this

The main use of invokespecial is to invoke an object's instance initialization method, <*init*>, during the construction phase for a new object. For example, when you write in Java:

```
new StringBuffer()
```

code like the following is generated:

```
new java/lang/StringBuffer      ; create a new StringBuffer
dup                             ; make an extra reference to the new instance
                               ; now call an instance initialization method
invokespecial java/lang/StringBuffer/<init>()V
                               ; stack now contains an initialized StringBuffer.
```

invokespecial is also used by the Java language by the "super" keyword to access a superclass's version of a method. For example, in the class:

```
class Example {
    // override equals
        public boolean equals(Object x) {
            // call Object's version of equals
            return super.equals(x);
        }
}
```

the "super.equals(x)" expression is compiled to:

```
aload_0  ; push 'this' onto the stack
aload_1  ; push the first argument (i.e., x) onto the stack
; now invoke Object's equals() method.
invokespecial java/lang/Object/equals(Ljava/lang/Object;)Z
```

Finally, invokespecial is used to invoke a private method. Remember that private methods are only visible to other methods belonging the same class as the private method.

Before performing the method invocation, the class and the method identified by <*method-spec*> are resolved. See Chapter 4 for a description of how methods are resolved. See Chapter 7 for a discussion of method dispatch.

invokespecial first looks at the *descriptor* given in <*method-spec*>, and determines how many argument words the method takes (this may be zero). It pops these arguments off the operand stack. Next it pops *objectref* (a reference to an object) off the operand stack. *objectref* must be an instance of the class named in `<method-spec>`, or one of its subclasses. The interpreter searches the list of methods defined by the class named in `<method-spec>`, looking for a method called *methodname* whose descriptor is *descriptor*. This search is not based on the runtime type of *objectref*, but on the compile time type given in `<method-spec>`.

Once a method has been located, `invokespecial` calls the method. First, if the method is marked as `synchronized`, the monitor associated with *objectref* is entered. Next, a new stack frame structure is established on the call stack. Then the arguments for the method (which were popped off the current method's operand stack) are placed in local variables of the new stack frame structure. arg1 is stored in local variable 1, arg2 is stored in local variable 2 and so on. *objectref* is stored in local variable 0 (the local variable used for the special Java variable this). Finally, execution continues at the first instruction in the bytecode of the new method.

Methods marked as `native` are handled slightly differently. For native methods, the runtime system locates the platform-specific code for the method, loading it and linking it into the JVM if necessary. Then the native method code is executed with the arguments popped from the operand stack. The exact mechanism used to invoke native methods is implementation-specific.

When the method called by `invokespecial` returns, any single (or double) word return result is placed on the operand stack of the current method. If the invoked method was marked as `synchronized`, the monitor associated with *objectref* is exited. Execution continues at the instruction that follows `invokespecial` in the bytecode.

Exceptions

- NullPointerException — *objectref* is `null`
- StackOverflowError — no more space in callstack for a new stack frame

Bytecode

In bytecode, after the `invokespecial` opcode is a 16-bit unsigned integer *index*. This is the index of an entry in the constant pool. The entry is tagged as a CONSTANT_Methodref entry. This entry has two fields. One field points to a CONSTANT_Class entry in the constant pool whose name is the *classname* from `<method-spec>`, and the other points to a CONSTANT_NameAndType entry in the constant pool whose name is the *methodname* from `<method-spec>` and whose descriptor is the type *descriptor* from `<method-spec>`.

Type	Description
u1	invokespecial opcode = 0xB7 (183)
u2	index

See Also

invokevirtual, invokeinterface, invokestatic

Notes

In Java Virtual Machine implementations prior to version JDK 1.02, this instruction was called invokenonvirtual, and was less restrictive than invokespecial—it wasn't limited to invoking only superclass, private or <init> methods. The class access flag ACC_SUPER (see Chapter 12, *Class File Reference*), is used to indicate which semantics are used by a class. In older class files, the ACC_SUPER flag is unset. In all new classes, the ACC_SUPER flag should be set, indicating that the restrictions enforced by invokespecial are obeyed. (In practice, all the common uses of invokenonvirtual continue to be supported by invokespecial, so this change should have little impact on JVM users.)

invokestatic invoke a class (static) method

Jasmin Syntax

```
invokestatic <method-spec>
```

<method-spec> is a method specification. It is a single token made up of three parts: a *classname*, a *methodname* and a *descriptor*. e.g.,

```
java/lang/System/exit(I)V
```

is the method called "exit" in the class called "java.lang.System", and it has the descriptor "(I)V" (i.e., it takes an integer argument and returns no result). In Jasmin, the characters up to the "(" character in <method-spec> form the *classname* and *methodname* (the *classname* is all the characters up to the last "/" character, and the *methodname* is all the characters between the last "/" and the "(" character). The characters from "(" to the end of the string are the *descriptor*. This is illustrated in the following diagram:

```
foo/baz/Myclass/myMethod(Ljava/lang/String;)V
---------------          --------------------
      |            --------           |
      |               |               |
  classname       methodname      descriptor
```

Stack

Before	After
argN	[result]
...	...
arg3	
arg2	
arg1	

Description

Calls a static method (also known as a class method). For example, if you write in Java:

```
System.exit(1);
```

this is compiled into the JVM code:

```
iconst_1        ; push 1 onto the stack.
                ; now call System.exit()
invokestatic java/lang/System/exit(I)V
```

Before performing the method invocation, the class and the method identified by <method-spec> are resolved. See Chapter 4 for a description of how methods are resolved. See Chapter 7 for a discussion of method dispatch.

invokestatic looks at the *descriptor* given in <method-spec>, and determines how many argument words the method takes (this may be zero). It pops these arguments off the operand stack. Then it searches the list of static methods defined by the class, locating the method *methodname* with a descriptor *descriptor*.

Once the method has been located, invokestatic calls the method. First, if the method is marked as synchronized, the monitor associated with the class object for the method's class is entered. Next, a new stack frame structure is established on the call stack. Then the arguments for the method (which were popped off the current method's operand stack) are placed in local variables of the new stack frame structure. arg1 is stored in local variable 0, arg2 is stored in local variable 1 and so on. Finally, execution continues at the first instruction in the bytecode of the new method.

Methods marked as native are handled slightly differently. For native methods, the runtime system locates the platform-specific code for the method, loading it and linking it into the JVM if necessary. Then the native method code is executed with the arguments that were popped from the operand stack. The exact mechanism used to invoke native methods is implementation-specific.

When the method called by invokestatic returns, any single (or double) word return result is placed on the operand stack of the current method. If the invoked method was marked as synchronized, the monitor associated with the class named in *<method-spec>* is exited. Execution continues at the instruction that follows invokestatic in the bytecode.

Exceptions

* StackOverflowError—no more space in callstack for a new stack frame

Bytecode

In bytecode, after the invokestatic opcode is a 16-bit unsigned integer *index*. This is the index of an entry in the constant pool. The entry is tagged as a CONSTANT_Methodref entry. This entry has two fields. One field points to a CONSTANT_Class entry in the constant pool whose name is the *classname* from *<method-spec>*, and the other points to a CONSTANT_NameAndType entry in the constant pool whose name is the *methodname* from *<method-spec>* and whose descriptor is the type *descriptor* from *<method-spec>*.

Type	Description
u1	invokestatic opcode = 0xB8 (184)
u2	index

See Also

invokevirtual, invokespecial, invokeinterface

---

invokevirtual call an instance method

Jasmin Syntax

```
invokespecial <method-spec>
```

<method-spec> is a method specification. It is a single token made up of three parts: a *classname*, a *methodname* and a *descriptor*, for example:

```
java/lang/StringBuffer/charAt(I)C
```

is the method called "charAt" in the class called "java.lang.StringBuffer", and it has the descriptor "(I)C" (i.e., it takes an integer argument and returns a char result). In Jasmin, the characters up to the "(" character in *<method-spec>* form the *classname* and *methodname* (the *classname* is all the characters up to the last "/" character, and the *methodname* is all the characters between the last "/" and the "("

character). The characters from "(" to the end of the string are the *descriptor*. This is illustrated in the following diagram:

```
foo/baz/Myclass/myMethod(Ljava/lang/String;)V
---------------        --------------------
       |         --------         |
       |            |             |
   classname   methodname    descriptor
```

Stack

Before	After
arg1	[result]
arg2	...
...	
argN	
objectref	
...	

Description

Dispatches a Java method. It is used in Java to invoke all methods except interface methods (which use invokeinterface), static methods (which use invokestatic), and the few special cases handled by invokespecial.

For example, when you write in Java:

```
Object x;
...
x.equals("hello");
```

this is compiled into something like:

```
aload_1        ; push local variable 1 (i.e., 'x') onto stack
ldc "hello"    ; push the string "hello" onto stack

; invoke the equals method
invokevirtual java/lang/Object/equals(Ljava/lang/Object;)Z
; the boolean result is now on the stack
```

Note that the actual method run depends on the runtime type of the object invokevirtual is used with. So in the example above, if x is an instance of a class that overrides Object's equal method, then the subclasses' overridden version of the equals method will be used.

Before performing the method invocation, the class and the method identified by <method-spec> are resolved. See Chapter 4 for a description of how methods are resolved. See Chapter 7 for a discussion of method dispatch.

invokevirtual looks at the *descriptor* given in <method-spec>, and determines how many argument words the method takes (this may be zero). It pops these arguments off the operand stack. Next it pops *objectref* off the stack. *objectref* is a reference to the object whose method is being called. invokevirtual retrieves the Java class for *objectref*, and searches the list of methods defined by that class and then its superclasses, looking for a method called *methodname*, whose descriptor is *descriptor*.

Once a method has been located, invokevirtual calls the method. First, if the method is marked as synchronized, the monitor associated with *objectref* is entered. Next, a new stack frame structure is established on the call stack. Then the arguments for the method (which were popped off the current method's operand stack) are placed in local variables of the new stack frame structure. arg1 is stored in local variable 1, arg2 is stored in local variable 2 and so on. *objectref* is stored in local variable 0 (the local variable used for the special Java variable this). Finally, execution continues at the first instruction in the bytecode of the new method.

When the method called by invokevirtual returns, any single (or double) word return result is placed on the operand stack of the current method and execution continues at the instruction that follows invokevirtual in the bytecode.

Exceptions

- NullPointerException—*objectref* is null
- StackOverflowError—no more space in callstack for a new stack frame

Bytecode

In bytecode, after the invokevirtual opcode is a 16-bit unsigned integer *index*. This is the index of an entry in the constant pool. The entry is tagged as a CONSTANT_Methodref entry. This entry has two fields. One field points to a CONSTANT_Class entry in the constant pool whose name is the *classname* from <method-spec>, and the other points to a CONSTANT_NameAndType entry in the constant pool whose name is the *methodname* from <method-spec> and whose descriptor is the type *descriptor* from <method-spec>.

Type	Description
u1	invokevirtual opcode = 0xB6 (182)
u2	index

See Also

invokespecial, invokestatic, invokeinterface

Notes

invokevirtual cannot be used to invoke the special methods `<init>` or `<clinit>`—see invokespecial.

---

ior integer bitwise or

Jasmin Syntax

```
ior
```

Stack

Before	After
value1	result
value2	...
...	

Description

Computes the bitwise or of *value1* and *value2* (which must be ints). The int result replaces *value1* and *value2* on the stack.

Example

```
; This is like the Java code:
;       int x;
;       x |= 2;
;
iload_1          ; load local variable 1 onto stack
iconst_2         ; push the integer 2 onto the stack
ior              ; compute the bitwise or
istore_1         ; store the result in local variable 1
```

Bytecode

Type	Description
u1	ior opcode = 0x80 (128)

See Also

ishl, ishr, iushr, lshl, lshr, lushr, iand, land, lor, ixor, lxor

---

irem remainder of two integers

Jasmin Syntax

```
irem
```

Stack

Before	After
value1	result
value2	...
...	

Description

Pops two ints off the operand stack, divides *value2* by *value1* (i.e., value2/value1), computes the remainder and pushes the int remainder back onto the stack. The remainder is (value2 – ((value1/value2) * value2)). This is used by the % operator in Java.

Exceptions

*   ArithmeticException—the divisor (*value1*) is zero

Bytecode

Type	Description
u1	irem opcode = 0x70 (112)

See Also

lrem, frem, drem

ireturn return from method with integer result

Jasmin Syntax

```
ireturn
```

Stack

Before	After
return-value	n/a
...	

Description

Pops an int from the top of the stack and pushes it onto the operand stack of the invoker (i.e., the method which used `invokevirtual`, `invokespecial`, `invokestatic` or `invokeinterface` to call the currently executing method). All other items on the current method's operand stack are discarded. If the current method is marked as synchronized, then an implicit monitorexit instruction is executed. Then the current method's frame is discarded, the invoker's frame is reinstated, and control returns to the invoker. This instruction can only be used in methods whose return type is int.

Bytecode

Type	Description
u1	ireturn opcode = 0xAC (172)

See Also

lreturn, freturn, dreturn, areturn, return

---

ishl integer shift left

Jasmin Syntax

```
ishl
```

Stack

Before	After
value1	result
value2	...
...	

Description

Pops two ints off the stack. Shifts *value2* left by the amount indicated in the five low bits of *value1*. The int result is then pushed back onto the stack.

This is the same as computing the expression:

x * 2^s

where s is value1 and x is value2.

Example

```
; This is like the Java code:
;       int x;
;       x <<= 3;
;
iload_1          ; push integer in local variable 1 onto stack
iconst_3         ; push the integer 3 onto the stack
ishl             ; shift left
istore_1         ; store the result in local variable 1
```

Bytecode

Type	Description
u1	ishl opcode = 0x78 (120)

See Also

ishr, iushr, lshl, lshr, lushr, iand, land, ior, lor, ixor, lxor

ishr integer arithmetic shift right

Jasmin Syntax

```
ishr
```

Stack

Before	After
value1	result
value2	...
...	

Description

Pops two ints off the stack. Shifts *value1* right by the amount indicated in the five low bits of *value2*. The int result is then pushed back onto the stack. *value1* is shifted arithmetically (preserving the sign extension).

This is the same as computing the expression:

x / 2^s

where s is value1 and x is value2.

Example

```
; This is like the Java code:
;       int x;
;       x >>= 3;
;
iload_1          ; load local variable 1 onto stack
iconst_3         ; push the integer 3 onto the stack
ishr             ; arithmetic shift right
istore_1         ; store the result in local variable 1
```

Bytecode

Type	Description
u1	ishr opcode = 0x7A (122)

See Also

ishl, iushr, lshl, lshr, lushr, iand, land, ior, lor, ixor, lxor

istore   store integer in local variable

Jasmin Syntax

```
    istore <varnum>
or
    wide
    istore <varnum>
```

In the first form, <*varnum*> is an unsigned integer in the range 0 to 0xFF. In the second (wide) form, <*varnum*> is an unsigned integer in the range 0 to 0xFFFF.

Stack

Before	After
value	...
...	

Description

Pops an in off the stack and stores it in local variable <*varnum*>. The istore instruction takes a single parameter, <*varnum*>, an unsigned integer which indicates which local variable should be used. <*varnum*> must be a valid local variable number in the current frame.

Example

```
  bipush 10      ; push 10 onto the stack
  istore 3       ; pop 10 off of the stack and store it in local variable 3
```

Bytecode

For local variable numbers in the range 0-255, use:

Type	Description
u1	istore opcode = 0x36 (54)
u1	<varnum>

There is also a `wide` format for this instruction, which supports access to all local variables from 0 to 65535:

Type	Description
u1	wide opcode = 0xC4 (196)
u1	istore opcode = 0x36 (54)
u2	<varnum>

See Also

lstore, fstore, dstore, astore, wide

istore_<n> store integer in local variable *<n>*

Jasmin Syntax

```
        istore_0
   or
        istore_1
   or
        istore_2
   or
        istore_3
```

Stack

Before	After
value	...
...	

Description

Pops an int off the stack and stores it in local variable *<n>*, where *<n>* is 0, 1, 2, or 3. *<n>* must be a valid local variable number in the current frame.

"istore_*<n>*" is functionally equivalent to "istore *<n>*", although it is typically more efficient and also takes fewer bytes in the bytecode.

Example

```
   istore_0        ;store integer in local variable 0
   istore_1        ;store integer in local variable 1
   istore_2        ;store integer in local variable 2
   istore_3        ;store integer in local variable 3
```

Bytecode

Type	Description
u1	istore_0 opcode = 0x3B (59)
u1	istore_1 opcode = 0x3C (60)
u1	istore_2 opcode = 0x3D (61)
u1	istore_3 opcode = 0x3E (62)

See Also

lstore, fstore, dstore, astore

---

isub subtract two integers

Jasmin Syntax

```
isub
```

Stack

Before	After
value1	result
value2	...
...	

Description

Pops two ints off the operand stack, subtracts the top one from the second (i.e., computes *value2 – value1*), and pushes the int result back onto the stack.

Bytecode

Type	Description
u1	isub opcode = 0x64 (100)

See Also

lsub, fsub, dsub

---

iushr integer logical shift right

Jasmin Syntax

```
iushr
```

Stack

Before	After
value1	result
value2	...
...	

Description

Pops two ints off the operand stack. Shifts *value1* right by the amount indicated in the five low bits of *value2*. The int result is then pushed back onto the stack.

value1 is shifted logically (ignoring the sign extension—useful for unsigned values).

Example

```
; This is like the Java code:
;      int x;
;      x >>>= 3;
;
iload_1            ; load local variable 1 onto stack
iconst_3           ; push the integer 3 onto the stack
iushr              ; logical shift right
istore_1           ; store the result in local variable 1
```

Bytecode

Type	Description
u1	iushr opcode = 0x7C (124)

See Also

ishl, ishr, lshl, lshr, lushr, iand, land, ior, lor, ixor, lxor

---

ixor   integer bitwise exclusive or

Jasmin Syntax

```
ixor
```

Stack

Before	After
value1	result
value2	...
...	

Description

Pops two integers off the operand stack. Computes the bitwise exclusive or of *value1* and *value2*. The integer result replaces *value1* and *value2* on the stack.

Example

```
; This is like the Java code:
;        int x;
;        x ^= 2;
;
iload_1             ; load local variable 1 onto stack
iconst_2            ; push the integer 2 onto the stack
ixor                ; compute the bitwise exclusive or
istore_1            ; store the result in local variable 1
```

Bytecode

Type	Description
u1	ixor opcode = 0x82 (130)

See Also

ishl, ishr, iushr, lshl, lshr, lushr, iand, land, ior, lor, lxor

---

jsr jump to subroutine

Jasmin Syntax

```
jsr <label>
```

`<label>` is a label name. To define the location of the label, use the `<label>` name followed by a colon:

```
<label>:
```

then becomes associated the address of the following instruction. Labels can only be assigned one location in a method. On the other hand, a single <label> can be the target of multiple branch instructions.

Stack

Before	After
...	return-address
	...

Description

Calls a local subroutine defined within the body of a method. It is used to implement Java's finally clause.

jsr first pushes the address ($pc + 3$) onto the operand stack, where pc is the address of this jsr instruction in the bytecode. The address ($pc + 3$) is the address of instruction that immediately follows the jsr instruction in bytecode—it is used used by the ret instruction to return from the subroutine.

Next, execution branches to the address ($pc + branchoffset$), where pc is the address of the jsr opcode in the bytecode and *branchoffset* is the 16-bit signed integer parameter following the jsr opcode in the bytecode. If you are using Jasmin, *branchoffset* is computed for you from the address of <label>.

Example

```
; This example method uses a PrintMe subroutine to invoke the
: System.out.println() method.

.method usingSubroutine()V
    ldc "Message 1"
    jsr PrintMe          ; print "Message 1"

    ldc "Message 2"
    jsr PrintMe          ; print "Message 2"

    ldc "Message 3"
    jsr PrintMe          ; print "Message 3"

    return    ; now return from usingSubroutine

; define the PrintMe subroutine ...
PrintMe:
    astore_1             ; store return-address in local variable 1
    ; call System.out.println()
    getstatic java/lang/System/out Ljava/io/PrintStream;
```

```
    invokevirtual java/io/PrintStream/println(Ljava/lang/String;)V

    ret 1                    ; return to the return-address in local variable 1
.end method
```

Bytecode

Type	Description
u1	jsr opcode = 0xA8 (168)
s2	*branchoffset*

See Also

jsr_w, ret, goto, goto_w

Notes

1. Addresses are measured in bytes from the start of the bytecode (i.e., address 0 is the first byte in the bytecode of the currently executing method).
2. Subroutines complicate the work of the class file verifier, so extensive use of subroutines may slow down verification speeds

---

jsr_w jump to subroutine using wide offset

Jasmin Syntax

```
jsr_w <label>
```

<label> is a label name. To define the location of the label, use the *<label>* name followed by a colon:

```
<label>:
```

<label> then becomes associated the address of the following instruction. Labels can only be assigned one location in a method. On the other hand, a single *<label>* can be the target of multiple branch instructions.

Stack

Before	After
...	return-address
	...

Description

Calls a local subroutine defined within the body of a method. It is used to implement Java's `finally` clause.

`jsr_w` first pushes the address ($pc + 5$) onto the operand stack, where pc is the address of this `jsr_w` instruction in the bytecode. The address ($pc + 5$) is the address of instruction that immediately follows the `jsr_w` instruction in bytecode—it is used used by the `ret` instruction to return from the subroutine.

Next, execution branches to the address ($pc + branchoffset$), where pc is the address of the `jsr_w` opcode in the bytecode and *branchoffset* is the 32-bit signed integer parameter following the `jsr_w` opcode in the bytecode. If you are using Jasmin, *branchoffset* is computed for you from the address of <`label`>.

Bytecode

Type	Description
u1	jsr_w opcode = 0xC9 (201)
s4	*branchoffset*

See Also

jsr, ret, goto, goto_w

Notes

1. `jsr_w` is identical to the `jsr` instruction except that it uses a 32-bit `wide` offset instead of a 16-bit `wide` offset.
2. Addresses are measured in bytes from the start of the bytecode (i.e., address 0 is the first byte in the bytecode of the currently executing method). The maximum address in a method is 65535.
3. In Jasmin, `jsr` and `jsr_w` are synonymous, since the Jasmin assembler automatically decides which version of the instruction to use, based on the address of the<`label`>.

---

l2d convert long to double

Jasmin Syntax

```
l2d
```

Stack

Before	After
long-word1	double-word1
long-word2	double-word2
...	...

Description

Pops a long integer off of the stack, casts it into a double precision floating point number, and pushes the double back onto the stack. Notice that this can cause loss of precision (the significand in a double is 54 bits, compared to 64 bits for the long) though not loss of magnitude (since the range of a double is greater than the range of a long). Rounding is done using the IEEE 754 round-to-nearest mode.

Bytecode

Type	Description
u1	l2d opcode = 0x8A (138)

See Also

l2i, l2f

l2f convert long to float

Jasmin Syntax

```
l2f
```

Stack

Before	After
long-word1	float
long-word2	...
...	

Description

Pops a long integer off of the stack, casts it into a single precision floating point number, and pushes the single *float* back onto the stack. Notice that this can cause loss of precision (the significand in a float is 24 bits, compared to 64 bits for the long) though not loss of magnitude (since the range of a float is greater than the range of a long). Rounding is done using the IEEE 754 round-to-nearest mode.

Bytecode

Type	Description
u1	l2f opcode = 0x89 (137)

See Also

l2i, l2d

---

l2i long to integer conversion

Jasmin Syntax

```
l2i
```

Stack

Before	After
long-word1	integer
long-word2	...
...	

Description

Pops a long integer off of the stack, discards the most significant 32 bits, and pushes the low 32 bits onto the stack as an int. This may cause the magnitude or sign of the value to change.

Bytecode

Type	Description
u1	l2i opcode = 0x88 (136)

See Also

12f, 12d

ladd add two long integers

Jasmin Syntax

```
ladd
```

Stack

Before	After
value1-word1	result-word1
value1-word2	result-word2
value2-word1	...
value2-word2	
...	

Description

Pops two long integers from the operand stack, adds them and then pushes the result back onto the stack. On overflow, ladd produces a result whose low order bits are correct, but whose sign bit may be incorrect.

Bytecode

Type	Description
u1	ladd 0x61 (97)

See Also

iadd, fadd, dadd

laload retrieve long integer from array

Jasmin Syntax

```
laload
```

Stack

Before	After
index	value-word1
arrayrefref	value-word2
...	...

Description

Retrieves a long integer from a long integer array and places it on the stack. *arrayref* is a reference to an array of long integers. *index* is an int. The *arrayref* and *index* are removed from the stack, and the long integer entry at the given *index* in the array is pushed onto the stack.

Example

```
; This is like the Java code:
;     long x = arr[0];
; where x is local variable 2 and arr is an array of longs in local variable 1
aload_1       ; load local variable 1 onto the stack
iconst_0      ; push the integer 0 onto the stack
laload        ; retrieve the entry
lstore_2      ; store the entry in local variables 2 and 3
```

Exceptions

- NullPointerException—*arrayref* is null
- ArrayIndexOutOfBoundsException—*index* is < *0 or* >= *arrayref.length*

Bytecode

Type	Description
u1	laload opcode = 0x2F (47)

See Also

iaload, faload, daload, aaload, baload, caload, saload, iastore, lastore, fastore, dastore, aastore, bastore, castore, sastore

land long integer bitwise and

Jasmin Syntax

```
land
```

Stack

Before	After
value1-word1	result-word1
value1-word2	result-word2
value2-word1	...
value2-word2	
...	

Description

Pops two long integers off the stack. Computes the bitwise and of *value1* and *value2*. The long integer result replaces *value1* and *value2* on the stack.

Example

```
; This is like the Java code:
;       long x;
;       x &= 1;
;
lload_1             ; push the long integer in local variable 1
lconst_1            ; push the integer 1 onto the stack
land                ; compute the bitwise and
lstore_1            ; store the long result in local variable 1
```

Bytecode

Type	Description
u1	land opcode = 0x7F (127)

See Also

ishl, ishr, iushr, lshl, lshr, lushr, iand, ior, lor, ixor, lxor

lastore store in long integer array

Jasmin Syntax

```
lastore
```

Stack

Before	After
value-word1	...
value-word2	
index	
arrayref	
...	

Description

Takes a two-word long integer from the stack and stores it in an array of long integers. *arrayref* is a reference to an array of long integers. *index* is an int. *value* is the long integer value to be stored in the array. *arrayref, index* and *value* are removed from the stack, and *value* is stored in the array at the given *index*.

Exceptions

* NullPointerException—*arrayref* is null
* ArrayIndexOutOfBoundsException—*index* is < *0* or >= *arrayref.length*

Bytecode

Type	Description
u1	lastore opcode = 0x50 (80)

See Also

iastore, fastore, dastore, aastore, bastore, castore, sastore, iaload, laload, faload, daload, aaload, baload, caload, saload

lcmp long integer comparison

Jasmin Syntax

    lcmp

Stack

Before	After
value1-word1	int-result
value1-word2	...
value2-word1	
value2-word2	
...	

Description

Takes two two-word long integers off the stack and compares them. If the two integers are the same, the int 0 is pushed onto the stack. If *value2* is greater than *value1*, the int 1 is pushed onto the stack. If *value1* is greater than *value2*, the int −1 is pushed onto the stack.

Example

```
; This is like the Java expression:
;      (x > 0)
; where x is a long.

lload_1        ; push the long int in local variable 1
lconst_0       ; push the long integer 0 onto the stack
lcmp           ; compare the two long integers

; The integer result on the stack is:
;      0 if local variable 1 equals 0
;      -1 if local variable 1 is less than 0
;      1 if local variable 1 is greater than 0
```

Bytecode

Type	Description
u1	lcmp opcode = 0x94 (148)

See Also

fcmpl, fcmpg, dcmpl, dcmpg

lconst_<l> push the long integer 0 or 1

Jasmin Syntax

```
      lconst_0
 or
      lconst_1
```

Stack

Before	After
...	\<l>-word1
	\<l>-word2
	...

Description

Represents the two opcodes lconst_0, lconst_1 that are used to push the constant long integers 0 and 1 onto the stack. For example, to push the long integer zero onto the stack, use:

```
  lconst_0 ; push long integer 0 onto the stack
```

Note that you could also use:

```
  ldc2_w 0    ; push the long integer 0 onto the stack
```

although this instruction takes more space in the class file and is also slower.

Example

```
  lconst_0    ; push the long int 0 onto the stack
  lconst_1    ; push the long int 1 onto the stack
```

Bytecode

Type	Description
u1	lconst_0 opcode = 0x09 (9)
u1	lconst_1 opcode = 0x0A (10)

See Also

bipush, sipush, ldc, ldc_w, ldc2_w, aconst_null, iconst_m1, iconst_<n>, fconst_<f>, dconst_<d>

---

ldc push single-word constant onto stack

Jasmin Syntax

```
ldc <value>
```

<value> is an int, a float, or a quoted (i.e., literal) string.

Stack

Before	After
...	<value>
	...

Description

Pushes a one-word constant onto the operand stack. ldc takes a single parameter, *<value>*, which is the value to push. The following Java types can be pushed using ldc:

- int
- float
- String

Pushing a String causes a reference to a java.lang.String object to be constructed and pushed onto the operand stack. Pushing an int or a float causes a primitive value to be pushed onto the stack.

Example

```
ldc "Hello World"    ; push string "Hello World" onto stack
ldc 10               ; push the integer 10
ldc 1.54             ; push the single-precision float 1.54
```

Exceptions

- OutOfMemoryError—not enough memory to allocate a reference to a String

Bytecode

In bytecode, the `ldc` opcode is followed by an 8-bit unsigned integer. This integer is the index of an entry in the constant pool of the current class. The entry is tagged as a CONSTANT_Integer, a CONSTANT_Float or a CONSTANT_String entry. The data field of the entry contains *<value>* (in the case of a CONSTANT_String, the entry identifies a CONSTANT_Utf8 entry that contains the characters of the string).

Type	Description
u1	ldc opcode = 0x12 (18)
u1	index

See Also

bipush, sipush, ldc_w, ldc2_w, aconst_null, iconst_m1, iconst_*<n>*, lconst_*<1>*, fconst_*<f>*, dconst_*<d>*

Notes

1. Where possible, it's more efficient to use one of `bipush`, `sipush`, or one of the const instructions instead of `ldc`.
2. If the same string constant (i.e., a string with the same sequence of characters) appears in several different class files, only one String instance is built for that constant. The String.intern() method can be used to retrieve the instance used for a given sequence of characters.

ldc2_w push two-word constant onto stack

Jasmin Syntax

```
ldc2_w <value>
```

<value> is a long integer or a double-precision floating-point number.

Stack

Before	After
...	<value>-word1
	<value>-word2
	...

Description

Pushes a two-word constant value onto the operand stack. ldc2_w takes a single parameter, *<value>*, which is the two-word item to push. The following Java types can be pushed using ldc2_w:

*   long
*   double

Example

```
ldc2_w 10        ; push the long integer 10
ldc2_w 1.54      ; push the double precision float 1.54
```

Bytecode

In bytecode, the ldc2_w opcode is followed by a 16-bit unsigned integer. This integer is the index of an entry in the constant pool. The entry is tagged either as a CONSTANT_Double or a CONSTANT_Long entry, and has a data field which contains *<value>*.

Type	Description
u1	ldc2_w opcode = 0x14 (20)
u2	index

See Also

bipush, sipush, ldc, ldc_w, aconst_null, iconst_m1, iconst_<n>, lconst_<l>, fconst_<f>, dconst_<d>

---

ldc_w push single-word constant onto stack (wide index)

Jasmin Syntax

```
ldc_w <value>
```

<value> is an int, a float, or a quoted string.

Stack

Before	After
...	<value>
	...

Description

Pushes a one-word constant onto the operand stack. ldc_w takes a single parameter, <value>, which is the value to push. The following Java types can be pushed using ldc_w:

- int
- float
- String

Pushing a String causes a reference to a java.lang.String object to be constructed and pushed onto the stack. Pushing an int or a float causes a primitive value to be pushed onto the stack.

ldc_w is identical to ldc except that, in bytecode, ldc_w uses a 16-bit index rather than an 8-bit index.

Exceptions

- OutOfMemoryError—not enough memory to allocate a reference to a String

Bytecode

In bytecode, the ldc_w opcode is followed by a 16-bit unsigned integer. This integer is the index of an entry in the constant pool of the current class. The entry is tagged as a CONSTANT_Integer, a CONSTANT_Float or a CONSTANT_String entry. The data field of the entry contains <value> (in the case of a CONSTANT_String, the entry identifies a CONSTANT_Utf8 entry that contains the characters of the string).

Type	Description
u1	ldc_w opcode = 0x13 (19)
u2	index

See Also

bipush, sipush, ldc, ldc2_w, aconst_null, iconst_m1, iconst_<n>, lconst_<l>, fconst_<f>, dconst_<d>

Notes

1. Where possible, it's more efficient to use one of bipush, sipush, or one of the const instructions instead of ldc_w.
2. If the same string constant (i.e., a string with the same sequence of characters) appears in several different class files, only one String instance is built for that constant. The String.intern() method can be used to retrieve the instance used for a given sequence of characters.

3. The Jasmin assembler automatically determines whether to use `ldc` or `ldc_w`, so in Jasmin assembly files these two instructions are synonymous.

ldiv divide a long integer

Jasmin Syntax

```
ldiv
```

Stack

Before	After
value1-word1	result-word1
value1-word2	result-word2
value2-word1	...
value2-word2	
...	

Description

Pops the top two two-word long integers from the stack and divides by the top long integer (i.e., computes *value2 / value1*). The result is rounded to the nearest integer, with rounding going towards 0. The long integer quotient result is pushed back onto the stack.

Exceptions

*   ArithmeticException—the divisor (*value2*) is zero

Bytecode

Type	Description
u1	ldiv opcode = 0x6D (109)

See Also

idiv, fdiv, ddiv

Notes

Because of the two's-complement representation used for negative numbers, dividing Long.MIN_VALUE by −1 produces Long.MIN_VALUE, not Long.MAX_VALUE as you might expect.

---

lload retrieve long from local variable

Jasmin Syntax

```
      lload <varnum>
  or
      wide
      lload <varnum>
```

In the first form, <*varnum*> is an unsigned integer in the range 0 to 0xFF. In the second (wide) form, <*varnum*> is an unsigned integer in the range 0 to 0xFFFE.

Stack

Before	After
...	result-word1
	result-word2
	...

Description

Retrieves a long integer held in a local variable and pushes it onto the operand stack.

Since long integers are 64-bits wide, and each local variable only holds up to 32 bits, Java uses two consecutive local variables, <*varnum*> and <*varnum*> + 1 to store a long. So lload <*varnum*> actually places the values of both <*varnum*> and <*varnum*> + 1 onto the operand stack.

Both <*varnum*> and <*varnum*> + 1 must be valid local variable numbers in the current frame, and together they must be holding a long.

Example

```
      lconst_1       ; push the long integer 1 onto the stack
      lstore 3       ; pop 1 off of the stack and store in local variables 3 and 4
      lload 3        ; push the value from local variables 3 and 4 (the long integer 1)
                     ; back onto the stack
```

Bytecode

For local variable numbers in the range 0-255, use:

Type	Description
u1	lload opcode = 0x16 (22)
u1	<varnum>

There is also a `wide` format for this instruction, which supports access to all local variables from 0 to 65534:

Type	Description
u1	wide opcode = 0xC4 (196)
u1	lload opcode = 0x16 (22)
u2	<varnum>

See Also

fload, iload, dload

---

lload_<n> retrieve long integer from local variables <n> and <n> + 1

Jasmin Syntax

```
    lload_0
or
    lload_1
or
    lload_2
or
    lload_3
```

Stack

Before	After
...	result-word1
	result-word2
	...

Description

Retrieves the two-word long integer stored in local variables <n> and <n> + 1 and pushes it onto the operand stack. Both <n> and <n> + 1 must be valid local variable numbers in the current frame, and together they must be holding a long.

See the description of lload for more information on how longs are retrieved from local variables.

"lload_<n>" is functionally equivalent to "lload <n>", although it is typically more efficient and also takes fewer bytes in the bytecode.

Example

```
lload_0          ;push long integer in local variable 0 and 1 onto stack
lload_1          ;push long integer in local variable 1 and 2 onto stack
lload_2          ;push long integer in local variable 2 and 3 onto stack
lload_3          ;push long integer in local variable 3 and 4 onto stack
```

Bytecode

Type	Description
u1	lload_0 opcode = 0x1E (30)
u1	lload_1 opcode = 0x1F (31)
u1	lload_2 opcode = 0x20 (32)
u1	lload_3 opcode = 0x21 (33)

See Also

fload, iload, dload

lmul multiply two longs

Jasmin Syntax

```
lmul
```

Stack

Before	After
value1-word1	result-word1
value1-word2	result-word2
value2-word1	...

Before	After
value2-word2	
...	

Description

Pops the top two long integers from the operand stack, multiplies them, and then pushes the long integer result back onto the stack. On overflow, lmul produces a result whose low order bits are correct, but whose sign bit may be incorrect.

Bytecode

Type	Description
u1	lmul opcode = 0x69 (105)

See Also

imul, fmul, dmul

lneg negate a long

Jasmin Syntax

```
lneg
```

Stack

Before	After
value-word1	result-word1
value-word2	result-word2
...	...

Description

Removes the top long integer from the operand stack, negates it, and pushes the negated result back onto the stack. This is the same as multiplying the long integer by −1, which is the same as (˜value) + 1.

Bytecode

Type	Description
u1	lneg opcode = 0x75 (117)

See Also

ineg, fneg, dneg

Notes

Because of the two's-complement representation used for negative numbers, negating Long.MIN_VALUE actually produces Long.MIN_VALUE, not Long.MAX_VALUE as you might expect.

lookupswitch   match key in table and jump

Jasmin Syntax

```
lookupswitch
    <key1>    : <label1>
    <key2>    : <label2>
    ...
    <keyN>    : <labelN>
    default : <labelDefault>
```

<key1>, <key2> etc. are 32-bit integers. <label1>, <label2>, etc. are label names.

To define the location of the label, use the <label> name followed by a colon:

```
<label>:
```

then becomes associated the address of the following instruction. Labels can only be assigned one location in a method. On the other hand, a single <label> can be the target of multiple branch instructions.

Stack

Before	After
item	...
...	

Description

Performs an efficient compare-and-jump, as might be needed for a switch statement. The table used by lookupswitch is given after the lookupswitch opcode in bytecode.

lookupswitch works as follows. First, an int, *item*, is taken from the top of the stack. Then, lookupswitch searches the table looking for an entry whose *<key>* field matches *item*. If a match is found, execution branches to the address of the corresponding *<label>*. If no match is found, execution branches to *<labelDefault>*.

Example

```
; this is like the Java code:
;       switch (i) {
;              case 1:     return(10);
;              case 10:    return(100);
;              default:    return(0);
;       }
    iload_1    ; push local variable 1 onto the stack (i.e., i)

    ; switch based on the value on the stack
    lookupswitch
        1       : Label1
        10      : Label2
        default : Dlabel
Label1:                 ; local variable 1 holds the value 1
    bipush 10
    ireturn    ; return 10

Label2:                 ; local variable 1 holds the value 10
    bipush 100
    ireturn    ; return 100

Dlabel:                 ; local variable 1 holds something else
    bipush 0
    return     ; return 0
```

Bytecode

lookupswitch is a variable length instruction. After the lookupswitch opcode, between 0 to 3 bytes of padding zeros are inserted, so that the *default_offset* parameter starts at an offset in the bytecode which is a multiple of 4. Next, a 32-bit int n >= 0 is given, indicating the number of key/value integer pairs in the table. This is followed by n pairs of ints. For each pair, the first 32-bit int value is the key, and the second 32-bit int value is the relative offset to jump to if that key is matched. (the offset is relative to the address of the lookupswitch instruction in bytecode).

Type	Description
u1	lookupswitch opcode = 0xAB (171)
-	...0-3 bytes of padding ...
s4	default_offset
s4	n
s4	key_1
s4	offset_1
s4	key_2
s4	offset_2
...	...
s4	key_n
s4	offset_n

See Also

tableswitch

Notes

1. Addresses are measured in bytes from the start of the bytecode (i.e., address 0 is the first byte in the bytecode of the currently executing method).
2. Addresses given in the table are relative—the values in the table are added to the current pc (i.e., the address of this lookupswitch instruction) to obtain the new value for pc.
3. Keys in the table must be sorted in increasing order, so <*key1*> is less than <*key2*>, and so on up to <*keyN*>. Jasmin performs this sorting automatically.
4. Even though offsets in the table are given as 32-bit ints, the maximum address in a Java method is limited by other factors to 65535.

lor long integer bitwise or

Jasmin Syntax

```
lor
```

Stack

Before	After
value1-word1	result-word1
value1-word2	result-word2
value2-word1	...
value2-word2	
...	

Description

Pops two long integers off the stack. Computes the bitwise or of *value1* and *value2*. The long integer result replaces *value1* and *value2* on the stack.

Example

```
; This is like the Java code:
;       long x;
;       x |= 1;
;
lload_1            ; load long integer in local variable 1 onto stack
lconst_1           ; push the integer 1 onto the stack
lor                ; compute the bitwise or
lstore_1           ; store the long result in local variable 1
```

Bytecode

Type	Description
u1	lor opcode = 0x81 (129)

See Also

ishl, ishr, iushr, lshl, lshr, lushr, iand, land, ior, ixor, lxor

---

lrem modulus of two longs

Jasmin Syntax

```
lrem
```

Stack

Before	After
value1-word1	result-word1
value1-word2	result-word2
value2-word1	...
value2-word2	
...	

Description

Pops two long integers off the operand stack, divides *value2* by *value1*, computes the remainder and pushes the long integer remainder back onto the stack. The remainder is (value2 − ((value1/value2) * value2)). This is used by the % operator in Java.

Exceptions

*   ArithmeticException—the divisor (*value1*) is zero

Bytecode

Type	Description
u1	lrem opcode = 0x71 (113)

See Also

irem, frem, drem

---

lreturn return from method with long result

Jasmin Syntax

```
lreturn
```

Stack

Before	After
value-word1	n/a
value-word2	...
...	

Description

Pops a two-word long integer from the top of the stack and pushes it onto the operand stack of the invoker (i.e., the method which used invokevirtual, invoke-special, invokestatic or invokeinterface to call the currently executing method). All other items on the current method's operand stack are discarded. If the current method is marked as synchronized, then an implicit monitorexit instruction is executed. Then the current method's frame is discarded, the invoker's frame is reinstated, and control returns to the invoker. This instruction can only be used in methods whose return type is long.

Bytecode

Type	Description
u1	lreturn opcode = 0xAD (173)

See Also

ireturn, freturn, dreturn, areturn, return

lshl long integer shift left

Jasmin Syntax

    lshl

Stack

Before	After
value1	result-word1
value2-word1	result-word2
value2-word2	...
...	

Description

Pops a long integer and an int from the stack. Shifts *value2* (the long integer) left by the amount indicated in the low six bits of *value1* (an int). The long integer result is then pushed back onto the stack.

This is the same as computing the expression:

$x * 2^s$

where s is value1 and x is value2.

Example

```
; This is like the Java code:
;       long x;
;       x <<= 3;
;
lload_1            ; load long integer in local variable 1 onto stack
iconst_3           ; push the integer 3 onto the stack
lshl               ; shift left
lstore_1           ; store the long result in local variable 1
```

Bytecode

Type	Description
u1	lshl opcode = 0x79 (121)

See Also

ishl, ishr, iushr, lshr, lushr, iand, land, ior, lor, ixor, lxor

lshr long integer arithmetic shift right

Jasmin Syntax

```
lshr
```

Stack

Before	After
value1	result-word1
value2-word1	result-word2
value2-word2	...
...	

Description

Pops an int and a long integer from the stack. Shifts *value2* (the long integer) right by the amount indicated in the low six bits of *value1* (an int). The long integer result is then pushed back onto the stack. The value is shifted arithmetically (preserving the sign extension).

This is the same as computing the expression:

x / 2^s

where s is value1 and x is value2.

Example

```
; This is like the Java code:
;       long x;
;       x >>= 3;
;
lload_1             ; load long in local variable 1 onto stack
iconst_3            ; push the integer 3 onto the stack
lshr                ; arithmetic shift right
lstore_1            ; store the long result in local variable 1
```

Bytecode

Type	Description
u1	lshr opcode = 0x7B (123)

See Also

ishl, ishr, iushr, lshl, lushr, iand, land, ior, lor, ixor, lxor

---

lstore store long integer in local variable

Jasmin Syntax

```
      lstore <varnum>
  or
      wide
      lstore <varnum>
```

In the first form, <*varnum*> is an unsigned integer in the range 0 to 0xFF. In the second (wide) form, <*varnum*> is an unsigned integer in the range 0 to 0xFFFE.

Stack

Before	After
long-word1	...
long-word2	
...	

Description

Pops a two-word long integer off the operand stack and stores it in a local variable. It takes a single parameter, <*varnum*>, an unsigned integer indicating which local variable to use.

Since long integers are 64-bits wide, and each local variable can only hold up to 32 bits Java uses two consecutive local variables, <*varnum*> and <*varnum*> + 1 to store a long. So lstore <*varnum*> actually modifies the values of both <*varnum*> (which is set to *long-word1*) and <*varnum*> + 1 (which is set to *long-word2).*

Both <*varnum*> and <*varnum*> + 1 must be valid local variable numbers in the current frame, and together they must be holding a long.

Example

```
ldc2_w 10        ; push the long integer 10 onto the stack
lstore 3         ; pop 10 off of the stack and store it in local variables 3 and 4
```

Bytecode

For local variable numbers in the range 0-255, use:

Type	Description
u1	lstore opcode = 0x37 (55)
u1	<varnum>

There is also a wide format for this instruction, which supports access to all local variables from 0 to 65534:

Type	Description
u1	wide opcode = 0xC4 (196)
u1	lstore opcode = 0x37 (55)
u2	<varnum>

See Also

istore, fstore, dstore, astore, wide

lstore_<n> store long in local variables *<n>* and *<n>* + 1

Jasmin Syntax

```
    lstore_0
or
    lstore_1
or
    lstore_2
or
    lstore_3
```

Stack

Before	After
value-word1	...
value-word2	
...	

Description

Retrieves the long integer stored in local variables *<n>* and *<n>* + 1 and pushes it onto the operand stack. Both *<n>* and *<n>* + 1 must be valid local variable numbers in the current frame, and together they must be holding a long.

See the description of lstore for more information on how doubles are retrieved from local variables.

"lstore_*<n>*" is functionally equivalent to "lstore *<n>*", although it is typically more efficient and also takes fewer bytes in the bytecode.

Example

```
    lstore_0        ;store long in local variable 0 and 1
    lstore_1        ;store long in local variable 1 and 2
    lstore_2        ;store long in local variable 2 and 3
    lstore_3        ;store long in local variable 3 and 4
```

Bytecode

Type	Description
u1	lstore_0 opcode = 0x3F (63)
u1	lstore_1 opcode = 0x40 (64)
u1	lstore_2 opcode = 0x41 (65)
u1	lstore_3 opcode = 0x42 (66)

See Also

astore, istore, dstore, fstore

lsub subtract two longs

Jasmin Syntax

```
lsub
```

Stack

Before	After
value1-word1	result-word1
value1-word2	result-word2
value2-word1	...
value2-word2	
...	

Description

Pops two long integers from the stack, subtracts the top one from the second (i.e., computes *value2 – value1*), and pushes the result back onto the stack.

Bytecode

Type	Description
u1	lsub opcode = 0x65 (101)

See Also

isub, fsub, dsub

---

lushr long integer logical shift right

Jasmin Syntax

```
lushr
```

Stack

Before	After
value1	result-word1
value2-word1	result-word2
value2-word2	...
...	

Description

Pops an integer and a long integer and from the stack. Shifts *value2* (the long integer) right by the amount indicated in the low six bits of *value1* (an int). The long integer result is then pushed back onto the stack. The value is shifted logically (ignoring the sign extension—useful for unsigned values).

Example

```
; This is like the Java code:
;       long x;
;       x >>>= 3;
;
lload_1          ; load long in local variable 1 onto stack
iconst_3         ; push the integer 3 onto the stack
lushr            ; logical shift right
lstore_1         ; store the long result in local variable 1
```

Bytecode

Type	Description
u1	lushr opcode = 0x7D (125)

See Also

ishl, ishr, iushr, lshl, lshr, iand, land, ior, lor, ixor, lxor

lxor long integer bitwise exclusive or

Jasmin Syntax

```
lxor
```

Stack

Before	After
value1-word1	result-word1
value1-word2	result-word2
value2-word1	...
value2-word2	
...	

Description

Pops two long integers off the stack. Computes the bitwise exclusive or of *value1* and *value2*. The long integer result replaces *value1* and *value2* on the stack.

Example

```
; This is like the Java code:
;       long x;
;       x ^= 1;
;
lload_1          ; load long in local variable 1 onto stack
lconst_1         ; push the integer 1 onto the stack
lxor             ; compute the bitwise exclusive or
lstore_1         ; store the long result in local variable 1
```

Bytecode

Type	Description
u1	lxor opcode = 0x83 (131)

See Also

ishl, ishr, iushr, lshl, lshr, lushr, iand, land, ior, lor, ixor

---

monitorenter   enter synchronized region of code

Jasmin Syntax

```
monitorenter
```

Stack

Before	After
objectref	...
...	

Description

Coordinates access to an object among multiple threads when used by the Java synchronized statement. For example, when you write in Java code:

```
static void Sort(int [] array) {
    // synchronize this operation so that some other thread can't
    // manipulate the array while we are sorting it. This assumes that other
    // threads also synchronize their accesses to the array.
    synchronized(array) {
        // now sort elements in array
    }
}
```

then JVM code like the following is generated:

```
.method static Sort([I)V
    aload_0
    monitorenter     ; lock object in local variable 0

    ; now sort elements in array

    aload_0
    monitorexit      ; finished with object in local variable 0
    return
.end method
```

monitorenter obtains an exclusive lock on the object referenced by *objectref*. There are three possible scenarios.

1. If no other thread has locked the object, a new lock is established on the object, and execution continues at the next instruction.
2. If the object is currently locked by another thread, monitorenter blocks, waiting for the other thread to unlock the object.
3. If the current thread already owns a lock on the object, a counter is incremented —the lock will only be released when the counter returns to zero (see monitorexit).

Exceptions

*   NullPointerException—the object reference on the stack is null

Bytecode

Type	Description
u1	monitorenter opcode = 0xC2 (194)

See Also

*   monitorexit
*   The Java Language Specification provides a full account of how locks and threads are managed.

Notes

1. Methods which are marked as synchronized implicitly perform a monitorenter when invoked, and a monitorexit when they return.
2. Java's wait(), notify() and notifyAll() methods also interact with locks on objects.

monitorexit leave synchronized region of code

Jasmin Syntax

```
monitorexit
```

Stack

Before	After
objectref	...
...	

Description

Releases an exclusive lock that was previously obtained using monitorenter for the object *objectref.* If other threads are waiting for the object to become unlocked, one of the waiting threads will be able to acquire a lock on the object and proceed.

Note that a single thread can lock an object several times—the runtime system maintains a count of the number of times that the object was locked by the current thread, and only unlocks the object when the counter reaches zero (i.e., when the number of monitorenters and monitorexits applied to a given object are equal).

The monitorenter/monitorexit mechanism is used by the Java synchronized statement to coordinate access to an object among multiple threads.

Exceptions

*   NullPointerException—*objectref* is null
*   IllegalMonitorStateException—*objectref* was not previously locked by the current thread

Bytecode

Type	Description
u1	monitorexit opcode = 0xC3 (195)

See Also

monitorenter

---

multianewarray allocate multi-dimensional array

Jasmin Syntax

```
multianewarray <type> <n>
```

<type> is the type descriptor of the array, e.g., for an array holding arrays of integers <type> is [[I. <n> is an integer in the range 1–255.

Stack

Before	After
sizeN	arrayref
—	...
size3	

Before	After
size2	
size1	
...	

Description

Allocates a multi-dimensional array. In Java, a multi-dimensional array is structured as an array of arrays, i.e., an array whose elements are references to array objects. So constructing an array like:

```
new int [3][2]
```

produces a structure in memory like:

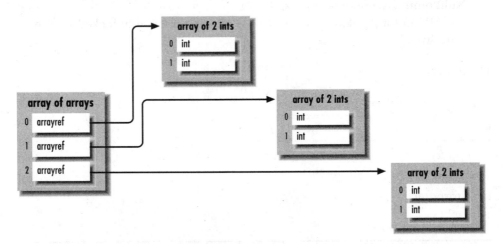

In this particular example the top level array is an array containing three 32-bit references. Each of these references identifies a two-element int array.

The same general approach applies to higher dimension arrays. For example, a three-dimensional array is structured as a top level array of arrayrefs, each of which refers to an array of arrayrefs, each of which refers to an array of items.

The lengths of each array within the multi-dimensional array are given as positive ints on the operand stack. The number of ints taken from the stack is specified by the unsigned byte parameter <n>. The type of the array is given as an array type descriptor by the <type> parameter.

The <type> is first resolved to a Java class (see Chapter 4 for a description of how array type descriptors are resolved). multianewarray then allocates the first <n> dimensions of a multidimensional array from the heap. If <n> is one, only the top-level array is created.

So the statement:

```
new int [3][]
```

generates JVM code like:

```
bipush 3
multianewarray [[I 1      ; construct first dimension of the 2-D array
```

in this case only the three-element top-level array is created.

To construct both the top-level array and its sub-arrays, e.g., to fully construct

```
new int [3][2]
```

use the JVM code:

```
bipush 3
bipush 2
multianewarray [[I 2      ; construct both dimensions of the 2-D array
```

Here the second parameter given to multianewarray is 2, so the first and second dimensions are created (i.e., the top-level array and the array objects within the top-level array).

<n> must be less than or equal to the dimensionality given in the array's descriptor—i.e., it must be less than or equal to the number of "[" characters at the start of <type>.

The elements within the array are initialized to zero (for numeric and boolean arrays), or null for arrays of references. multianewarray leaves a reference to the newly constructed array on the operand stack.

Example

```
; to allocate an array like:
;     new String[2][5]

    bipush 2
    bipush 5
    multianewarray [[Ljava/lang/String; 2    ; construct both dimensions
    ; stack now hold a reference two the new two dimensional array.

;
; multianewarray can be used to allocate only some of the
; dimensions of an array. For example, you write:
;
;     x = new int[6][3][]
;
; using:

    bipush 6
    bipush 3
```

```
    multianewarray [[[I 2   ; allocate 2 of the 3 dimensions
    astore_1                ; store array in local variable 1

; then you can create the final dimensions later using
; newarray or anewarray. e.g.,
;
;    x[0][1] = new int[50];
;
; would be:

    aload_1            ; push the array
    iconst_0
    aaload             ; get x[0] - an array of arrays of ints

    iconst_1
    bipush 50
    newarray int       ; allocate an array of 50 ints
    aastore            ; store this in x[0][1]

;
; You can also use multianewarray to create
; single-dimensional arrays. e.g.,

    bipush 50
    multianewarray [Ljava/lang/Thread; 1

; is the same as writing:

    bipush 50
    anewarray java/lang/Thread

; except that the latter is more efficient.
```

Exceptions

- NegativeArraySizeException - size is less than zero
- OutOfMemoryError - insufficient memory to allocate the array

Bytecode

In bytecode, after the multianewarray opcode is a 16-bit unsigned integer *index*. This is the index of an entry in the constant pool of the current class. The entry at that index is tagged a CONSTANT_Class entry. The name field of the entry is a string containing the characters given by <*type*> in Jasmin.

After the index is a single unsigned byte, <*n*>, the number of dimensions of the array to allocate.

Type	Description
u1	multianewarray opcode = 0xC5 (197)
u2	index
u1	<n>

See Also

newarray, anewarray, new.

Notes

You can use multianewarray to allocate single-dimension arrays, though using anewarray or newarray is more efficient.

new create an object

Jasmin Syntax

```
new <class>
```

<class> is the name of the class to use, e.g., java/lang/String.

Stack

Before	After
...	objectref
	...

Description

Creates object instances.

new takes a single parameter, <class>, the name of the class of object you want to create. <class> is resolved into a Java class (see Chapter 4 for a discussion of how classes are resolved). Then new determines the size in bytes of instances of the given class and allocates memory for the new instance from the garbage collected heap. The fields of the instance are set to the initial value 0 (for numeric and boolean fields), or null (for reference fields). Next, a reference to the new object is pushed onto the operand stack.

Note that the new object is uninitialized—before the new object can be used, one of its <init> methods must be called using invokespecial, as shown in the example below.

Example

```
; This example creates a new StringBuffer object. This is like the Java code:
;
;     StringBuffer x = new StringBuffer();

; 1. use new to create a new object reference
new java/lang/StringBuffer

; 2. dup the object reference and call its constructor
dup
invokespecial java/lang/StringBuffer/<init>()V

; 3. assign object reference on the stack to a local variable
astore_1
; local variable 1 now contains a StringBuffer object,
; ready for use


; the following example shows how to call a non-default
; constructor. It is like the Java code:
;
;     StringBuffer x = new StringBuffer(100);
new java/lang/StringBuffer
dup
bipush 100
invokespecial java/lang/StringBuffer/<init>(I)V
astore_1
```

Exceptions

- OutOfMemoryError—not enough memory to allocate a new instance
- InstantiationError—The class named by `<type>` is an abstract class or an interface

Bytecode

In bytecode, after the new opcode is a 16-bit unsigned integer *index*. This integer is the index of an entry in the constant pool of the current class. The entry is tagged a CONSTANT_Class entry (see Chapter 4). The name field of the entry is a string given by the `<type>` parameter in Jasmin.

Type	Description
u1	new opcode = 0xBB (187)
u2	index

See Also

anewarray, newarray, multianewarray

newarray allocate new array for numbers or booleans

Jasmin Syntax

```
newarray <type>
```

where `<type>` is one of: boolean, char, float, double, byte, short, int or long.

Stack

Before	After
n	arrayref
...	...

Description

Allocates single-dimension arrays of booleans, chars, floats, doubles, bytes, shorts, ints or longs. For example, when you write the Java code:

```
new int[10];
```

this is compiled into:

```
bipush 10          ; push the int 10 onto the stack
newarray int       ; make an array of 10 ints. The new array is left on the stack
```

newarray pops a positive int, n, off the stack, and constructs an array for holding n elements of the type given by `<type>`. Initially the elements in the array are set to zero. A reference to the new array object is left on the stack.

Example

```
; This is like the Java code:
;     short x[] = new short[2];

iconst_2           ; push 2 onto the stack
newarray short     ; call newarray to make a 2-element short array
astore_1           ; store the reference to the array in local variable 1
```

Exceptions

- NegativeArraySizeException—n is less than zero
- OutOfMemoryError—insufficient memory to allocate the array

Bytecode

Type	Description
u1	newarray opcode = 0xBC (188)
u1	array-type (see below)

In bytecode, the type of the array is specified by the array-type byte immediately following the newarray opcode, which has one of the following values:

Array Type	Value
boolean	4
char	5
float	6
double	7
byte	8
short	9
int	10
long	11

See Also

anewarray, multianewarray, new

Notes

The Java boolean **false** is represented in the JVM by the integer 0; **true** is represented by the integer 1. Boolean arrays are actually treated as byte arrays and are initialized to false (0). You should use the baload and bastore instructions to load and store values in boolean arrays.

nop do nothing

Jasmin Syntax

```
nop
```

Stack

Before	After
...	...

Description

Has no effect—compilers sometimes generate nop's for debugging, testing or timing purposes.

Example

```
nop              ; do nothing
```

Bytecode

Type	Description
u1	nop opcode = 0x0 (0)

pop discard top word on stack

Jasmin Syntax

```
pop
```

Stack

Before	After
item	...
...	

Description

Pops the top single-word item off the stack and discards it.

Example

```
invokevirtual Myclass/test()Z  ; call boolean Myclass.test();
pop                            ; discard the boolean result
```

Bytecode

Type	Description
u1	pop opcode = 0x57 (87)

See Also

pop2

Notes

1. Use pop2 to remove long integers and doubles from the stack (using pop when the top item on the stack is a long integer or double will cause a verification error).
2. Note there is no matching "push" instruction. Use bipush or sipush.

pop2 discard top two words on stack

Jasmin Syntax

```
pop2
```

Stack

Before	After
item1	...
item2	
...	

Description

Removes two single-word items from the stack (e.g., two integers, or an integer and an object reference) or one two-word item (i.e., a double or a long).

Example

```
invokemethod Myclass/foo()D    ; call double Myclass.foo();
pop2                           ; discard the double result
```

Bytecode

Type	Description
u1	pop2 opcode = 0x58 (88)

See Also

pop

---

putfield set value of object field

Jasmin Syntax

```
putfield <field-spec> <descriptor>
```

`<field-spec>` is composed of two parts, a *classname* and a *fieldname*. The *classname* is all of the characters in the `<field-spec>` up to the last "/" character, and the *fieldname* is the rest of the characters after the last "/". For example:

```
foo/baz/AnotherClass/aVeryLongFieldName
-- classname -------/-- fieldname -----
```

`<descriptor>` is the Java type descriptor for the field, for example `Ljava/io/PrintStream;`.

In Jasmin, the `.field` directive is used to add a field to a class. See Appendix C for a description of this and other Jasmin directives.

Stack

Before	After
value	...
objectref	
...	

or, for fields holding doubles or longs, see the following table.

Before	After
value-word1	...
value-word2	
objectref	
...	

Description

Sets the value of the field identified by *<field-spec>* in *objectref* (a reference to an object) to the single or double word value on the operand stack. For example, if you have the class:

```
package xyz;
class Point {
    public int xCoord, yCoord;
};
```

Then, assuming p is an instance of the class Point, writing the Java expression:

```
p.xCoord = 10;
```

generates JVM code like:

```
aload_1                    ; push object in local varable 1 (i.e., p) onto
                           ; the stack
bipush 10                  ; push the integer 10 onto the stack
putfield xyz/Point/xCoord I ; set the value of the integer field p.xCoord to 10
```

In Jasmin, putfield takes two parameters, *<field-spec>* and *<descriptor>*. *<field-spec>* provides *classname*, the name of the class that defines the field, as well as *fieldname*, the name of the field. In the example above, the *<field-spec>* is "xyz/Point/xCoord", indicating that the *classname* is called "xyz/Point" and the *fieldname* is "xCoord". *<descriptor>* indicates the type of data held in the field, and is a standard Java type descriptor (see Chapter 4). In the example above, *<descriptor>* is "I", since the field holds an integer.

putfield first resolves *classname* to a Java class. Then it locates *fieldname* in that class, determining the *size* of the field (in bytes) and its *offset* (in bytes) from the base of the object data. The type of the field must match *<descriptor>*. See Chapter 4 for a full discussion of how fields are resolved.

To set the value of the field, putfield pops either a 4-byte or 8-byte quantity off the stack (depending on the field descriptor), and truncates it to be *width* bytes long. Then it sets the bytes starting at *offset* and extending for *width* bytes in *objectref*'s instance data to the new value.

Exceptions

* NullPointerException—*objectref* is null

Bytecode

In bytecode, the putfield opcode is followed by a 16-bit unsigned integer *index*. This is the index of an entry in the constant pool of the current class. The entry is tagged a CONSTANT_Fieldref entry. The fieldref entry lists a CONSTANT_Class entry in the constant pool whose name is the *classname* given in `<field-spec>`, as well as a CONSTANT_NameAndType entry in the constant pool, whose name is the *fieldname* given in `<field-spec>`, and whose descriptor is the string given by `<descriptor>`.

Type	Description
u1	putfield opcode = 0xB5 (181)
u2	index

See Also

getfield, putstatic, getstatic

Notes

Fields cannot be overriden, although they can be 'shadowed'. For example, with the two classes:

```
class A {int x; }
```
and
```
class B extends A {int x; }
```

instances of B will have storage for both the field "A/x" and the field "B/x". Which field is accessed is determined by the class name given in `<field-spec>`.

---

putstatic set value of static field

Jasmin Syntax

```
putstatic <field-spec> <descriptor>
```

`<field-spec>` is composed of two parts, a *classname* and a *fieldname*. The *classname* is all of the characters in the `<field-spec>` up to the last "/" character, and the *fieldname* is the rest of the characters after the last "/".

For example:

```
foo/baz/AnotherClass/aVeryLongFieldName
-- classname -------/-- fieldname -----
```

<descriptor> is the Java type descriptor for the field, for example "Ljava/io/PrintStream;".

In Jasmin, the .field directive is used to add a field to a class. See Appendix C for a description of this and other Jasmin directives.

Stack

Before	After
value	...
...	

or, for static fields holding longs or doubles:

Before	After
value-word1	...
value-word2	
...	

Description

Sets the value of the static field (also known as a class field) identified by <field-spec> to the single or double word value on the operand stack. For example, when you write the Java expression:

```
java.lang.System.out = myStream;
```

this generates a call to getstatic like:

```
aload_1     ; push object reference in local variable 1 (i.e., myStream) onto stack
            ; now use putstatic to assign it to System.out
putstatic java/lang/System/out Ljava/io/PrintStream;
```

In Jasmin, putstatic takes two parameters, <field-spec> and <descriptor>. <field-spec> provides *classname*, the name of the class that defines the static field, as well *fieldname*, as the name of the field. In the example above, the <field-spec> is "java/lang/System/out", indicating that the *classname* is "java/lang/System" and the *fieldname* is "out". <descriptor> indicates the type of data held in the field, and is a standard Java type descriptor (see Chapter 4). In the example above, <descriptor> is "Ljava/io/PrintStream;", i.e., an instance of the PrintStream class.

putstatic first resolves *classname* into a Java class. Then it locates the *fieldname* in that class, determining the *width* of the field (in bytes) and its *offset* (in bytes) from the base of the class's static data. The type of the field must match `<descriptor>`. See Chapter 4 for more on how fields are resolved.

To set the value of the field, putstatic pops either a 4-byte or 8-byte quantity off the stack (depending on the field descriptor), and truncates it to be *wodth* bytes long. Then it sets the bytes starting at *offset* and extending for *width* bytes in the class's static data to the new value.

Bytecode

In bytecode, the putstatic opcode is followed by a 16-bit unsigned integer *index*. This is the index of an entry in the constant pool of the current class. The entry is tagged a CONSTANT_Fieldref entry. The fieldref entry lists a CONSTANT_Class entry in the constant pool whose name is the *classname* given in `<field-spec>`, as well as a CONSTANT_NameAndType entry in the constant pool, whose name is the *fieldname* given in `<field-spec>`, and whose descriptor is the string given by `<descriptor>`.

Typo	Doooription
u1	putstatic opcode = 0xB3 (179)
u2	index

See Also

putfield, getfield, getstatic

Notes

Fields cannot be overriden, although they can be 'shadowed'. For example, with the two classes:

```
    class A {static int X; }
  and
    class B extends A {static int X; }
```

then the runtime system will allocate storage for both the static field "A/X" and the static field "B/X". Which field is accessed is determined by the class name given in `<field-spec>`.

ret   return from subroutine

Jasmin Syntax

```
    ret <varnum>
or
    wide
    ret <varnum>
```

In the first form, `<varnum>` is an unsigned integer in the range 0 to 0xFF. In the second (wide) form, `<varnum>` is an unsigned integer in the range 0 to 0xFFFF.

Stack

Before	After
...	...

Description

Returns from a subroutine that was invoked by `jsr` or `jsr_w`. It takes a single 8parameter, `<varnum>`, an unsigned integer which local variable is holding the returnAddress for this subroutine. Execution continues at the address stored in that local variable.

Return addresses are left on the stack by the `jsr` and `jsr_w` instructions. Methods are expected to immediately store the return address in a local variable, ready for use with `ret`.

Example

```
; This example method uses a PrintMe subroutine to invoke the
; System.out.println() method.

.method usingSubroutine()V
    ldc "Message 1"
    jsr PrintMe          ; print "Message 1"

    ldc "Message 2"
    jsr PrintMe          ; print "Message 2"

    ldc "Message 3"
    jsr PrintMe          ; print "Message 3"

    return    ; now return from usingSubroutine

; define the PrintMe subroutine ...
PrintMe:
    astore_1             ; store return-address in local variable 1
```

```
    ; call System.out.println()
    getstatic java/lang/System/out Ljava/io/PrintStream;
    invokevirtual java/io/PrintStream/println(Ljava/lang/String;)V

    ret 1                   ; return to the return-address in local variable 1
.end method
```

Bytecode

For local variable numbers in the range 0-255, use:

Type	Description
u1	ret opcode = 0xA9 (169)
u1	<varnum>

There is also a **wide** format for this instruction, which supports access to all local variables from 0 to 65535:

Type	Description
u1	wide opcode = 0xC4 (196)
u1	ret opcode = 0xA9 (169)
u2	<varnum>

See Also

jsr, jsr_w, goto, goto_w, wide

Notes

The asymmetry between jsr (which pushes a returnAddress onto the stack) and ret (which gets the returnAddress from a local variable) is intentional—the byte-code verifier relies on this structure (see Chapter 5, *Security*) .

return return from method

Jasmin Syntax

```
return
```

Stack

Before	After
...	...

Description

Returns from a method whose return type is void.

All items on the current method's operand stack are discarded. If the current method is marked as synchronized, then an implicit monitorexit instruction is executed. Then the current method's frame is discarded, the invoker's frame is reinstated, and control returns to the invoker.

Example

```
; the following method takes no parameters, performs no actions,
; and returns no results.
.method identity()V
    return  ; simply return with no result
.end method
```

Bytecode

Type	Description
u1	return opcode = 0xB1 (177)

See Also

lreturn, freturn, dreturn, areturn, ireturn

saload retrieve short from array

Jasmin Syntax

```
saload
```

Stack

Before	After
index	value
arrayref	...
...	

Description

Retrieves a short from an array of shorts and places it on the stack. *arrayref* is a reference to an array of shorts. *index* is an int. The *arrayref* and *index* are removed from the stack, and the 16-bit signed short at the given *index* in the array is retrieved, sign-extended to an int, and pushed onto the stack.

Example

```
; This is like the Java code:
;       short x = arr[0];
; where x is local variable 2 and arr is
; an array in local variable 1
aload_1         ; load local variable 1 onto the stack
iconst_0        ; push the integer 0 onto the stack
saload          ; retrieve the entry
istore_2        ; store the entry in local variable 2
```

Exceptions

- NullPointerException—*arrayref* is null
- ArrayIndexOutOfBoundsException—*index* is < 0 or >= *arrayref.length*

Bytecode

Type	Description
u1	saload opcode = 0x35 (53)

See Also

iaload, laload, faload, daload, aaload, baload, caload, iastore, lastore, fastore, dastore, aastore, bastore, castore, sastore

---

sastore store in short array

Jasmin Syntax

```
sastore
```

Stack

Before	After
value	...
index	
arrayref	
...	

Description

Takes an int from the stack, truncates it to a signed 16-bit short, and stores it in an array of shorts. *arrayref* is a reference to an array of 16-bit signed shorts. *index* is an int. *value* is the int to be stored in the array. *arrayref, index* and *value* are removed from the stack, and *value* is stored in the array at the given *index*.

Exceptions

- ArrayIndexOutOfBoundsException—*index* is < *0* or >= *arrayref.length*
- NullPointerException—*arrayref* is null

Bytecode

Type	Description
u1	sastore opcode = 0x56 (86)

See Also

iastore, lastore, fastore, dastore, aastore, bastore, castore, iaload, laload, faload, daload, aaload, baload, caload, saload

---

sipush   push two-byte signed integer

Jasmin Syntax

```
sipush <n>
```

<n> is a signed integer in the range –32768 to 32767.

Stack

Before	After
...	value
	...

Description

Takes a single parameter, <n> (a 16-bit signed integer), sign extends it to a 32-bit int, and pushes the resulting int onto the operand stack.

sipush is typically more efficient than ldc. It also occupies fewer bytes in the class file.

Example

```
sipush    0x10     ; push the value 0x10 (16)
                   ; onto the operand stack
```

Bytecode

The sipush opcode is followed in the bytecode by a 16-bit signed short specifying the integer value to push.

Type	Description
u1	sipush opcode = 0x11 (17)
s2	<n>

See Also

bipush, ldc, ldc_w, ldc2_w, aconst_null, iconst_m1, iconst_<n>, lconst_<l>, fconst_<f>, dconst_<d>

---

swap swap top two stack words

Jasmin Syntax

```
swap
```

Stack

Before	After
word1	word2
word2	word1
...	...

Description

Swaps the top two single-word items on the stack. word1/word2 cannot belong to a long or double.

Bytecode

Type	Description
u1	swap opcode = 0x5F (95)

Notes

There is no swap2, although to achieve the same effect, you could use:

```
dup2_x2
pop2
```

tableswitch jump according to a table

Jasmin Syntax

```
tableswitch  <low> [<high>]
             <label1>
             <label2>
             . . .
             <labelN>
    default : <defaultLabel>
```

<low> is a 32-bit signed integer. *<label1>*, *<label2>*, etc. are label names. *<high>* is a 32-bit signed integer which is greater than or equal to *<low>*. There must be *<high>*-*<low>*+1 labels given in the table. If *<high>* is omitted, Jasmin calculates it for you based on the number of entries in the table.

To define the location of the label, use the *<label>* name followed by a colon:

```
<label>:
```

then becomes associated the address of the following instruction. Labels can only be assigned one location in a method. On the other hand, a single <label> can be the target of multiple branch instructions.

Stack

Before	After
val	...
...	

Description

Performs computed jump. The jump table used by tableswitch is given in the bytecode after the tableswitch opcode.

An integer, *val*, is popped off the top of the operand stack. If this value is less than <low>, or if it is greater than <high>, execution branches to the address (*pc* + *default_offset*), where *pc* is the address of the tableswitch opcode in the bytecode, and *default_offset* is taken from the bytecode and is the relative address of the instruction at <defaultLabel>.

If val is in the range <low> to <high>, execution branches to the i'th entry in the table, where i is (*val* − <low>) and the first entry in the table is *index* 0. i.e., *pc* becomes the address (*pc* + table[*val* − <low>]).

The following pseudo-code illustrates the computation performed by tableswitch:

```
int val = pop();            // pop an int from the stack
if (val < low || val > high) { // if it's less than <low> or greater than <high>,
    pc += default;          // branch to default
} else {                    // otherwise
    pc += table[val - low]; // branch to entry in table
}
```

Notice that all addresses stored in the table are relative to the address of the tableswitch opcode in the bytecode. If you are using Jasmin, these addresses are computed for you from the address of the given labels.

Example

```
iload_1 ; push local variable 1 onto the stack

; if the variable contains 0, jump to ZeroLabel
; if the variable contains 1, jump to OneLabel
; if the variable contains 2, jump to TwoLabel
; otherwis jump to DefaultLabel
tableswitch 0 2
    ZeroLabel
```

```
        OneLabel
        TwoLabel
     default: DefaultLabel

ZeroLabel:
    ; the variable contained 0 ...
    ldc 100
    ireturn   ; return the result 100

OneLabel:
    ; the variable contained 1 ...
    bipush 200
    ireturn   ; return the result 200

TwoLabel:
    ; the variable contained 2 ...
    bipush 300
    ireturn   ; return the result 300

DefaultLabel:
    ; the variable contained something else ...
    bipush 0
    ireturn   ; return the result 0
```

Bytecode

tableswitch is a variable length instruction. Immediately after the tableswitch opcode, between 0 to 3 bytes of padding zeros are inserted, so that the *default_offset* parameter starts at an offset in the bytecode which is a multiple of 4. Next, two signed 32-bit integers are given—low and high, followed by (low – high + 1) 32-bit integer offsets.

Type	Description
u1	tableswitch opcode = 0xAA (170)
—	...0–3 bytes of padding ...
s4	*default_offset*
s4	\<low>
s4	\<low> + N – 1
s4	offset_1
s4	offset_2
...	...
s4	offset_N

See Also

lookupswitch

Notes

Addresses are measured in bytes from the start of the bytecode (i.e., address 0 is the first byte in the bytecode of the currently executing method).

---

wide next instruction uses 16-bit index

Jasmin Syntax

```
wide

<instruction> <parameter> [<parameter>]
```

Note that the Jasmin assembler automatically widens instructions as necessary —so the wide instruction is optional in Jasmin.

Stack

Before	After
...	...

Description

When placed in front of an instruction that accesses a local variable, extends the range of local variables available to the instruction from 8 bits (i.e., 0–255) to 16 bits (i.e., 0–65535). In addition, for iinc, it increases the increment range. wide is used in conjunction with one of the following opcodes: aload, dload, iload, fload, lload, astore, dstore, istore, fstore, lstore, iinc and ret. See the reference pages of those instructions for more details.

Bytecode

There are two bytecode formats. For aload, dload, iload, fload, lload, astore, dstore, istore, fstore, lstore, and ret, use:

Type	Description
u1	wide opcode = 0xC4 (196)
u1	<opcode>
u2	<varnum>

or, for `iinc`, use:

Type	Description
u1	wide opcode = 0xC4 (196)
u1	<opcode>
u2	<varnum>
u2	<n>

See Also

aload, iload, fload, dload, lload, astore, istore, fstore, dstore, lstore, iinc, ret

Notes

The opcode that follows `wide` cannot be the target of a branch.

In this appendix:
- *Data Operations*
- *Arithmetic and Type Conversion*
- *Flow Control*
- *Odds and Ends*

Instructions by Function Group

Data Operations

The Stack

Pushing constants onto the stack

    bipush
    sipush
    ldc
    ldc_w
    ldc2_w
    aconst_null
    iconst_m1
    iconst_<n>
    lconst_<l>
    fconst_<f>
    dconst_<d>

Stack manipulation

    nop
    pop
    pop2
    dup
    dup2
    dup_x1
    dup2_x1
    dup_x2
    dup2_x2
    swap

Local Variables

Pushing local variables onto the stack

iload
iload_<n>
lload
lload_<n>
fload
fload_<n>
dload
dload_<n>
aload
aload_<n>

Popping stack values into local variables

istore
istore_<n>
lstore
lstore_<n>
fstore
fstore_<n>
dstore
dstore_<n>
astore
astore_<n>

Miscellaneous local variable instructions

iinc
wide

Arrays

Creating arrays

newarray
anewarray
multianewarray

Retrieving values from arrays

iaload
laload
faload
daload
aaload

baload
caload
saload

Storing values in arrays

iastore
lastore
fastore
dastore
aastore
bastore
castore
sastore

Miscellaneous array instructions

arraylength

Objects

Creating objects

new

Manipulating object fields

putfield
getfield
putstatic
getstatic

Miscellaneous object operations

checkcast
instanceof

Arithmetic and Type Conversion

Arithmetic

iadd
ladd
fadd
dadd
isub
lsub
fsub

dsub
imul
lmul
fmul
dmul
idiv
ldiv
fdiv
ddiv
irem
lrem
frem
drem
ineg
lneg
fneg
dneg

Logical

ishl
ishr
iushr
lshl
lshr
lushr
iand
land
ior
lor
ixor
lxor

Conversions

i2l
i2f
i2d
l2I
l2f
l2d
f2I
f2l
f2d
d2I
d2l

d2f
i2b
i2c
i2s

Flow Control

Control Transfer

Conditional branches

ifeq
ifnull
iflt
ifle
ifne
ifnonnull
ifgt
ifge
if_icmpeq
if_icmpne
if_icmplt
if_icmpgt
if_icmple
if_icmpge

Comparisons

lcmp
fcmpl
fcmpg
dcmpl
dcmpg

Unconditional branches and subroutines

goto
goto_w
jsr
jsr_w
ret
ret_w

Table jumping

lookupswitch
tableswitch

Methods

Method invocation

invokevirtual
invokespecial
invokestatic
invokeinterface

Method return

ireturn
lreturn
freturn
dreturn
areturn
return

Odds and Ends

Exceptions

athrow

Debugging

breakpoint

Monitors

monitorenter
monitorexit

Instructions by Opcode

Standard Opcodes

0	nop	25	aload	50	aaload	75	astore_0
1	aconst_null	26	iload_0	51	baload	76	astore_1
2	iconst_m1	27	iload_1	52	caload	77	astore_2
3	iconst_0	28	iload_2	53	saload	78	astore_3
4	iconst_1	29	iload_3	54	istore	79	iastore
5	iconst_2	30	lload_0	55	lstore	80	lastore
6	iconst_3	31	lload_1	56	fstore	81	fastore
7	iconst_4	32	lload_2	57	dstore	82	dastore
8	iconst_5	33	lload_3	58	astore	83	aastore
9	lconst_0	34	fload_0	59	istore_0	84	bastore
10	lconst_1	35	fload_1	60	istore_1	85	castore
11	fconst_0	36	fload_2	61	istore_2	86	sastore
12	fconst_1	37	fload_3	62	istore_3	87	pop
13	fconst_2	38	dload_0	63	lstore_0	88	pop2
14	dconst_0	39	dload_1	64	lstore_1	89	dup
15	dconst_1	40	dload_2	65	lstore_2	90	dup_x1
16	bipush	41	dload_3	66	lstore_3	91	dup_x2
17	sipush	42	aload_0	67	fstore_0	92	dup2
18	ldc	43	aload_1	68	fstore_1	93	dup2_x1
19	ldc_w	44	aload_2	69	fstore_2	94	dup2_x2
20	ldc2_w	45	aload_3	70	fstore_3	95	swap
21	iload	46	iaload	71	dstore_0	96	iadd
22	lload	47	laload	72	dstore_1	97	ladd
23	fload	48	faload	73	dstore_2	98	fadd
24	dload	49	daload	74	dstore_3	99	dadd

100	isub	126	iand	152	dcmpg	178	getstatic
101	lsub	127	land	153	ifeq	179	putstatic
102	fsub	128	ior	154	ifne	180	getfield
103	dsub	129	lor	155	iflt	181	putfield
104	imul	130	ixor	156	ifge	182	invoke-virtual
105	lmul	131	lxor	157	ifgt	183	invoke-special
106	fmul	132	iinc	158	ifle	184	invokestatic
107	dmul	133	i2l	159	if_icmpeq	185	invoke-interface
108	idiv	134	i2f	160	if_icmpne	186	xxxunusedxxx
109	ldiv	135	i2d	161	if_icmplt	187	new
110	fdiv	136	l2i	162	if_icmpge	188	newarray
111	ddiv	137	l2f	163	if_icmpgt	189	anewarray
112	irem	138	l2d	164	if_icmple	190	arraylength
113	lrem	139	f2i	165	if_acmpeq	191	athrow
114	frem	140	f2l	166	if_acmpne	192	checkcast
115	drem	141	f2d	167	goto	193	instanceof
116	ineg	142	d2i	168	jsr	194	monitorenter
117	lneg	143	d2l	169	ret	195	monitorexit
118	fneg	144	d2f	170	tableswitch	196	wide
119	dneg	145	i2b	171	lookup-switch	197	multianew-array
120	ishl	146	i2c	172	ireturn	198	ifnull
121	lshl	147	i2s	173	lreturn	199	ifnonnull
122	ishr	148	lcmp	174	freturn	200	goto_w
123	lshr	149	fcmpl	175	dreturn	201	jsr_w
124	iushr	150	fcmpg	176	areturn		
125	lushr	151	dcmpl	177	return		

"Quick" Opcodes

203	ldc_quick	217	invokestatic_quick
205	ldc2_w_quick	218	invokeinterface_quick
206	getfield_quick	219	invokevirtualobject_quick
207	putfield_quick	221	new_quick
208	getfield2_quick	222	anewarray_quick
209	putfield2_quick	223	multianewarray_quick
211	putstatic_quick	224	checkcast_quick
212	getstatic2_quick	225	instanceof_quick
213	putstatic2_quick	226	invokevirtual_quick_w
214	invokcvirtual_quick	227	getfield_quick_w
215	invokenonvirtual_quick	228	putfield_quick_w
216	invokesuper_quick		

Reserved Opcodes

202	breakpoint
254	impdep1
255	impdep2

C

Jasmin User Guide

What Is Jasmin?

Jasmin is an assembler for the Java Virtual Machine. It takes ASCII descriptions of Java classes, written in a simple assembler-like syntax using the Java Virtual Machine instruction set. It converts them into binary Java class files, suitable for loading by a Java runtime system.

Jasmin was created as a companion to the book *Java Virtual Machine*, written by Jon Meyer and Troy Downing and published by O'Reilly & Associates.

About this Document

This document describes the rules and syntax used in Jasmin, and also explains how to run Jasmin. Note that this document doesn't explain the Java Virtual Machine itself, or give syntax notes for every instruction known to Jasmin. Readers are expected to be familiar with the Java class file format, and have some knowledge of the JVM instruction set.

Jasmin Design

Jasmin is designed as a simple assembler. It has a clean, easy-to-learn syntax, with few bells and whistles. Where possible, Jasmin adopts a one-to-one mapping between its syntax and the conventions followed by Java class files. For example, package names in Jasmin are delimited with the "/" character (e.g., "java/lang/String") used by the class file format, instead of the "." character (java.lang.String) used in the Java language.

The Jasmin assembler does little compile-time processing and checking of the input code. For example, it doesn't check that classes you reference actually exist, or that your type descriptors are well formed. Jasmin also lacks many of the features found in full macro assemblers. For example, it doesn't inline mathematical expressions, perform variable substitutions, or support macros.

On the other hand, using Jasmin, you can quickly try out nearly all of the features of the Java Virtual Machine, including methods, fields, subroutines, exception handlers, and so on. The Jasmin syntax is also readable and compact.

Running Jasmin

The `jasmin` command runs Jasmin on a file. For example:

```
% jasmin myfile.j
```

assembles the file *myfile.j*. Jasmin looks at the .class directive contained in the file to decide where to place the output class file. So if *myfile.j* starts with:

```
.class mypackage/MyClass
```

then Jasmin will place the output class file *MyClass.java* in the subdirectory *mypackage* of the current directory. It will create the *mypackage* directory if it doesn't exist.

You can use the *-d* option to tell Jasmin to place the output in an alternative directory. For example,

```
% jasmin -d /tmp myfile.j
```

will place the output in */tmp/mypackage/MyClass.class*.

Finally, you can use the *-g* option to tell Jasmin to include line number information (used by debuggers) in the resulting .class file. Jasmin will number the lines in the Jasmin source file that JVM instructions appear on. Then, if an error occurs, you can see what instruction in the Jasmin source caused the error. Note that specifying *-g* causes any .line directives within the Jasmin file to be ignored.

Statements

Jasmin source files consist of a sequence of newline-separated statements. There are three types of statement:

- directives
- instructions
- labels

Directives and instructions can take *parameters*. These parameters are placed on the same line as the directive or instruction, separated by spaces.

Directives

Directive statements are used to give Jasmin meta-level information. Directive statements consist of a directive name, zero or more parameters separated by spaces, and a newline.

All directive names start with a "." character. The directives in Jasmin are:

.catch	.line
.class	.method
.end	.source
.field	.super
.implements	.throws
.interface	.var
.limit	

Some example directive statements are:

```
.limit stack 10
.method public myMethod()V
.class Foo
```

The parameters used by each directive are described in detail later in this chapter.

Instructions

An instruction statement consists of an instruction name, zero or more parameters separated by spaces, and a newline.

Jasmin uses the standard mnemonics for JVM opcodes as instruction names. For example, aload_1, bipush and iinc are all Jasmin instruction names.

Here are some examples of instruction statements:

```
ldc     "Hello World"
iinc    1 -1
bipush 10
```

Labels

A Jasmin label statement consists of a name followed by a ":", and a newline. For example:

```
Foo:
Label:
```

Label names cannot start with a numeric digit, and cannot contain any of the special characters: = : . " -

You cannot use directive names or instruction names as labels. Other than that, there are few restrictions on label names. For example, you could use the label:

```
#_1:
```

Labels can be used only within method definitions. The names are local to that method.

Tokens

Jasmin tokenizes its input stream, splitting the stream into tokens by looking for whitespace characters (spaces, tabs, and newlines). The tokenizer looks for:

- directive names
- instruction names
- labels
- comments
- type descriptor names
- class names
- numbers and quoted strings

Comments

A comment is a token that starts with a ";" character, and terminates with the newline character at the end of the line.

Note that the semicolon must be the first character in the token (i.e., embedded semicolons are ignored). For example,

```
abc;def
```

is treated as a single token "abc;def", and

```
Ljava/lang/String;
```

is the token "Ljava/lang/String;", whereas

```
foo ; baz ding
```

is the token "foo" followed by a comment "baz ding".

Numbers and Strings

In Jasmin, only simple decimal and integer numeric formats are recognized. Floats in scientific or exponent format are not yet supported. Character codes and octal aren't currently supported, either. This means you can have:

```
1, 123, .25, 0.03, 0xA
```

but not

```
1e-10, a, \u123
```

Quoted strings are also very basic. The full range of backslash escape sequences are not yet supported, although "\n" and "\t" are.

Class Names

Class names in Jasmin should be written using the Java class file format conventions, so java.lang.String becomes java/lang/String.

Type Descriptors

Type information is also written as it appears in class files (e.g., the descriptor "I" specifies an integer, "[Ljava/lang/Thread;" is an array of Threads, etc.).

Methods

Method names are specified using a single token, for example:

```
java/io/PrintStream/println(Ljava/lang/String;)V
```

is the method called "println" in the class java.io.PrintStream, which has the type descriptor "(Ljava/lang/String;)V" (i.e., it takes a String and returns no result). In general, a method specification is formed of three parts. The characters before the last "/" form the class name. The characters between the last "/" and "(" are the method name. The rest of the string is the type descriptor for the method.

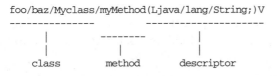

As another example, you would call the Java method:

```
class mypackage.MyClass {
    int foo(Object a, int b[]) {... }
}
```

using:

```
invokevirtual mypackage/MyClass/foo(Ljava/lang/Object;[I)I
```

Fields

Field names are specified in Jasmin using two tokens, one giving the name and class of the field, the other giving its descriptor. For example:

```
getstatic mypackage/MyClass/my_font    Ljava/awt/Font;
```

gets the value of the field called "my_font" in the class mypackage.MyClass. The type of the field is "Ljava/awt/Font;" (i.e., a Font object).

File Structure

Jasmin files start by giving information on the class being defined in the file—such as the name of the class, the name of the source file that the class originated from, the name of the superclass, etc.

Typically, a Jasmin file starts with the following three directives:

```
.source <source-file>
.class  <access-spec> <class-name>
.super  <class-name>
```

For example, the file defining MyClass might start with these directives:

```
.source MyClass.j
.class  public MyClass
.super  java/lang/Object
```

.source Directive

The .source directive is optional. It specifies the value of the "SourceFile" attribute for the class file. (This is used by Java to print out debugging information if something goes wrong in one of the methods in the class.) If you generated the Jasmin file automatically (e.g., as the result of compiling a file written in another syntax), you should use the .source directive to tell Java the name of the originating file. Note that the source filename should not include any pathname. Use *foo.src* but not */home/user/foo.src*.

If no .source directive is given, the name of the Jasmin file you are compiling is used instead as the SourceFile attribute.

.class and .super Directives

The .class and .super directive tell the JVM the name of this class and its super-class. These directives take parameters as follows:

<class-name>

>   is the full name of the class, including any package names. For example, foo/baz/MyClass.

<access-spec>

>   defines access permissions and other attributes for the class. This is a list of zero or more of the following keywords: public, final, super, interface, and abstract.

.interface Directive

Note that, instead of using the directive .class, you can use the directive .interface. This has the same syntax as the .class directive, but indicates that the Jasmin file is defining a Java interface, for example:

```
.interface public foo
```

.implements Directive

After .source, .class, and .super, you can list the interfaces that are implemented by the class you are defining, using the .implements directive. The syntax of .implements is:

```
.implements <class-name>
```

where <class-name> has the same format used by .class and .super. For example:

```
.class foo
.super java/lang/Object
.implements Edible
.implements java/lang/Throwable
```

Field Definitions

After the header information, the next section of the Jasmin file is a list of field definitions.

A field is defined using the .field directive:

```
.field <access-spec> <field-name> <descriptor> [ = <value> ]
```

where:

<access-spec>

is zero or more of the following keywords: public, private, protected, static, final, volatile, and transient.

<field-name>

is the name of the field.

<descriptor>

is its type descriptor.

<value>

is an integer, a quoted string, or a decimal number, giving the initial value of the field (for final fields).

For example, the Java field definition:

```
public int foo;
```

becomes

```
.field public foo I
```

whereas the constant:

```
public static final float PI = 3.14;
```

becomes

```
.field public static final PI F = 3.14
```

Method Definitions

After listing the fields of the class, the rest of the Jasmin file lists methods defined by the class.

A method is defined using the basic form:

```
.method <access-spec> <method-spec>
        <statements>
    .end method
```

where:

<access-spec>

is zero or more of the following keywords: public, private, protected, static, final, synchronized, native, and abstract.

<method-spec>

    is the name and type descriptor of the method.

<statements>

    is the code defining the body of the method.

Method definitions cannot be nested. Also, Jasmin does not insert an implicit "return" instruction at the end of a method. It is up to you to ensure that your methods return cleanly. So the most basic Jasmin method looks something like:

```
.method foo()V
    return     ; must give a return statement
.end method
```

Method Directives

The following directives can be used only within method definitions:

.limit stack <integer>

    sets the maximum size of the operand stack required by the method.

.limit locals <integer>

    sets the number of local variables required by the method.

.line <integer>

    is used to tag the subsequent instruction(s) with a line number. Debuggers use this information, together with the name of the source file (see .source above) to show at what line in a method things went wrong. If you are generating Jasmin files by compiling a source file, this directive lets you indicate what line numbers in the source file produced corresponding Jasmin instructions. For example:

```
.method foo()V
.line 5
    bipush 10    // these instructions generated from line 5
    istore_2     // of the source file.
.line 6
    ...
```

.var <var-number> is <name> <descriptor> from <label1> to <label2>

    The .var directive is used to define the name, type descriptor, and scope of a local variable number. This information is used by debuggers, so that they can be more helpful when printing out the values of local variables (rather than printing just a local variable number, the debugger can actually print the name of the variable). For example:

```
.method foo()V
    .limit locals 1
```

```
; declare variable 0 as an "int Count;"
; whose scope is the code between Label1 and Label2
;
.var 0 is Count I from Label1 to Label2

Label1:
    bipush 10
    istore_0
Label2:

    return
.end method
```

.throws <classname>

indicates that this method can throw exceptions of the type indicated by <classname>, for example:

```
.throws java/io/IOException
```

This information isn't required by Java runtime systems, but it is used by the Java compiler to check that methods either catch exceptions they can cause, or declare that they throw them.

.catch <classname> from <label1> to <label2> using <label3>

appends an entry to the end of the exceptions table for the method. The entry indicates that when an exception which is an instance of <classname> or one of its subclasses is thrown while executing the code between <label1> and <label2>, then the runtime system should jump to <label3>, for example:

```
.catch java/io/IOException from L1 to L2 using IO_Handler
```

If classname is the keyword "all", then exceptions of any class are caught by the handler.

Abstract Methods

To declare an abstract method, write a method with no body, for example:

```
.method abstract myAbstract()V
.end method
```

Note that abstract methods can have .throws directives, for example:

```
.method abstract anotherAbstract()V
    .throws java/io/IOException
.end method
```

JVM Instructions

JVM instructions are placed between the .method and .end method directives. VM instructions can take zero or more parameters, depending on the type of instruction used. Some example instructions are:

```
iinc 1 -3     ; decrement local variable 1 by 3
bipush 10     ; push the integer 10 onto the stack
pop           ; remove the top item from the stack.
```

NOTE   See the instruction reference for more details on the syntax of instructions in Jasmin.

D

In this appendix:
- *Overview*
- *Working with JAS*
- *Writing HelloWorld in JAS*
- *Beyond the HelloWorld Example*

The JAS Library

Overview

This appendix contains a brief look at JAS, a publicly available Java package designed to make it easy to generate files in the Java class file format.[*] JAS is the library used by the Jasmin assembler to convert textual descriptions of Java Virtual Machine instructions into the binary bytecodes of a class file. However, JAS can also be used without Jasmin. For example, JAS could be used by a Java application to create new classes and methods dynamically.

This appendix gives you just the flavor of the JAS package. We assume you already know the Java programming language, and you should also be familiar with the overview material presented in Part I of this book. If you want more details about JAS, check out the JAS page, *http://www.blackdown.org/~kbs/jas.html*.

Working with JAS

To generate a class file using JAS, there are three basic steps:

1. Create and initialize a ClassEnv object.
2. Add Method and Field descriptions to the ClassEnv, using addMethod and addField.
3. Write out the class file for the ClassEnv by calling the write method.

The following section illustrates these three steps using the Hello World example.

---

[*] The creator of JAS is K.B. Sriram.

411

Writing HelloWorld in JAS

To illustrate using JAS, we are going to construct the canonical "Hello World" program from JAS primitives. You have already seen the program in Chapter 2, *Quick Tour*, so you should be familiar with it by now. The program, written in Java, is:

```
// class HelloWorld with one static method that prints "Hello World"

class public HelloWorld {
    static public void main(String args[]) {
        System.out.println("Hello World");
    }
};
```

The JAS code needed to generate the previous class is shown in the following code. Note that we've embellished the class a little bit by giving it two fields—this is to demonstrate how fields are declared using JAS.

```
//
// This is a program that makes calls into the JAS package
// to generate a class called HelloWorld that prints the string "Hello".
//
// Compiling and running this program will create a file, HelloWorld.class,
// containing the new class.

import jas.*;
import java.io.*;
import sun.tools.java.RuntimeConstants;

// N.B. JAS currently uses the sun.tools.java.RuntimeConstants to
// obtain definitions for the opcodes and other details of the JVM.

class Hworld implements RuntimeConstants
{
  public static void main(String argv[])
    throws jasError, IOException
  {
                              // Define the class
    ClassEnv myclass = new ClassEnv();
    myclass.setClass(new ClassCP("HelloWorld"));
    myclass.setSuperClass(new ClassCP("java/lang/Object"));
    myclass.setClassAccess((short)ACC_PUBLIC);

    // Add the field:
    //
    //      public int myfield;
    //
    myclass.addField(
        new Var((short)ACC_PUBLIC,
                new AsciiCP("myfield"),
                new AsciiCP("I"),
                null));
```

```
// Add the field:
//
//      public static final int MYCONSTANT = 10;
//
myclass.addField(
    new Var((short)(ACC_PUBLIC | ACC_STATIC | ACC_FINAL),
            new AsciiCP("MYCONSTANT"),
            new AsciiCP("I"),
            new ConstAttr(new IntegerCP(10))));

                            // Define the code for the <init> method
CodeAttr code = new CodeAttr();

// aload_0
code.addInsn(new Insn(opc_aload_0));

// invokenonvirtual java/lang/Object/<init>()V
code.addInsn(new Insn(opc_invokenonvirtual,
                    new MethodCP("java/lang/Object", "<init>", "()V")));

// return
code.addInsn(new Insn(opc_return));

                            // Add the <init> method to the class
myclass.addMethod((short)ACC_PUBLIC, "<init>", "()V", code, null);

                            // Define the code for the main() method
code = new CodeAttr();

// getstatic java.lang.System.out Ljava.io.PrintStream;
code.addInsn(new Insn(opc_getstatic,
                    new FieldCP("java/lang/System",
                                "out",
                                "Ljava/io/PrintStream;")));
// ldc "Hello World"
code.addInsn(new Insn(opc_ldc,
                    new StringCP("Hello World")));

// invokevirtual java/io/PrintString/println(Ljava/lang/String;)V
code.addInsn(new Insn(opc_invokevirtual,
                    new MethodCP("java/io/PrintStream",
                                "println",
                                "(Ljava/lang/String;)V")));

// return
code.addInsn(new Insn(opc_return));

                            // set the right sizes for code
code.setStackSize((short)3);
code.setVarSize((short)4);

                            // Add the main() method
myclass.addMethod((short)(ACC_PUBLIC|ACC_STATIC), "main",
                "([Ljava/lang/String;)V", code, null);
```

```
                                // Write it all out.
        myclass.write(new DataOutputStream
                (new FileOutputStream("HelloWorld.class")));
    }
}
```

Now let's look in more detail at what the program is doing.

Creating A ClassEnv Object

The first step in JAS is to create a ClassEnv object and initialize it. In Java, "new" is used to construct new instances of objects:

```
ClassEnv myclass = new ClassEnv();
```

This creates a new ClassEnv object and stores it in the variable called myclass.

The next step is to initialize various properties of myclass—such as its name and the name of its superclass. The following two lines achieve this:

```
myclass.setClass(new ClassCP("HelloWorld"));
myclass.setSuperClass(new ClassCP("java/lang/Object"));
```

The first line indicates that the name of the class being generated is "HelloWorld". The statement:

```
new ClassCP("HelloWorld")
```

generates a JAS reference to the class "HelloWorld". (In fact, this generates a new CONSTANT_Class entry in the Constant Pool—hence the name ClassCP. See Chapter 4, *Classes*, for more details on constant pool entry types.) Similarly,

```
new ClassCP("java/lang/Object")
```

is used in JAS to generate a reference to the java.lang.Object class. Note the use of "/" instead of "." to separate names. In Java class files, "/" is used as a separator for class, field, and method names.

You also need to specify the access mode for the class. The line

```
myclass.setClassAccess((short)ACC_PUBLIC);
```

tells JAS that myclass is a public class. See Chapter 12, *Class File Reference*, for a description of other class access flags.

Adding Fields

The HelloWorld class we are generating doesn't use any fields. However, for demonstration purposes, we've added two fields to the HelloWorld class:

```
public int myfield;
public static final int MYCONSTANT = 10;
```

You add fields to a class in JAS using the addField method. The addField method takes one argument—a Var object. To add the "myfield" field, for example, you use:

```
myclass.addField(
    new Var((short)ACC_PUBLIC,
            new AsciiCP("myfield"),
            new AsciiCP("I"),
            null));
```

The first argument to the Var constructor, (short)ACC_PUBLIC, specifies the access permissions for the field. See Chapter 12 for a list of valid values for this argument. In this particular case, the field is a public field—hence the use of ACC_PUBLIC.

The second and third arguments to the Var constructor give the name and type descriptor of the field. These should be specified as AsciiCP instances—in this case, the expression:

```
new AsciiCP("myfield")
```

takes a string and converts it into an AsciiCP instance. An AsciiCP refers to a Utf8 string entry in the constant pool. See Chapter 4 for a description of Utf8 string entries in the constant pool.

The fourth and final argument to the Var constructor gives the initial value for the field. Unless you are creating a constant static class field, this argument should be null.

To create a constant static class field, for example, to create the equivalent of:

```
public static final int MYCONSTANT = 10
```

use something like:

```
myclass.addField(
    new Var((short)(ACC_PUBLIC | ACC_STATIC | ACC_FINAL),
            new AsciiCP("MYCONSTANT"),
            new AsciiCP("I"),
            new ConstAttr(new IntegerCP(10))));
```

The expression:

```
new ConstAttr(new IntegerCP(10))
```

defines the value of the field—it takes an integer (10), converts it into an IntegerCP (a CONSTANT_Integer entry in the constant pool), and then converts this into a ConstAttr reference (i.e., a "ConstantValue" attribute—see Chapter 4 for a description of attributes).

Notice that in the second field, these are the access flags:

> ACC_PUBLIC | ACC_STATIC | ACC_FINAL

The field is a public static final field—the Java version of a global constant. As you can see, you can specify several access flags at once by *or*ing them together.

Methods

The HelloWorld class contains two methods: an initializer method and a static main() method.

Methods are added to a class in a slightly backward manner: You construct a CodeAttr object representing a block of code, add instructions to that block, and then register the CodeAttr object with the ClassEnv object as a new method.

The statement:

```
CodeAttr code = new CodeAttr();
```

creates a new CodeAttr object and stores it in the variable called code.

You can now add instructions to the Code block. You use the addInsn method to do this. Calls to addInsn usually look something like this:

```
code.addInsn(new Insn(<opcode>, ...));
```

where <opcode> is the opcode of the instruction you are adding, and "..." represents any additional arguments needed for that opcode. See the online documentation for information on the arguments to Insn.

For example, the first instruction of the initializer method,

```
aload_0
```

is added using:

```
code.addInsn(new Insn(opc_aload_0));
```

and the next instruction,

```
invokenonvirtual java/lang/Object/<init>()V
```

is added using:

```
code.addInsn(new Insn(opc_invokenonvirtual,
                 new MethodCP("java/lang/Object", "<init>", "()V")));
```

In this example:

```
new MethodCP("java/lang/Object", "<init>", "()V")
```

constructs a CONSTANT_Methodref entry in the constant pool identifying a method. The first argument is the name of the class, the second is the name of the method, and the third is the type descriptor for the method.

At the end of the method, you need to include a return instruction:

```
code.addInsn(new Insn(opc_return));
```

After you have added all the instructions, you need to assign the code block to a method in the class. You do this using the addMethod method. The method we are defining is the initializer for instances of the class—in JVM, initializers have the special name <init>, so the statement:

```
myclass.addMethod((short)ACC_PUBLIC, "<init>", "()V", code, null);
```

is used. The first argument to addMethod specifies the access mode for the method (in this case it's a public method). The second is the name of the method. The third is the type descriptor for the method. The fourth is the code block (a CodeAttr object). The last argument specifies an exception Catchtable— Catchtables are used to indicate how exceptions are handled in the method. In this case there is no Catchtable, so the last argument is null. See Chapter 4 for information on type descriptors. See the online documentation for JAS for more on Catchtables.

Now you have created a class containing a method. You add other methods using the same basic steps. After adding all the method definitions, you are ready to write the class file.

Writing the Class

The class file for the class specified in a ClassEnv can be written out using the write method:

```
myclass.write(new DataOutputStream
          (new FileOutputStream("HelloWorld.class")));
```

The write method takes a single argument—a java.io.DataOutputStream specifying where to write the data. In this example, the class file is written to the file called "HelloWorld.class".

Beyond the HelloWorld Example

The JAS package can be used to generate much more than just the simple class shown in this chapter. JAS supports all of the features of the Java Virtual Machine specification, including handling of exceptions, complex instructions (such as the lookupswitch and tableswitch), and debugging attributes (such as the LineNumberTable attribute and the LocalVariableTable attribute).

This appendix contained a very brief tour of the JAS API. For more examples of using JAS, you can look at the source code to the Jasmin compiler, or look at the JAS package itself—it is distributed with this book. JAS also comes with online reference documentation for all of its classes.

Index

About the Authors

Jon Meyer has been working with high-level languages and Virtual Machine architectures for the past nine years, primarily as a developer for Poplog, an advanced programming toolset developed by the University of Sussex and marketed commercially by Integral Solutions Ltd. In 1994, Jon moved to New York to join the New York University's Media Research Laboratory as a researcher, working under the direction of Professor Ken Perlin.

Jon's main research interests include real-time 2D and 3D computer graphics, multimedia, distributed systems, artificial intelligence, programming languages, and human computer interfaces. You can visit his homepage on the Web at *http://www.mrl.nyu.edu/meyer.*

Troy Downing is a research scientist and programmer specializing in Internet technologies at New York University's Media Research Lab. Troy is also adjunct faculty in the Information Technology Institute of NYU, teaching classes on Web Server Technologies, Java, CGI, and HTML authoring. Troy owns an Internet software development company that specializes in Web-based groupware called WebCal LLC that can be found online at: *http://www.webcal.com/.* He has been a primary force in WWW development at the Media Research Lab and has recently turned his focus to Java, working on porting many of the Media Research Lab's efforts to a Java platform. He has co-authored a number of Web related books including *HTML Web Publisher's Construction Kit* and *Java Primer Plus*. Besides his involvement in Internet technologies, Troy is also an avid mountain biker, homebrewer, and first-time father of his two-year-old daughter, Morgan.

Colophon

Edie Freedman designed the cover of this book, using an image from the CMCD PhotoCD Collection that she manipulated in Adobe Photoshop. The cover layout was produced with Quark XPress 3.3 using the Bodoni Black font from URW Software and BT Bodoni Bold Italic from Bitstream. The inside layout was designed by Nancy Priest.

Text was prepared by Erik Ray in SGML DocBook 2.4 DTD. The print version of this book was created by translating the SGML source into a set of gtroff macros using a filter developed at ORA by Norman Walsh. Steve Talbott designed and wrote the underlying macro set on the basis of the GNU troff -gs macros; Lenny Muellner adapted them to SGML and implemented the book design. The GNU groff text formatter version 1.09 was used to generate PostScript output. The heading font is Bodoni BT; the text font is New Baskerville. The illustrations that appear in the book were created in Macromedia Freehand 5.0 by Chris Reilley.

More Titles from O'Reilly

Java Programming

Exploring Java

By Patrick Niemeyer & Joshua Peck
1st Edition May 1996
426 pages, ISBN 1-56592-184-4

The ability to create animated World Wide Web pages has sparked the rush to Java. But what has also made this new language so important is that it's truly portable. *Exploring Java* introduces the basics of Java, the hot new object-oriented programming language for networked applications. The code runs on any machine that provides a Java interpreter, be it Windows 95, Windows NT, the Macintosh, or any flavor of UNIX.

But that's only the beginning! This book shows you how to quickly get up to speed writing Java applets (programs executed within web browsers) and other applications, including networking programs, content and protocol handlers, and security managers. *Exploring Java* is the first book in a new Java documentation series from O'Reilly that will keep pace with the rapid Java developments. Covers Java's latest Beta release.

Java in a Nutshell

By David Flanagan
1st Edition February 1996
460 pages, ISBN 1-56592-183-6

Java in a Nutshell is a complete quick-reference guide to Java, the hot new programming language from Sun Microsystems. This comprehensive volume contains descriptions of all of the classes in the Java 1.0 API, with a definitive listing of all methods and variables. It also contains an accelerated introduction to Java for C and C++ programmers who want to learn the language *fast*.

Java in a Nutshell introduces the Java programming language and contains many practical examples that show programmers how to write Java applications and applets. It is also an indispensable quick reference designed to wait faithfully by the side of every Java programmer's keyboard. It puts all the information Java programmers need right at their fingertips.

Java Virtual Machine

By Troy Downing & Jon Meyer
1st Edition March 1997
440 pages (est.), ISBN 1-56592-194-1

This book is a comprehensive programming guide for the Java Virtual Machine (JVM). It gives readers a strong overview and reference of the JVM so that they may create their own implementations of the JVM or write their own compilers that create Java object code. The book is divided into two sections: the first includes information on the semantics and structure of the JVM; the second is a reference of the JVM instructions, or "opcodes." The programming guide includes numerous examples written in Java assembly language. A Java assembler is provided with the book, so the examples can all be compiled and executed. The reference section offers a complete description of the instruction set of the VM and the class file format, including a description of the byte-code verifier.

Java Language Reference

By Mark Grand
1st Edition January 1997
448 pages, ISBN 1-56592-204-2

Java Language Reference is an indispensable tool for Java programmers. Part of O'Reilly's new Java documentation series, the book details every aspect of the Java programming language, from the definition of data types to the syntax of expressions and control structures.

Using numerous examples to illustrate various fine points of the language, this book helps you understand all of the subtle nuances of Java so you can ensure that your programs run exactly as expected. This edition describes Java Version 1.0.2. It covers the syntax (presented in easy-to-understand railroad diagrams), object-oriented programming, exception handling, multithreaded programming, and differences between Java and C/C++.

Java Programming *continued*

Java Fundamental Classes Reference

By Mark Grand
1st Edition May 1997 (est.)
880 pages (est.), ISBN 1-56592-241-7

The *Java Fundamental Classes Reference* provides complete reference documentation for the Java fundamental classes. These classes contain architecture-independent methods that serve as Java's gateway to the real world and provide access to resources such as the network, the windowing system, and the host filesystem. This book takes you beyond what you'd expect from a standard reference manual. Classes and methods are, of course, described in detail. But the book does much more. It offers tutorial-style explanations of the important classes in the Java Core API and includes lots of sample code to help you learn by example.

Java AWT Reference

By John Zukowski
1st Edition March 1997 (est.)
1100 pages (est.), ISBN 1-56592-240-9

With AWT, you can create windows, draw, work with images, and use components like buttons, scrollbars, and pulldown menus. *Java AWT Reference* covers the classes that comprise the java.awt, java.awt.image, and java.applet packages. These classes provide the functionality that allows a Java application to provide user interaction in a graphical environment.

The *Java AWT Reference* provides complete reference documentation on the Abstract Windowing Toolkit (AWT), a large collection of classes for building graphical user interfaces in Java. Part of O'Reilly's new Java documentation series, this edition describes Version 1.0.2 of the Java Developer's Kit. This book takes you beyond what you'd expect from a standard reference manual. It offers a comprehensive explanation of how AWT components fit together with easy-to-use reference material on every AWT class and lots of sample code to help you learn by example.

Java Threads

By Scott Oaks and Henry Wong
1st Edition January 1997
252 pages, ISBN 1-56592-216-6

Threaded programming being essential to Java, any new Java program that is at all substantial is multithreaded. The concept of threaded programming isn't new; however, as widespread as threads are, the number of developers who have worked with them is fairly small. *Java Threads* is a comprehensive guide to the intracacies of threaded programming in Java, covering everything from the most basic synchronization techniques to advanced topics like writing your own thread scheduler.

Java Threads uncovers the one tricky but essential aspect of Java programming and provides techniques, perhaps unfamiliar to most developers, for avoiding deadlock, lock starvation, and other topics. With many useful examples, you'll find this book essential if sophisticated Java programming is part of your future.

Java Network Programming

By Elliotte Rusty Harold
1st Edition February 1997
448 pages, ISBN 1-56592-227-1

Most Java programmers have yet to take advantage of Java's networking capabilities because they have limited themselves to relatively simple applets. *Java Network Programming* is a complete introduction to developing network programs, both applets and applications, using Java; covering everything from networking fundamentals to remote method invocation (RMI). It also covers what you can do without explicitly writing network code, how you can accomplish your goals using URLs and the basic capabilites of applets.

Java Network Programming includes chapters on TCP and UDP sockets, multicasting protocal and content handlers and servlets, part of the new Server API. Once you start taking advantage of Java's networking features, the possibilities are limited only by imagination!

How to stay in touch with O'Reilly

1. Visit Our Award-Winning Web Site

http://www.ora.com/

★ "Top 100 Sites on the Web" —*PC Magazine*
★ "Top 5% Web sites" —*Point Communications*
★ "3-Star site" —*The McKinley Group*

Our web site contains a library of comprehensive product information (including book excerpts and tables of contents), downloadable software, background articles, interviews with technology leaders, links to relevant sites, book cover art, and more. File us in your Bookmarks or Hotlist!

2. Join Our Email Mailing Lists

New Product Releases

To receive automatic email with brief descriptions of all new O'Reilly products as they are released, send email to: **listproc@online.ora.com**
Put the following information in the first line of your message (*not* in the Subject field):
subscribe ora-news "Your Name" of "Your Organization" (for example: subscribe ora-news Kris Webber of Fine Enterprises)

O'Reilly Events

If you'd also like us to send information about trade show events, special promotions, and other O'Reilly events, send email to: **listproc@online.ora.com**
Put the following information in the first line of your message (*not* in the Subject field):
subscribe ora-events "Your Name" of "Your Organization"

3. Get Examples from Our Books via FTP

There are two ways to access an archive of example files from our books:

Regular FTP

- ftp to:
  ftp.ora.com
  (login: anonymous
  password: your email address)
- Point your web browser to:
  ftp://ftp.ora.com/

FTPMAIL

- Send an email message to:
  ftpmail@online.ora.com
  (Write "help" in the message body)

4. Visit Our Gopher Site

- Connect your gopher to:
  gopher.ora.com

- Point your web browser to:
  gopher://gopher.ora.com/

- Telnet to:
  gopher.ora.com
  login: gopher

5. Contact Us via Email

order@ora.com
To place a book or software order online. Good for North American and international customers.

subscriptions@ora.com
To place an order for any of our newsletters or periodicals.

books@ora.com
General questions about any of our books.

software@ora.com
For general questions and product information about our software. Check out O'Reilly Software Online at **http://software.ora.com/** for software and technical support information. Registered O'Reilly software users send your questions to: **website-support@ora.com**

cs@ora.com
For answers to problems regarding your order or our products.

booktech@ora.com
For book content technical questions or corrections.

proposals@ora.com
To submit new book or software proposals to our editors and product managers.

international@ora.com
For information about our international distributors or translation queries. For a list of our distributors outside of North America check out:
http://www.ora.com/www/order/country.html

O'Reilly & Associates, Inc.
101 Morris Street, Sebastopol, CA 95472 USA
TEL   707-829-0515 or 800-998-9938
            (6am to 5pm PST)
FAX   707-829-0104

International Distributors

UK, Europe, Middle East and Northern Africa *(except France, Germany, Switzerland, & Austria)*

INQUIRIES

International Thomson Publishing
Europe
Berkshire House
168-173 High Holborn
London WC1V 7AA, United Kingdom
Telephone: 44-171-497-1422
Fax: 44-171-497-1426
Email: itpint@itps.co.uk

ORDERS

International Thomson Publishing
Services, Ltd.
Cheriton House, North Way
Andover, Hampshire SP10 5BE,
United Kingdom
Telephone: 44-264-342-832
  (UK orders)
Telephone: 44-264-342-806
  (outside UK)
Fax: 44-264-364418 (UK orders)
Fax: 44-264-342761 (outside UK)
UK & Eire orders: itpuk@itps.co.uk
International orders: itpint@itps.co.uk

France

Editions Eyrolles
61 bd Saint-Germain
75240 Paris Cedex 05
France
Fax: 33-01-44-41-11-44

FRENCH LANGUAGE BOOKS

All countries except Canada
Phone: 33-01-44-41-46-16
Email: geodif@eyrolles.com

ENGLISH LANGUAGE BOOKS

Phone: 33-01-44-41-11-87
Email: distribution@eyrolles.com

Australia

WoodsLane Pty. Ltd.
7/5 Vuko Place, Warriewood NSW 2102
P.O. Box 935, Mona Vale NSW 2103
Australia
Telephone: 61-2-9970-5111
Fax: 61-2-9970-5002
Email: info@woodslane.com.au

Germany, Switzerland, and Austria

INQUIRIES

O'Reilly Verlag
Balthasarstr. 81
D-50670 Köln
Germany
Telephone: 49-221-97-31-60-0
Fax: 49-221-97-31-60-8
Email: anfragen@oreilly.de

ORDERS

International Thomson Publishing
Königswinterer Straße 418
53227 Bonn, Germany
Telephone: 49-228-97024 0
Fax: 49-228-441342
Email: order@oreilly.de

Asia *(except Japan & India)*

INQUIRIES

International Thomson Publishing Asia
60 Albert Street #15-01
Albert Complex
Singapore 189969
Telephone: 65-336-6411
Fax: 65-336-7411

ORDERS

Telephone: 65-336-6411
Fax: 65-334-1617
thomson@signet.com.sg

New Zealand

WoodsLane New Zealand Ltd.
21 Cooks Street (P.O. Box 575)
Wanganui, New Zealand
Telephone: 64-6-347-6543
Fax: 64-6-345-4840
Email: info@woodslane.com.au

Japan

O'Reilly Japan, Inc.
Kiyoshige Building 2F
12-Banchi, Sanei-cho
Shinjuku-ku
Tokyo 160 Japan
Telephone: 81-3-3356-5227
Fax: 81-3-3356-5261
Email: kenji@ora.com

India

Computer Bookshop (India) PVT. LTD.
190 Dr. D.N. Road, Fort
Bombay 400 001
India
Telephone: 91-22-207-0989
Fax: 91-22-262-3551
Email: cbsbom@giasbm01.vsnl.net.in

The Americas

O'Reilly & Associates, Inc.
101 Morris Street
Sebastopol, CA 95472 U.S.A.
Telephone: 707-829-0515
Telephone: 800-998-9938 (U.S. &
Canada)
Fax: 707-829-0104
Email: order@ora.com

Southern Africa

International Thomson Publishing
Southern Africa
Building 18, Constantia Park
240 Old Pretoria Road
P.O. Box 2459
Halfway House, 1685 South Africa
Telephone: 27-11-805-4819
Fax: 27-11-805-3648

O'REILLY™

O'Reilly & Associates, Inc.
101 Morris Street
Sebastopol, CA 95472-9902
1-800-998-9938

Visit us online at:
http://www.ora.com/
orders@ora.com

O'REILLY WOULD LIKE TO HEAR FROM YOU

Which book did this card come from?

_____

Where did you buy this book?
- ❏ Bookstore
- ❏ Direct from O'Reilly
- ❏ Bundled with hardware/software
- ❏ Other _____
- ❏ Computer Store
- ❏ Class/seminar

What operating system do you use?
- ❏ UNIX
- ❏ Windows NT
- ❏ Other _____
- ❏ Macintosh
- ❏ PC(Windows/DOS)

What is your job description?
- ❏ System Administrator
- ❏ Network Administrator
- ❏ Web Developer
- ❏ Other _____
- ❏ Programmer
- ❏ Educator/Teacher

❏ Please send me O'Reilly's catalog, containing
a complete listing of O'Reilly books and
software.

Name _____ Company/Organization _____

Address _____

City _____ State _____ Zip/Postal Code _____ Country _____

Telephone _____ Internet or other email address (specify network) _____

Nineteenth century wood engraving
of a bear from the O'Reilly &
Associates Nutshell Handbook®
Using & Managing UUCP.

BUSINESS REPLY MAIL

FIRST CLASS MAIL   PERMIT NO. 80   SEBASTOPOL, CA

Postage will be paid by addressee

O'Reilly & Associates, Inc.
101 Morris Street
Sebastopol, CA 95472-9902